D1527003

THE GENETIC IMAGINARY:
DNA IN THE CANADIAN CRIMINAL JUSTICE SYSTEM

DNA testing and banking have become institutionalized in the Canadian criminal justice system. Their widespread use has been accepted with little critique or debate in a broad public forum on the potential infringement of individual rights and civil liberties. Neil Gerlach's *The Genetic Imaginary* addresses this deficiency, critically examining the social, legal, and criminal justice origins and effects of DNA testing and banking. Drawing on risk analysis, Gerlach explains why Canadians have accepted DNA technology with barely a ripple of public outcry.

Re-examining promises of better crime control and protections for existing privacy rights, Gerlach analyses police practices, courtroom decisions, and the changing role of scientific expertise in legal decision making and finds that DNA testing and banking have indeed led to a measurable erosion of individual rights. Biogovernance and the biotechnology of surveillance almost inevitably lead to the empowerment of state agent control and away from due process and legal protection. *The Genetic Imaginary* demonstrates that the overall effect of these changes to the criminal justice system has been to emphasize the importance of community security at the expense of individual rights. The privatization and politicization of biogovernance will certainly have profound future implications for all Canadians.

(Digital Futures)

NEIL GERLACH is an assistant professor in the Department of Sociology and Anthropology at Carleton University.

The Genetic Imaginary

DNA in the Canadian Criminal Justice System

NEIL GERLACH

UNIVERSITY OF TORONTO PRESS
Toronto Buffalo London

345.71
G37 g

© University of Toronto Press Incorporated 2004
Toronto Buffalo London
Printed in Canada

ISBN 0-8020-8784-1 (cloth)
ISBN 0-8020-8572-5 (paper)

Printed on acid-free paper

National Library of Canada Cataloguing in Publication Data

Gerlach, Neil, 1963–
 The genetic imaginary : DNA in the Canadian criminal justice
 system / Neil Gerlach.

 Includes bibliographical references and index.
 ISBN 0-8020-8784-1 (bound)   ISBN 0-8020-8572-5 (pbk.)

 1. DNA fingerprinting – Canada.   2. Evidence, Criminal – Canada.
 3. Criminal justice, Administration of – Canada.   I. Title.

 RA1057.55.G47 2004   345.71' 064   C2004-901334-3

UIL

University of Toronto Press acknowledges the financial assistance to its
publishing program of the Canada Council and the Ontario Arts Council.

This book has been published with the help of a grant from the Canadian
Federation for the Humanities and Social Sciences, through the Aid to
Scholarly Publications Programme, using funds provided by the Social
Sciences and Humanities Research Council of Canada.

University of Toronto Press acknowledges the financial support for its
publishing activities of the Government of Canada through the Book
Publishing Industry Development Program (BPIDP).

Contents

Acknowledgments

I wish to thank my wife, Sheryl Hamilton, for her tremendous support and patience throughout this project, and my daughter, Brigitte, for her inspiration.

I would like to thank the Social Sciences and Humanities Research Council of Canada and the Faculty Research Development Program of Concordia University for their generous support of this project.

I owe a debt of gratitude to a number of researchers without whom this book could not have been written. They include Laura Capobianco, Rachel Huggins, Nisrine Jaafar, Sarah Rayfield, and Lyle Robinson.

THE GENETIC IMAGINARY:
DNA IN THE CANADIAN CRIMINAL JUSTICE SYSTEM

1 Introduction: Risk, Biogovernance, and the Genetic Imaginary

In reality ... if any one age really attains, by eugenics and scientific education, the power to make its descendants what it pleases, all men who live after it are the patients of that power. They are weaker, not stronger: for though we may have put wonderful machines in their hands we have preordained how they are to use them ... Man's conquest of Nature, if the dreams of some scientific planners are realized, means the rule of a few hundreds of men over billions upon billions of men. There neither is nor can be any simple increase of power on Man's side. Each new power won by man is a power over man as well. Each advance leaves him weaker as well as stronger. In every victory, besides being the general who triumphs, he is also the prisoner who follows the triumphal car.

C.S. Lewis, The Abolition of Man (1947)

Imagine a society where violent crime rates have quadrupled over the past century, inexorably rising to levels that would be incomprehensible to previous generations. Imagine that the nature of violent crime seems to have changed, taking a turn toward casual sociopathy where the representative crime has become calculated serial murder rather than the one-off crime of passion. Imagine the resulting level of public fear, rampant to the point where civic-mindedness is replaced by a fortress mentality, walled communities, pervasive video surveillance, and electronic monitoring as the public sphere is virtually abandoned as too risky. In this imaginary society, the fearful public turns angrily upon its government, howling for more decisive action and demanding to know why traditional practices of crime control are not controlling crime.

Faced with the political consequences of admitting that the state cannot actually control crime, governments respond with massively greater numbers of prisons and police officers, tougher sentences, three-strikes laws, the elimination of parole, and relaxed restrictions on the use of deadly force in apprehending suspects. In other words, all of the traditional modes of crime control are strengthened. Yet crime rates do not fall. Prison populations begin to swell to the point that one must speak of the proportion of the total population that is incarcerated, rather than actual numbers. When traditional methods do not work, attention turns to the nature of criminality and the forms of expertise charged with understanding and rehabilitating criminals. Where, our imaginary government asks, have our criminologists, psychologists, sociologists, social workers, and prison managers gone wrong? Why can we not predetect potential criminals and contain them? And why can we not rehabilitate those who have committed crimes? Imagine that at just this moment, the 'experts' declare that they have found a link between genetic make-up and a tendency toward violent crime.

This scenario, I suggest, is not fictional. In fact, it reflects the assumptions, feelings, knowledges, and anticipations that constitute our 'sense' of the current social condition and the state of crime and crime management in our society. Also, it describes the enabling conditions for a new form of crime management premised on a governmental shift toward authorizing biological science to map, test, code, bank, and ultimately predict criminality in individuals and aggregate populations. Biotechnology is providing the most recent approach to the problem of managing risky populations and populations at risk, this time at the genetic level. DNA data banks and DNA testing are the tools presently available for this purpose, and since the late 1980s they have had a strong impact on the methods of the criminal justice system and on conceptions of social control. In this book I examine how DNA data banks for criminal offenders and the DNA testing of suspects have become part of Canadian criminal justice, how they have been defined and normalized in the public sphere, and how they participate in a broader set of governmental processes currently under construction to manage the social definitions and impacts of biotechnology in general.

DNA data banks and DNA testing are part of a broader biotechnological revolution, one that is causing many members of the public, government decision makers, business people, and scholars to ask: Are we becoming a civilization of the gene? At the beginning of the twenty-first century, we are struggling to make sense of the rivers of reports flowing out of biological science. The human genome has been mapped, and we now await the knowledge and practical applications that will result. Italian scientists have announced that an undisclosed European country has established the facilities for research that will soon lead to the cloning of a human being. A Quebec-based cult, the Raelians, has already announced the birth of the first human clone. (However, its leaders refuse to allow independent testing to verify the truth of this claim.) Meanwhile, a number of animals have been cloned, including sheep, cows, goats, cats, and mice. New reproductive technologies continue to proliferate, with more and more children being born through the intervention of biological science. Basic food crops such as canola, corn, and tomatoes are being genetically altered to resist pests and environmental conditions. International conferences of government and corporate representatives are convening to discuss the patentability of genetically altered life forms. Gene therapy looms on the horizon as a treatment for many diseases once considered untreatable. DNA matching and data banks are enabling law enforcement to apprehend a number of violent criminals and exonerate the wrongly convicted. Organizations are forming and mobilizing to oppose and politicize biotechnological innovations.

To past generations, most if not all of these developments would sound very much like science fiction. Yet we are only at the beginning of this transformation. Many of these new genetically based biotechnologies are already available to researchers, but they are still only experimental and the full extent of their social impact remains to be seen. Nevertheless, we have begun developing a 'genetic imaginary' – that is, a set of social concepts for thinking and speaking about the civilization of the gene and its future direction. Much of the discussion simply assumes that the genetic revolution is already a full-blown fact rather than a potential one. That is, a sort of 'hyperreality' wherein future possibilities are treated as present realities and as such are shaping our current actions. Why are we producing the genetic future before it arrives? Through what processes is this future unfolding? Who are the actors involved in producing the genetic imaginary?

Now, in the early twenty-first century, is the time to ask these questions. The civilization of the gene is still under construction and lacks conceptual edges. Ways of knowing it and speaking about it have not yet become part of everyday discourse. So far at least, we have not developed a framework of ideas, tropes, and metaphors for exercising the knowledge and power to order genetic knowledge. The genetic imaginary is still open, though it will not be for much longer. Already, approaches to biotechnology are being delimited so as to subsume the new science within a standardized regime of governance. As early as 1995, Dorothy Nelkin and M. Susan Lindee examined popular culture sources to suggest that a 'genetic essentialism' was forming:

> Increasing popular acceptance of genetic explanations and the proliferation of genetic images reflects, in part, highly publicized research in the science of genetics. Such research, however, occurs in a specific cultural context, one in which heredity and natural ability have often seemed important to formulations of social policy and social practice. Old ideas have been given new life at a time when individual identity, family connections, and social cohesion seem threatened and the social contract appears in disarray. (3)

Nelkin and Lindee focus on popular culture as the site where the genetic imaginary manifests itself. I wish to add to their analysis by examining another site – social governance. In this book I will refer to emerging governmental techniques for managing biotechnology as *biogovernance* – that is, the social ordering of the civilization of the gene. The central issue dealt with in this book is going to be the production of biogovernance in relation to the Canadian criminal justice system.

In December 1998 the Canadian government passed the DNA Identification Act, which established a national DNA data bank in Ottawa for storing biological samples and digital information from offenders convicted of designated offences. The road the government took to reach this point was neither smooth nor straight. It involved ten years of grappling with the issues raised by this new technology. The first criminal case involving DNA evidence arose in England in 1986, shortly after British scientist Alec Jeffreys announced that he and his team of geneticists at the University of Leicester had developed a method for matching DNA samples. After that, DNA testing spread quickly to other countries. The first reported Canadian case, *R. v. Bourguignon*, was in 1988. But Canadian law was uncertain about how to treat this new technology. Some courts excluded DNA evidence as a violation of the Charter of Rights and Freedoms, while others accepted it. Police found themselves rummaging through garbage cans and ashtrays looking for DNA samples because there was no common law or statutory authority to seize samples directly from suspects – a situation perpetuated in 1994 by *R. v. Borden*, the first Supreme Court decision on the matter.

In response to that decision and the public outcry surrounding it, the government moved quickly to establish a DNA identification system. In 1995, after public consultation, the Criminal Code was amended to provide for DNA warrants in the investigation of designated offences. Police were empowered to seize hair roots, saliva, and blood samples without regard to the bodily integrity of citizens. A series of Charter challenges inevitably followed, mainly on section 7 (which guarantees life, liberty, and security of the person) and section 8 (which guarantees the right against unreasonable search and seizure). However, the courts upheld the new laws as justifiable in a free and democratic society.

With the DNA warrant scheme having shown its durability, the government embarked on the second stage of its DNA policy – the creation of a DNA data bank for convicted offenders. Further public consultation was held in 1996, with heated debates between advocates of individual rights and advocates of public safety. In the end, the DNA Identification Act took the form originally proposed by the government. Those convicted of designated offences would have their biological samples, and digital information from those samples, entered into a convicted offenders' index. A second index of crime scene samples was also established. The offenders' samples would be kept indefinitely and would be compared with crime scene samples to determine matches. The act also expanded the list of designated offences, as did a 1999 Senate bill, which added designated military offences to the list. In July 2000 the data bank officially began full operations.

Obviously, a new technology does not simply move from the research laboratory directly to practical application. It must first pass through a social context of existing power relations and structures of meaning that set limits on when, where, and how it may be applied and that order it in terms of what it means for society. Processes such as these are potentially dangerous for institutionalized authorities, because public reaction cannot be gauged with certainty. The public must be convinced that the new technology is safe, beneficial, necessary, and even inevitable. A central argument of this book is that Canadian governmental authorities have been highly successful in constructing DNA testing and banking technologies as secure.

Because of various technological, social, and legal factors that have smoothed the entry of this technology into Canada, and because of hegemonic processes of framing the meanings of DNA testing and banking within criminal justice, these technologies inspire little controversy in the public sphere, unlike some other forms of biotechnology. The consequence is expanded state power: state agents have gained the right to enter the citizen's body. A new form of surveillance has been added to the existing array of surveillance technologies; as one result, the rituals of justice are now increasingly being performed behind laboratory doors instead of on the public stage of the courtrooms. Furthermore, the government's authority has been enhanced because the public sees it making progress in the 'war on crime.' As well, the authority of science is being enhanced at a time of increasing public reflexivity toward science and of calls for public oversight of scientific research and technological development, especially biotechnological development. Together, government and science are holding out the promise of better crime detection and perhaps even predetection of criminal tendencies through genetic screening. How did scientific and government authorities produce this security? And what are its implications for Canadian criminal justice, social control, and individual rights?

There are plenty of good reasons to use DNA testing and banking for a case study of how a new biotechnology enters our social institutions and the public sphere. First, although more and more social science research is focusing on the current and potential social impacts of biotechnologies, this research has tended to concentrate on biomedical, reproductive, and food-related technologies. Most such studies have been about reproduction and production. I suggest that biotechnology also has surveillance capacities and that in the present day, surveillance is probably the most widespread use of genetic-based biotechnologies. It is likely that so far, more people have been subjected to DNA matching and banking than to any other aspect of genetic technology. Yet matching and banking have not received the attention they deserve in the social sciences. These technologies administer individual bodies; they also intervene at the level of the social body to form an aggregate database on the criminal population of a country.

There have been few social science studies of DNA data banks in criminal justice. Cynthia Benjamin and Dean Weston (2000), in a criminology textbook chapter, have provided an interesting but necessarily brief overview of the privacy issues involved in implementing the Canadian DNA data bank. In a number of articles, various scholars have analysed how scientific knowledge about DNA matching is constructed and how scientific expertise is authorized to make legally significant pronouncements about those matches. For example, Daemmrich (1998) and Thompson (1997) have analysed the conflicts of interest that arise when private-sector forensic scientists perform DNA tests for prosecutors in the United States and how the courts have been instrumental in legitimating expert witnesses from these organizations. Jasanoff (1998) focuses on the O.J. Simpson trial, characterizing it as an event in which visual authority on DNA evidence had to be created in terms of whose vision was authorized as expert, and under what conditions a lay person's vision might take precedence over expert vision. Derksen (2000) examines the forms of negotiation that occur in laboratories and courts to render representations of the natural world 'objective' and, therefore, useful in court in terms of DNA matching.

Much more work has been done in critical legal analysis. Harlan Levy's 1996 book *And the Blood Cried Out* is the most comprehensive work dealing with the development and institutionalization of DNA testing technology in the American criminal justice system. It is a narrative account, written by a lawyer, of the events, debates, and controversies – both inside and outside American courtrooms – that led to the widespread use of DNA technologies. Levy clearly favours the use of DNA analysis in criminal cases; other legal scholars do not. Much of the analysis in law journals focuses on the potential rupture points and problematic social effects of DNA testing in criminal justice. Law journals have published articles by social scientists (Friedland, 1998) and biologists (Maienschein et al., 1998) that raise critical questions about the impact of a genetic justice system; but throughout the 1990s and into the 2000s most such journals focused on defence strategies for questioning DNA evidence. In Canada, these articles have taken three approaches: they have detailed common law sources for arguing against the legality of seizing biological samples (e.g., Bassan, 1996; Federico, 1990; Pomerance, 1995); they have outlined strategies for arguing against the constitutionality of seizing biological samples (e.g., Astroff, 1996); or they have presented courtroom tactics for challenging and discrediting DNA evidence and expert witnesses (e.g., Brodsky, 1993; Lussier, 1992).

Yet another area of social scientific discussion relates to genetically based assumptions about the nature of criminality. Much of this literature reviews the decades-old discourse around eugenics and compares it either implicitly or explicitly with the contemporary language emerging around genetics and behaviour (e.g., Hubbard and Wald, 1993; Kevles, 1997; Lewontin, 1995; Nelkin and Lindee, 1995). Other work views the question of criminality not as a discursive process, but rather as a potentially biological one that has implications for the sociobiology of crime (e.g., Fishbein, 1990; Gibbs, 1995; Kaplan, 2000). In the past, the generally accepted social science explanation for crime causation was a socio-economic one. Today, criminologists are increasingly moving away from that type of explanation. For example, in Canada, the statistical data do not indicate a strong correlation between socio-economic status and criminality among youths (National Council of Welfare, 2000). This shift in perspective certainly opens the door for genetic explanations of criminal tendencies; it is a continuation of the back-and-forth nature/nurture debate.

Clearly, in the study of biotechnology in criminal justice, a number of gaps remain. Research into how genetic science knowledge is legitimated in the courtroom is becoming well developed; however, the political and legal processes by which DNA testing and banking, as biotechnologies, enter into public knowledge remain largely unexplored. Legal scholars focus on courtroom strategies for managing genetic evidence; questions about the more general power/knowledge relations behind these arguments do not enter into their analyses. Finally, although it is difficult to avoid the nature/nurture debate about criminal causation, it is important for social science to step outside the box of that debate and begin to consider the new biotechnologies in terms of governmental processes with certain identifiable characteristics. This book seeks to address these gaps.

A second reason for looking at DNA technology in criminal justice is to ask why it has enjoyed such an easy passage into Canadian society. In the public sphere, other biotechnologies are much more controversial. Commercial products such as Calgene's FlavrSavr tomato (with the gene responsible for decay genetically engineered to be non-functional) and Monsanto's Posilac (a genetically engineered bovine growth hormone injected into cattle to increase milk production) have received considerable public attention. Politicization has been much more extensive in food biotechnologies than in DNA testing and banking. I suggest this is due in part to the distinction between technologies that *intervene* in the body and technologies that *administer* the body. Other factors are involved, however, including fear of crime and the level of comfort our society already has with surveillance technologies. These social enabling factors have helped open the door to genetic surveillance of criminals; they have also helped depoliticize the broader social implications of new surveillance technologies in Canadian society, especially since September 11th.

A third reason for focusing on the DNA data bank and DNA matching is that these technologies have been used in Canada since the late 1980s and have already had a strong impact on criminal justice and social control. Certain fundamental common law principles about the bodily integrity of citizens have been overturned by legislation that allows agents of the state to enter citizens' bodies. This has never been permissible before in Canadian law. DNA sweeps of entire communities have thrown the presumption of innocence into question. Additionally, during the period between the passage of the DNA warrant provisions in the Criminal Code in 1995, and the official opening of the National DNA Data Bank (NDDB) in 2000, there was a significant expansion of the number of designated offences for which an offender might be entered into the data bank. The state cannot help but be tempted to expand the use of this technology for broader surveillance. It is important to maintain a critical social science perspective on these developments in order to analyse their ongoing impact on individual rights and social institutions.

Finally, a significant reason for examining DNA banking and matching as techniques of biogovernance is their role in producing the genetic imaginary. It is interesting to note the mode of critique raised by those groups and individuals who are more concerned about the potential of the technology than they are about its present impact. Specifically, they frame the issue this way: Will the presence of DNA data banks allow researchers to one day identify a genetic complex that produces violent criminality in individuals? This is not possible under the present DNA testing and banking system, but much of the critical discussion focuses on whether it one day could be. Framing the primary critical question in this way moves critique and political reaction into the future and glosses over the current power implications of these practices. It also contributes to the redefinition of criminality as based in nature, not nurture – a redefinition that is already well underway in biological science, government policy, and popular culture.

Risk Society: The Governmental Context

How can social science make theoretical sense of the nascent genetic imaginary – the feeling that we are already living within the future potentials of genetic technology – and the processes now being developed to manage it? Genetic-based biotechnologies are relatively new and are therefore possible rupture points around which existing social

conditions may be called into question. It can be argued that new reproductive technologies are producing new kinship relations and family
structures. New international relationships are forming between governments that wish to control biotechnological developments on the
one hand, and corporate and scientific organizations that wish to have
a free hand in developing the technology on the other hand. New discourses are developing outside of governmental institutions. For example, social movements are being formed to oppose genetically modified
foods, and these movements are resorting to the language of rights and
justice in rejecting the economic rationales of government and business.
New types of actors are appearing as a result of powerful new techniques of knowing and acting; for example, cults and 'rogue' scientists
are actively pursuing human cloning technologies despite official scientific and governmental disapproval, and criminals are developing techniques to circumvent the technologies of DNA identification. In other
words, the new biotechnologies present risks to existing forms of institutional authority. So the question arises: How can we govern the intersection of biotechnology, the public, and the state? The challenges
posed by biotechnology are made even stronger by the increasing role
the notion of 'risk' plays within the governmental rationality of Western
nations. To understand biogovernance, we must first understand the
role that risk management plays in contemporary social governance.

Late modern consciousness has replaced the notion of danger with
that of risk. Danger is characterized by a relatively exact location – one
that allows us to take measures to avert it. Dangers come and go; they
are accidental and external to human effort; they are disturbances outside the otherwise smooth pursuit of our objectives. In contrast, as
Zygmunt Bauman (1999) points out, risks are

> endemic features of our own actions; they are present in and arise from
> whatever we do; they may be perhaps reduced in size, but never extin-
> guished completely. From an 'either-or' situation we have passed to the
> 'and-and' or 'yes, but' condition, the condition of permanent trade-off,
> when gains never come unless accompanied by losses, when we must
> choose not between good and bad solutions, but between greater and
> lesser evils. First and foremost, we may try to calculate the risk involved
> in our undertakings – but no more than in probability terms, which
> means that we can never be quite sure what the outcome of our actions
> will in fact be and whether the precautions we take will not in the end
> bring more harm than benefit. (146–7)

Risk is internal to our actions and is a product of their indeterminate outcomes. Society today is characterized by an increasing governmental preoccupation with the distribution of risks rather than with the management and distribution of social wealth. To show the impact of this development, I explore a set of problematics central to risk society: the origins of risk society, changing perspectives on expert knowledge, a changing relationship between the individual and social institutions, and changing forms of social control.

In terms of origins, risk society emerged from a fundamental process of modernity – the uprooting of local, everyday knowledge and its replacement by technical, expert knowledge systems and symbolic media of exchange. As a result of this process, social relations were removed from their specific time and space contexts and relocated in abstract, distant systems on which virtually everyone has now come to rely. At the end of the twentieth century, these systems became increasingly global in nature at the same time that social, economic, political, and technological change was accelerating. Contrary to the expectations established in early modernity, the more that knowledge developed, the more complex, contradictory, and indeterminate it became. Utopian promises of progress through increasingly certain knowledge and rational control gave way to a permanent sense of anxiety as people pondered the sheer scale of potential calamity if uncertain globalized technological, scientific, and economic systems should fail. Chernobyl, Bhopal, global warming, holes in the ozone layer, reductions in biodiversity, the fires of Kuwaiti oil fields, the AIDS epidemic, and other environmental and human calamities and threats have undermined science's promise to control the impacts of technology and channel them toward progressive outcomes.

In other words, we no longer face dangers so much as risks. As a result, social governance has become a matter of addressing public anxieties rather than public needs. Institutional cohesion and capitalist profitability depend on the use of technologies that are inherently risky. So it is not simply a matter of eliminating the risk-producing qualities of technologies; it must also be determined where responsibility will fall if the risks lead to actual catastrophes. One element of risk society is a shift toward a language of responsibility for risk and away from a language of rights and justice, both of which are about addressing problems of distribution of wealth and power. Risk society also entails a reverse in relations of causation among past, present, and future. The present is no longer determined by the past, but rather by the future and its projected risks. Anxiety about risk results in a preoccupation with future security.

The second problematic of risk analysis is the anxiety-producing relationship between expert knowledge systems and the public at large. According to Ulrich Beck, late modernity is characterized by a general awareness of the contingency of expert knowledge and governmental action. Knowledge is constantly being revised, practitioners are constantly in disagreement, and this erodes trust in our abstract systems of knowledge. Beck and Anthony Giddens refer to this awareness and the cynicism it breeds as 'reflexivity.' Through reflexivity, scientific expertise loses its extra-political status and science becomes an arena for public contention. As science becomes more high-risk, it exposes itself to claims for democratic accountability and societal responsibility.

Intimately tied to the notion of reflexivity is that of trust. When local traditions and knowledge systems were uprooted at the beginning of modernity, trust came to be placed in the abstract systems of knowledge that now dominate modern life. This relationship is characterized by uncertainty; if these systems fail, the repercussions will be monumental. Expert knowledge must win people's trust; that is, it must be aware of risk, and it must demonstrate reliability in the face of contingent outcomes. The public at large has little understanding of the technical details of science and must make a leap of faith when dealing with expert knowledge. But as Giddens (1990) argues, to facilitate that leap of faith, experts must help establish a sense of ontological security, a feeling of confidence in the continuation of self-identity and the social and material environments. Without this psychological (i.e., emotional) basis for security, people will be unable to trust expertise and will face global risks which paralyze action through anxiety and against which they have no local resources to buffer themselves. It is also important to remember Jürgen Habermas's (1971) caution regarding modernity's tendency to separate moral from technical expertise. He argues that this helps reduce public trust in experts; it does so by bringing their motives into question. When scientists no longer couch their pronouncements in a moral language of the social good, when they resort only to the technical language of discovery for its own sake, for technological innovation, or for profit and market competitiveness, how can the public trust scientists to have a proper regard for risk?

A third problematic of risk society relates to the individualization of risk management. In discussing individualization, Beck (1992) is not referring to alienation, but rather to the requirement to produce one's own biography in the face of the breakdown of obligatory and traditional norms and their structuring institutions. Early modernity was driven in part by a rebellion against the authority of premodern traditions and customs; in the same way, late modernity is in part a reaction against the traditions and customs formed through two centuries of modern institutional operation. It entails an apparent freeing of social roles based on gender, class, ethnicity, age, and sexuality through processes of mass education, feminism, changes in the labour market, and so on. Freed from these predetermined roles, the individual becomes more thoroughly self-determined, makes himself or herself the centre of the conduct of life, and assumes multiple and mutable subjectivities. Thus, people face the burden of making more complex and difficult decisions about every aspect of life – sexual identity, work, and family relationships, to name only three.

With the collapse of so many certainties around gender, class, age, ethnicity, and other identity-forming positionings, new risks open up, including unemployment and unstable marriage and family life. These risks are accompanied by intense anxiety and deep insecurity. Life becomes less certain even as it comes under the individual's own control. Social inequalities and class, gender, and ethnicity barriers are still present in the risk society, but they are pushed into the background. As a consequence of individualization and the pervasiveness of a language of responsibility, people increasingly come to feel that their weakened position in society is a result of personal inadequacies, poor decisions, and the inability to cope with the pressures of self-management.

None of this means that institutionalized forms of social control have disappeared. Understanding the changing bases for social control constitutes the fourth problematic of risk analysis. Bauman (1987), writing about developments in class within late modernity, points out that a process of polarization is underway and is producing a class of the 'seduced' and a class of the 'suppressed.' As the task of social co-ordination is transferred more and more to the market, the significant class distinction comes to fall between those who have the capital to participate in the consumer economy and who are seduced into active participation as perpetually unfulfilled consumers, and those who do not have the capital or who are not needed in the economy. This latter group is then circulated to the margins of society, where it remains under government management.

The margins, however, are not what they used to be. No longer are they dangerous and unexplored territories. Developments in information technology and administration make it possible to control population processes that in the past were indeterminable. Colin Gordon (1991) suggests that authorities have improved their ability to identify and code all members of society who manifest a combination of specific factors that have been defined as risky to individuals and/or groups. This enables the state to organize marginality as a zone into which deviants and the underclass can be directed. A number of techniques have emerged for institutionally containing the suppressed class, for fixing its members in space and time, and for directing their energies toward non-risky activities. It is here that risk society converges with the 'crimefare' state (in which the underclass is managed through the criminal justice system; Andreas, 1998) and with the 'workfare' state (in which the underclass is managed through an endless cycle of job-training programs; Shragge, 1997). The remnants of the welfare state are becoming increasingly oppressive as well; the underclass can now be managed through welfare payments conditional on ever tighter surveillance (Fraser and Gordon, 1992).[1]

The suppressed are managed through direct institutional coercion and forms of panopticism; the seduced are managed through the regulation of individual choices. According to Gordon (1991), the aim is to produce self-regulation among autonomous citizens who have been allowed to enter the centres of society. People have more choices when constructing their biographies, but they are still required to exercise power over themselves in their efforts to achieve a state of normality, which is along the route to health and happiness. Normality is defined by forms of expertise that collect aggregate data, which are then used to advise individuals on the proper conduct of their lives. As expert knowledge about risk proliferates, so do the risk avoidance strategies individuals must practise on themselves. To resist these strategies becomes a form of deviance, a declaration of irresponsibility or inability in the care of the self. In this way, risk avoidance becomes a moral enterprise of self-control, self-knowledge, and self-improvement.

More and more, risk avoidance is also something that must be purchased in the marketplace; state welfare-based expertise is becoming market-based expertise. Nikolas Rose (1993) points out that late modernity can be defined in part by the neoliberal strategy of relocating experts from government institutions to market institutions. Today, neoliberalism disciplines individuals and populations by working through market mechanisms and individual consumer choice. Although governments still have a role to play in state processes, the market plays an ever-greater role in eliciting effort, distributing rewards, and positioning people within fields of social power.

A final characteristic of social control in risk society is that a division of labour is developing between knowledge-based expertise and administrative expertise. Robert Castel (1991) argues that the management of individual pathologies and deviance takes on a particular form in risk society. Knowledge experts – or, to use his terminology, therapeutic experts – who work face to face with clients, are relegated to objectifying the characteristics of these individuals through standardized processes of coding. Administrative information managers are now responsible for decisions about the disposition of coded individuals. Decisions are based on the presence or absence of codes that signify risk, and individuals are circulated either to zones of seduction or to zones of suppression according to their codes. In effect, the individual as a unitary subject produced through social, historical, and bodily experience is decontextualized by a set of codes that operate to enhance risk-based decision making on the part of administrative systems.

In summary, risk theorists characterize late modern societies as risk societies distinguished by constant anxiety as public trust in expert knowledge systems decreases through reflexive awareness of the impacts that scientific developments may have on society and nature. Many factors heighten the sense of ontological insecurity that characterizes our time: the social distance between expert knowledge systems and everyday life; the increasingly technical nature of expert knowledge and the gulf between experts and lay people; the inability of research to lead to fixed forms of knowledge on which social utopias could be based; the ongoing separation of moral expertise from technical and administrative expertise; the destabilization of institutions that at one time were instrumental in determining self-identity and life choices; and the individualization of those choices during an era of social, economic, and technological upheaval. At the same time, risk society is characterized by ongoing developments in social control: the polarization of society into classes of seduced and suppressed based on access to the consumer economy; the proliferation of aggregate containment strategies for those defined as marginal; the social management of the seduced through regulation of individual choice by market-based expertise; and the importance of techniques of coding for risk factors in determining the social trajectories of individuals.

Biogovernance

The problematics of risk society frame the governmental context of state approaches to biotechnological developments. Biogovernance arises from the intersection of risk management and biotechnology to produce techniques of state management of biotechnological risks. From this perspective, biotechnologies become the practical modalities through which science operates to mediate, diagnose, manage, and manipulate biological objects. I use the term biotechnology to refer specifically to new technologies that intervene directly at the molecular and genetic levels. These new developments do more than mediate between nature and culture; they have the potential to reshape natural processes in humanity's image.

Biogovernance operates through risk rationality; this means that its core project is not to manage biotechnology, but rather to manage the *risks* of biotechnology. Biogovernance organizes a cluster of pertinent social processes; through these processes and their related techniques, biotechnology and its risks increasingly fall under a system of governance. Biogovernance manifests itself as a set of social practices and leaves its traces in techniques and texts such as government policy statements, media coverage, corporate marketing, scientific publications, and legal analyses relating to a broad array of biotechnologies. My review of these traces suggests that the social processes characterizing biogovernance include the following: privatization, which prescribes the location and management rationality of genetic research and development; politicization, through which often conflictual forces work out issues produced by reflexivity and ontological insecurity; objectification, which defines a set of techniques that open up the gene as a field of intervention and management; normalization, which mobilizes a set of hegemonically negotiated frames that establish the possibilities of meaning; and responsibilization, which individualizes social responsibility for genetic pathologies and defines new forms of subjectivity. It is not inevitable that these processes should come to define the framework and techniques for incorporating biotechnology into society, but these processes flow out of the specific governmental rationality of late modernity.

Privatization

Privatization is a biogovernmental process that defines the proper locus of biotechnological development. As an industry, biotechnology has developed almost completely in the private sector; it is profit-driven in an era of global economic competition. In neoliberal societies, privatization is a generalized process that involves a shifting of expertise to the marketplace. It also involves the state assigning powers of social coordination to market processes. This means that the laws of supply and demand – and those who enforce those laws – determine the disposition of more and more social resources. It also means that corporate models of organizational restructuring (i.e., profit-maximizing models) are generalized to other social institutions, including government departments, educational institutions, health care facilities, prisons, and scientific laboratories. Within neoliberal discourse and current corporate philosophy, market-based institutions are potentially more flexible than government institutions and are better able to manage the risks of the new global economic order. Profitability becomes a defence to accusations of socially and ethically questionable corporate and entrepreneurial practices. Governments undergo a further shift toward purely economic rationality to the exclusion of broader, long-term social planning. Employees are redefined as entrepreneurs who must draw from their own internal resources to produce value on behalf of the corporation. Individual consumers are redefined as 'entrepreneurial customers' operating on a strict instrumental rationality; they are made fully responsible for their life choices, which they must now make in the context of their own consumption practices.

In terms of biotechnology, developments are firmly under corporate control. Biological scientists generally operate as private entrepreneurs located in the market. Even when biotechnological innovations are developed within semipublic institutions such as hospitals and universities, the innovations can be patented by individual scientist-entrepreneurs or by the organization for which they work. The result is a booming genomics industry comprising a number of sectors, some of which are simply potentials at the moment. These sectors include companies that produce computing systems for analysing gene sequences, software service companies that sell databases of genetic information to drug companies and researchers, research companies producing hybridized and cloned plants and animals, and pharmaceutical companies attempting to develop drugs related to gene therapy. This latter group of companies is also involved in 'gene prospecting' – that is, the search for indigenous populations, remote islanders, and traditional religious communities that are geographically or socially isolated and genetically homogenous. Ethnically diverse populations are difficult to study because their greater genetic variation makes it difficult to identify which genes may be involved in disease causation. Homogeneous populations have less genetic 'background noise'; this allows for faster identification of disease-bearing genes.

In one of the best-known examples of gene prospecting, Iceland has recently sold access to its gene pool to deCode Genetics. This Iceland-based genetic research firm will collect data on Icelanders' genetic sequences for the Swiss drug manufacturer Roche Holding, which is paying for the research. Also recently, the South Pacific island nation of Tonga sold the rights to its gene pool to an Australian genetic research firm. Other Pacific nations are poised to cut similar deals. In today's global economy, national gene pools have become just one more commodity to help prop up economically marginal nations.

In the privatization process, the primary technique is biopatenting – that is, placing patents on human and non-human gene sequences that may be involved in disease production or the production of certain physical and behavioural traits. Biopatenting can also mean patenting genetically engineered animals and plants. The number of genetic patents granted increases every year. In 1990, roughly 300 patents for genetic material were granted around the world; in 1999, the number was around 4,200 (Regalado, 2000: 55). Various patents related to the following years, among others, the Alzheimer's gene (patented by Duke University, licensed to Glaxo Wellcome); the blindness gene (patented by Axys Pharmaceuticals); and the obesity gene (patented by Millennium Pharmaceuticals, licensed to Hoffmann–La Roche). Even certain life forms have been patented, including a number of genetically engineered seeds and certain transgenic animals.

One of the most highly publicized Canadian cases of patenting involves the 'Oncomouse' or 'Harvard mouse.' In the early 1980s, researchers at Harvard University developed a process for producing genetically modified mice that are prone to developing cancer and licensed those mice to Du Pont, Inc., for use in cancer research. In 1988 the U.S. Patent Office granted a patent on the mice and their offspring; the European Union and Japan followed suit shortly afterwards. In Canada, however, the case dragged on until finally, in 1995, the Canadian Commissioner of Patents ruled that Harvard could patent the process for producing the mice but could not patent the mice themselves. Harvard appealed that decision to the Federal Court Trial Division, which upheld the Commissioner of Patents' ruling. Harvard then appealed to the Federal Court of Appeal, which in 2000 overturned the findings of the previous hearings and ruled that non-human higher life forms are patentable in Canada. Finally, in December 2002, the Supreme Court of Canada ruled that under the current Patent Act, higher life forms could not be patented. The matter is currently in the hands of Parliament, which will probably act quickly to bring Canada into line with the United States, Europe, and Japan.

From a legal perspective, the issue was the definition of the term 'invention' within the Patent Act. Can living beings be considered 'compositions of matter' and thus subject to invention? From an industry perspective, the argument is that patents are needed to spur innovation and to protect companies and their investors during the R&D phases of innovation. Without patents, there will be no innovations in genetic engineering in Canada. From an ethical perspective, there are concerns that patenting life forms could lead to a weakening of respect for life, generate unforeseen environmental and health risks, and further concentrate economic power in large agribusiness and pharmaceutical corporations. Clearly, Canada needs to clarify its laws and policies relating to the patenting of life forms. However, responsibility for managing the risks of biotechnological development has been placed firmly in the hands of the private sector, and governments are generally loathe to interfere in market processes. The role of government is to create agencies that will promote the biotechnology industry and that will also promote Canadian biotechnological competitiveness in the global economy.[2]

Politicization

Issues relating to public reflexivity, to trust and ontological security, and to private-sector scientific experimentation are addressed through the politicization process. Authority and agency around biotechnology are currently in flux; governments, corporations, the scientific and legal communities, activist organizations, and the public at large are typing to negotiate the social meanings of biotechnologies, produce relations of trust, legitimate biotechnological security, and distribute responsibility for biotechnological risk. This is where agency manifests itself in ways that cannot be completely managed by the state. An alliance of government, business, and scientific elites has initiated the coming genetic revolution, but that alliance has not yet earned complete public trust. As result, political reaction to biotechnology is arising from the public, through citizens' groups, rather than from threatened ruling elites. This constitutes a break from society's past experience with scientific developments. Reflexivity, combined with higher levels of education than in the past, means that people today are better able to imagine the potential impacts of biotechnologies on health, food, and the environment. Also, public opinion today has a greater impact on how science and social issues are discussed. Changing notions of democracy, and instruments such as the Charter of Rights and Freedoms, have done much to produce a political culture in Canada in which individuals and groups are more aware of their right to promote their own views on scientific and social questions, be it through legal mechanisms or through activism.

Reflexivity also means that scientific truth claims based strictly on scientific evidence and proof are no longer adequate to win public trust. Activists are mobilizing conflicting expertise, including scientific expertise which contradicts that of the biotechnology industry. The increasingly technical nature of scientific research and the decrease in ethical expertise has robbed scientists of a language for responding to hypothetical risks proposed by public interest groups. For example, one genetic scientist responded in this way to concerns over patenting and the use of animals in genetic experimentation:

> Objections to the production or the patenting of transgenic animals are based largely on metaphysical convictions or on purely hypothetical dangers, and they have so far not been persuasive to most Americans or their elected representatives. This powerful new approach to improving livestock has produced transgenic fish, mice, rabbits, swine, sheep, goats, and cattle, and more will follow. A more serious impediment to the benefits of genetic engineering is the growth of an animal welfare movement that presses for excessively stringent regulation of research with animals, and an animal rights movement that objects to all use of animals to serve human society – now in research, tomorrow no doubt in agriculture. (Loew, 1991: 129)

The 'metaphysical' and 'hypothetical' concerns raised by critics of certain types of genetic science applications are here dismissed as frivolous, poorly informed, unpopular, and contrary to the need for efficiency in livestock production.

Such dismissals may be premature. Recent polls suggest that Canadians continue to be uneasy about the most highly publicized forms of biotechnological innovation. For example, 68 per cent of Canadians stated they would be less likely to buy food products labelled as having genetically modified ingredients (McIlroy, 2000: A2). Also, a 'vast majority' of Canadians oppose cloning humans, although around 75 per cent of respondents to a survey considered it acceptable to clone organs for transplantation (Canadian Press, 2001). Many activist groups are calling for democratic accountability and for public review processes for genetic research. Biological science has become an arena of contention as a result of public concern over the potential intimate contact it implies and its presence in the everyday worlds of medical practice, reproductive decision making, food consumption, and criminal justice.

There are two main reasons why issues surrounding the politicization of genetic science have not yet been resolved. The first relates to the different languages used by the parties in conflict – that is, by activists and by science/government/industry. Activists employ a language of rights and justice when pressing their interest in biotechnological controls; they draw from essentialist moral claims. In contrast, science, government, and industry employ the risk-based language of responsibility and focus on practical questions of how to distribute the risks of biotechnology. When these frameworks collide, little dialogue ensues.[3]

A second reason relates to the absence of an appropriate forum for mediating political conflicts around biotechnologies. Neither legislatures nor the courts are addressing the issues in definitive ways. One could argue that this is for the best, since the issues as presented by competing interests often become fundamental ontological questions of life and death, nature and culture. Neoliberal governments, with their economic frame of decision-making, may well not be the best bodies for addressing these questions. The legal system may also be inappropriate because it operates on a case-by-case basis and tends to make decisions according to technical legal rules, at least when a clear policy direction from government is lacking. Furthermore, as Christian Byk (1999) points out, legal systems are currently undermined by four processes: the increasingly broad diversity of interests to be taken into account; the loss of moral authority of legal doctrine and its substitution by the concept of expertise; the binding rules of international agreements; and international diversity regarding how these rules are enforced in different forums. These developments certainly apply in the case of biotechnology, which involves a global industry, a number of competing claims, and scientific expertise in conflict with legal expertise.

Conflicting language frames and the lack of a forum mean there is little mediation of the growing conflict over biotechnological development. Instead, this conflict manifests itself as a series of incidents between activist organizations on the one hand and corporate and governmental organizations on the other. Often, conferences to discuss international agreements on biotechnological conventions (or simply general trade talks) become arenas for clashes between the two groups. Their interaction is mainly with the media rather than with each other; the two sides stage spectacles and declare their positions in incompatible languages and images. At present, politicization as an element of biogovernance is limited to an oppositional politics with little room for dialogue.[4]

Objectification

I employ the notion of objectification to describe the epistemological production of biogovernance – that is, the means by which biogovernmental knowledge is produced. This involves a set of techniques for rendering the gene visible and open to management, techniques that include mapping, testing, coding, banking, simulating, and predicting. Such techniques are quintessentially modern in their ends – knowledge and power, representing and intervening, understanding and reforming. These ends and means are built into the modern process of biogovernance. In his analysis of the implications of the Human Genome Project, Paul Rabinow (1992) argues that these techniques imply a rejection of the philosophy of naturalism inherited from the Hellenic Greeks. Naturalism elevates the productions of nature above those of humanity because nature has its own internal and automatic generation system. Human works do not, and require continual human manufacture in order to generate more. The divide between nature and human society is unbreached by human production. New biotechnologies promise to bridge that divide and to bring nature fully into culture by rendering the gene visible and opening it to artificial transformation to produce human-defined outcomes through automatic reproduction. At the very least, they promise to bring nature and culture together by industrializing both and subjecting them to the same techniques.

Bruce Mazlish (1993) referred to four scientific 'discontinuities' that decentred humanity and desacralized its inner and outer workings. This decentring is one of the defining characteristics of modernity and includes the following: Copernicus's heliocentric model of the solar system, which suggested that the earth is not central to creation and that the workings of the cosmos can be understood through a mechanical metaphor; Darwin's definition of the processes by which living creatures evolve over time, which ultimately overthrew the creationist model of the origins of life; Freud's mapping of the human psyche, which suggested that the mind can be understood by applying mechanistic principles; and the computer revolution, which has disprivileged humans in their relationship to machines and which holds out the possibility that there is a continuum between machine intelligence and human intelligence. I suggest that the genetic revolution is the fifth discontinuity, insofar as it paves the way for the direct manipulation of the fundamental organizing principles of all life.

The preliminary steps of the genetic revolution – mapping, testing, coding, banking, simulating, and predicting – are already well under way, and early forms of genetic transformation are beginning as well. Besides the obvious example of the Human Genome Project, which has completed mapping the human genome, scientists have begun to code a number of genetically based diseases, including Alzheimer's disease, Huntington's disease, and certain forms of cancer. They are even mapping certain behavioural problems such as the 'suicide gene.' In 2000, researchers at the Royal Ottawa Hospital announced that after ten years of research, they had discovered a genetic defect linked to suicidal thoughts. Their hope is that a simple blood test will identify people at risk of killing themselves (Kirkey, 2000: A17). The search is now on to determine how to manipulate genes in order to cure these diseases and their resulting behaviours. Carlos Novas and Nikolas Rose (2000) suggest that these processes of objectification are producing a 'molecular optic' through which to understand human subjectivity. This optic provides a means for surveying and predetecting human conditions, for determining future risk, and for reducing complex behaviours to visible biological 'facts' for both individuals and aggregates. This is the goal of objectification – to detect latent conditions and to predict possible outcomes. Only in this way can genetic risk be contained.

Normalization

Normalization describes a set of techniques employed by government, business, and science to manage public discussion and to render biotechnologies legitimate, normal, and secure. It includes practices of consulting, social marketing, and legislating. Consulting involves identifying experts and stakeholders and mobilizing them to build a consensus. This consensus may not be achieved, but it doesn't have to be; the real purpose of this effort is to reach a hegemonic consensus on the issues that frame the debate. In chapter 3, I will examine how the consultation processes around DNA warrants and DNA banking in Canada involved primarily experts from law enforcement, government, and the legal community; although these experts disagreed over the parameters of DNA technology in criminal justice, they never challenged the starting assumption that this technology should be employed. Those who did raise that issue – most notably women's groups – were quickly marginalized.

Social marketing involves establishing governmental and corporate agencies to manage public discussion through monologic marketing techniques while avoiding dialogic processes of public debate and full public consultation. Thus, in developing the Canadian Biotechnology Strategy report (1998), the Minister of Industry consulted mainly business and scientific stakeholders to produce a public document, which began with this statement: 'Biotechnology is one of the world's fastest-growing technologies. It offers significant economic benefits, particularly in exports and job creation, as well as important health, safety and environmental benefits' (Industry Canada, 1998: 1). The sentiments behind this report were echoed in a series of television and magazine advertisements in 2001 – ads prepared by the Council for Biotechnology Information. One magazine read: 'Biotechnology is helping him protect the land and preserve his family's heritage.' The went on to detail how soybean farmer Rod Gangwish was growing a new type of soybean that required less tilling and allowed him to preserve topsoil. It pointed out how other kinds of crops were benefiting from biotechnology and how we were all benefiting generally from developments in health-related biotechnology (in *Scientific American*, July 2001: 5).

Through legislating, governments fix definitions and regulations – but only if necessary. The pattern is that governments avoid making decisions until lobbyists force their hand. Governments see little short-term benefit to legislating on biotechnological issues. Regulation will bring down the wrath of the business community; non-regulation may well provoke a public that is already suffering from ontological insecurity about these new technologies. Often, however, an absence of action is a choice in itself. When the Canadian government refused to endorse the 1999 Biosafety Protocol in Cartagena, it was acting out of concern that a requirement to label genetically modified foods might hurt the profits of Canada's agriculture industry. Thus it refused to act; this benefited the industry although it failed to address the public's demand for labelling. The same seems to be happening with the Oncomouse case;

the legislature seems content to leave it up to the courts to regulate ownership of genetically modified higher life forms, despite calls from a number of parties – including the courts themselves – to legislate on the matter. The government has been accused of 'dragging its feet' on the Proposed Legislation for Governing Assisted Human Reproduction – legislation that would regulate and limit the types of technologies and procedures allowable for reproductive purposes (Gray, 2001).

Authorities use these normalizing techniques to mediate the risks of biotechnologies and to generate technological optimism. Normalization processes construct frames for understanding social impacts; they also place limits on public debate. However, this exclusion of the public is done in such a way that it is legitimate – representatives from the established hierarchy of knowledge mobilize to advocate use of the technology, while governments and corporations speak to representatives of public and expert interests to ensure that 'all' voices are heard. In this way, normalization is also a means for addressing calls for democratic process. The goal is to foster public trust by giving the appearance of risk awareness and sensitivity to the need for ontological security. To date, however, Canadian regulators have not inspired much public trust. A 1999 poll indicated that about 25 per cent of Canadians felt that the government was doing a 'poor' job of managing biotechnology, 55 per cent felt it was doing a 'fair' job; only 20 per cent felt it was doing a 'good' job. The same study also noted a decline in public perceptions of government performance in recent years (Pollara and Earnscliffe Research, reported in May 1999). Media analyst Edna Einsiedel (1997) conducted a national survey and found that the most trusted sources of information on biotechnology in Canada tend to be environmental and consumer organizations, university faculties, and medical professionals. Pollara and Earnscliffe found that Canadians do not trust the stakeholders involved in genetically modified food production to provide accurate information (reported in May 1999). The public tends to perceive scientists, businesspeople, and governments as influenced by corporate funding. Obviously, normalization of biotechnologies is a complex and ongoing hegemonic process that may always be incomplete.

Responsibilization

The term responsibilization was first coined by criminologists to define current policy initiatives around crime management (Garland, 1996; O'Malley, 1992). This view of crime is premised on the belief that the best way to control it is to simply assume that everyone is a potential criminal. This perspective flows out of neoliberal assumptions about human behaviour – that it is motivated by cost/benefit analysis. A person who sees an unchained bicycle on the sidewalk will consider whether the benefits of stealing it outweigh the consequences of being caught. If this is how criminality operates, the best means of controlling it must be to push responsibility for crime control onto each individual. It is the individual citizen's responsibility to ensure that he or she does not create the conditions for being victimized. Bicycles must always be chained, dangerous neighbourhoods must always be avoided, large amounts of money must never be carried, and women must never go out alone after dark. If you fail to take this responsibility, you are responsible for your own victimization.

I suggest that the concept of responsibilization can be profitably employed to describe an effect of biogovernance. The processes of privatization, politicization, objectification, and normalization operate together to individualize responsibility for managing genetic pathology; they do so by defining biotechnologies as questions of consumer choice, by calling into question institutional political responsibility for risk, and through processes of objectification that cast genetic risks as calculable and as present within the genetic sequences of individuals. Rabinow (1992) suggests that notions of individualized genetic responsibility will also lead to 'biosociality' – that is, new social groupings or communities of interest based on shared genetic coding, with their own specialists, laboratories, narratives, traditions, and pastoral keepers.

Since Rabinow's article was published, the World Wide Web has very quickly brought this prediction into effect. A random search for sites related to Huntington's disease, a genetically produced disease, turned up 289 websites. The sites are of a variety of types. For example, the Kansas University Medical Center, Department of Neurology, provides a site with information on the following issues: abuse of the patient, behaviour, communication strategies, disability, eating and swallowing, the genetics of Huntington's disease, home safety, safe sleeping arrangements, tube feeding, and help for school reports. It also has a link to 'Faces of Huntington's, a wonderful look at Huntington's disease through the words of people with Huntington's disease and those who are close to them.' A social worker, Catherine Kendall, offers e-therapy for Huntington's sufferers and their families on her website. She and her clients meet on-line on a regular basis in a secure chat room. Shana Martin, a young woman whose mother has Huntington's disease and who has a 50 per cent chance of acquiring the disease herself, has established a website on which she tells her story and provides information on the disease. These are some of the forms that biosociality, communication, and interaction can take as a result of new technologies and shared communities of interest.

A genetically defined form of subjectivity does not necessarily lead to fatalism; it can also generate an imperative to act in the present to manage future risks. The individual is not responsible for acquiring the genetic condition but *is* responsible for managing the personal and social impacts of that condition. If genetic therapy ever reaches the point where genetic disease can be eliminated through biotechnological intervention, other implications will follow. A potential risk here is the power to manipulate genes may lead to demands for a 'right to normalcy' (Rapp, 1999). This 'new eugenics' would empower expert definitions of normality and cast them in the language of individual biomedical rights. The belief that the 'normal' can be objectified and individually selected lies at the heart of eugenics. This belief is bound up with individual responsibility for arbitrating normality, and it contributes to an extreme reduction of all problematic differences to an individual and genetic basis.

To characterize the effects of biotechnology and biogovernance as eugenic may be alarmist, and it seems unlikely that new genetic technologies will lead to excesses such as institutionalization, sterilization, and even genocide – all of these the legacies of the early-twentieth-century eugenics movement. But if this does transpire, we may never even know, because the fallout will not occur within a top-down command model of state directives and police coercion, except within the containment zones of the suppressed. Rather, it will occur within a model of individual choice based on risk assessment, market opportunities, and the desire to be normal. Its records will not be centralized in state databases; rather, they will be diffused through the private and confidential databases of individual medical practitioners. Holocausts could occur and we would not even know, because they would be the result of millions of individual choices.

Through processes of privatization, politicization, objectification, normalization, and responsibilization, biogovernance produces a regime for managing the risks of biotechnology in the twenty-first century. These processes operate through a set of techniques that fix the gene as an ontological object; that place genetic expertise largely within the marketplace; that open political contestation over scientific, business, ethical, and human rights issues; that promote ontological security in terms of biotechnological innovation; and that produce a molecular optic that increasingly places responsibility for genetic risk on the individual/consumer. Within the Canadian criminal justice system, biogovernance takes on specific characteristics through DNA testing and banking technologies.

In the United States, privatization involves moving forensic DNA testing and banking into the corporate sector. In Canada the process is more subtle than this; it involves importing corporate rationales of efficiency, productivity, and flexibility into the management of the DNA data bank as well as searching for patentable intellectual property assets that can be developed through the operation of the data bank. In terms of politicization, the primary relationship regarding these technologies is not between the public and the scientific community or the government; rather, it is between competing legal and scientific forms of expertise within the criminal justice system. Objectification proceeds through the structuring of forensic DNA testing and population genetics as knowledge systems that promise to find the ultimate objective identifier – one that will allow us to circumvent the vagaries of testimony, memory, trustworthiness, self-interest, and courtroom tactics. Normalization proceeds through public policy statements and popular culture sources that represent DNA testing and banking as effective, objective, and secure – as the ultimate risk management technology in crime control. There has been little debate over whether these technologies should be employed; rather, the debate has been over how far should they go. Finally, responsibilization involves a growing tendency toward explaining crime through biological characteristics – a further individualization of crime management. Increasingly, the goal of criminal justice policy is to promote techniques of predetecting crime and responsibilizing the at-risk individual to manage any predisposition toward crime or any potential for being victimized. Although criminal genes may never be identified, I suggest that DNA testing and banking are the first steps toward the production of a genetic justice system that makes certain assumptions about criminality and that has certain future trajectories built into it.

A Methodological Note

How does one go about studying a set of processes of meaning making and representation when these processes are still very much under construction? What are the observable traces of the genetic imaginary, a set of cultural and social understandings that exist largely in the future? These are the methodological challenges of this book. Because I wish to examine a process of meaning making and representation largely through the textual traces of their production, I employ qualitative text-based methods as my primary entry into these questions. Specifically, I am interested in how ideas and images about genetic technologies are constructed within government, scientific, legal and media sites and in the possibilities of meaning they produce. This is a large question, of course, so I utilize a case study approach to focus on a particular site of biogovernance, the criminal justice system. However, I also argue that the characteristics of biogovernance that I have defined describe the fundamental processes by which biotechnologies of various sorts are entering into society.

My primary object of analysis is the textual productions of institutions and organizations involved in deployment of DNA technology in the Canadian criminal justice system in order to understand how they order knowledge. I utilize media framing analysis, critical legal analysis, archival research, and methods of literary analysis to read the public sphere texts produced by the actors involved in biogovernmental processes around DNA banking and testing in Canada. Through these methods, I develop a picture of the institutional and textual methods for framing the meanings around DNA banking and testing as they enter Canadian society.

This book explores the techniques of biogovernance at work within the Canadian criminal justice system. DNA data banking and testing, like other forms of biotechnology, reflect the techniques of privatization, politicization, normalization, objectification, and responsibilization either directly, through their presence, or more indirectly, through their absence. In chapter 2, I examine the DNA data bank and DNA testing procedures employed in forensic laboratories and discuss the technological, social, and legal contexts which form the enabling conditions that allow the Canadian state to implement these biogovernmental techniques. I consider why these techniques have entered into Canadian society in such an unproblematic and unheralded manner.

In chapter 3, I examine the normalizing techniques employed by the Canadian government in the process of implementing the DNA data bank, DNA warrants, and DNA testing. Who were the critical stakeholders in the policy process? How was a consensus reached on the problematics involved? What frames were invoked to delimit debate? In the case of the DNA data bank and warrants, the government has had to take more decisive action than with other biotechnologies, fixing them in legislation in order to ensure that past legal frameworks cannot override them. As a result, the discourse of criminal justice has moved farther away from individual rights and closer toward public safety.

In chapter 4, I argue that the government-sponsored normalization process described in chapter 3 was not about informing the public and did not have that effect, nor did news media coverage of the consultation process. Rather, DNA in criminal justice entered the public imaginary through popular media. Specifically, Canadians have learned about it through a series of sensational media events – the trials of Guy Paul Morin and David Milgaard. DNA testing and banking have been normalized primarily through popular media rather than through state-driven processes, and they are generally represented as a corrective to the inherent flaws of the adversarial legal system.

In chapter 5, I explain the functioning of the National DNA Data Bank at the RCMP forensics laboratory in Ottawa. What image of genetics is at work in defining the gene as something open to observation and intervention? How do laboratory techniques objectify DNA and convert it into evidence? How effective has the DNA data bank been in terms of the numbers of matches that have been made and the rate of arrests and prosecutions based on DNA evidence? What role do human operators play in producing DNA evidence? A tension exists between the narrative of objective DNA analysis and the role of human operators in interpreting results. How is this tension elided from the dominant narrative of DNA analysis to produce reliability?

In chapter 6 I examine the impact that biogovernmental processes are having on criminal justice in Canada. I argue that DNA testing and banking have rationalized the criminal justice system. This has occurred through the particular forms that politicization and privatization take around this particular kind of technology. Politicization involves a contest for institutional supremacy between scientific and legal expertise, with the objective forms of scientific knowledge gaining preference. Privatization involves importing corporate rationalities of efficiency, flexibility, and customer service into criminal justice. DNA technologies contribute to these processes, but is this an appropriate rationale for criminal justice?

In chapter 7, I conclude the book by returning to the genetic imaginary and examining how the enabling conditions and use of DNA technologies in criminal justice contribute to a shift in thinking about the origins of criminality. I suggest that in government, criminology, and popular culture, the thinking about the causes of criminality is shifting away from nurture and back toward nature. This is the ultimate effect of biogovernance in criminal justice. As a result of privatization, politicization, normalization, objectification, and responsibilization, responsibility for criminal justice is coming to be located in experts and institutions tasked with predetecting and containing criminal risk before it manifests itself as a danger. This is the future of crime control, and the DNA data bank is both a symbol of and a step toward that future.

Throughout these chapters, I tell the story of DNA testing and data banking in terms of their institutional development and also in terms of the processes of meaning making employed to manage the risks they pose to the Canadian public. I argue that through biogovernmental processes of privatization, politicization, objectification, normalization, and responsibilization, DNA testing and banking are coming to be defined as secure biotechnologies that will produce enhanced security from dangerous criminals. At the same time, they are contributing to an erosion of certain individual rights within the criminal justice system and opening the door to an increased level of surveillance and police power, the outcomes of which remain to be seen.

2 Creating the Conditions of Possibility: Scientific, Social, and Legal Contexts

In 1983, in a town in Leicester, England, a young woman was sexually assaulted and murdered. Three years later, in 1986, in a neighbouring town, another young woman suffered the same fate. In the intervening years, however, there had been a revolution in crime detection. In 1985, Alec Jeffreys and a team of geneticists at the University of Leicester reported a technique for DNA testing of forensic evidence. All men of a certain age range in the three surrounding communities were asked to submit to DNA testing, but no matches were found to the seminal material left at the crime scenes. The case was solved when someone overheard one man telling others in a pub that he had been paid to stand in for another man during the DNA testing. After questioning the witness from the pub, the police learned the identity of the man who had eluded the DNA net. His name was Colin Pitchfork, and he was apprehended and tested for a DNA match. He became the first person in the annals of criminal justice to be convicted through DNA matching.

In Britain and North America, DNA identification technology in criminal justice developed and spread within a set of contexts that enabled its rapid and unproblematic diffusion. By 'context' I mean the established values, beliefs, expectations, and cultural narratives concerning technology, crime, and law. In this chapter I identify three broad contexts – technological, social, and legal – within which DNA testing and banking technology entered Canadian society. These could have conflicted with one another, but ultimately they did not. The technology passed fairly smoothly into society, in contrast to some other types of biotechnology regarding which science, the public, and the law have competing definitions and expectations. Developments that preceded DNA testing and banking opened the way to their ready acceptance.

The Technological Context

For a number of reasons, DNA identification resonates powerfully in Western culture. This is partly because genetics is widely perceived as a prestigious and even 'charismatic' science. Like charismatic political authority as described by Max Weber, genetic science seems to have special powers to affect our relationship with our surroundings. The molecular scientists who manipulate these powers are seen as having a miraculous ability to create new forms of life and new ways of producing life that did not previously exist in nature. In the early twenty-first century, genetic science offers some of the benefits that religious belief held in other times and places. Nelkin and Lindee contend that in popular culture, DNA acts as

> a secular equivalent of the Christian soul. Independent of the body, DNA appears to be immortal. Fundamental to identity, DNA seems to explain individual differences, moral order, and human fate. Incapable of deceiving, DNA seems to be the locus of the true self, therefore relevant to the problems of personal authenticity posed by a culture in which the 'fashioned self' is the body manipulated and adorned with the intent to mislead. In many popular narratives, individual characteristics and the social order both seem to be direct transcriptions of a powerful, magical, and even sacred entity, DNA. (3)

The science that allows us to know our DNA holds a special place in our society. We live in an era of genetic optimism. Many of the promises that genetics makes have not yet come to pass, but neither have many of its pitfalls. In terms of detection and surveillance in criminal justice, DNA promises to provide the ultimate identifier – something that has been sought after since the very beginnings of modernity.

The Culture of the Trace

Before the late nineteenth century, the only generally available trace of an individual was his or her signature. But around that time, various systems of human classification were developed, each of them premised on the notion that science could use peripheral traces to find something unique about any individual. Ann Joseph and Alison Winter (1996) refer to this development as the beginnings of the 'culture of the trace' in crime detection. Behind this development lay the assumption that individuals are constantly shedding bodily clues that can be linked back to them and their actions by scientific experts. In the early nineteenth century, identification systems could only classify people into types; they could not be used to identify uniquely individual qualities. Such systems included physiognomy (the attribution of mental qualities to facial structure) and phrenology (the attribution of moral and intellectual characteristics based on skull contours).

In the 1870s, Alphonse Bertillon invented anthropometry. Bertillon was a clerk in the Parisian Sûreté, and his new system was a means for identifying individuals by measuring certain of their body parts, including the head (length and width), the left foot, the middle finger, and the ear (all length), and the chest. All of these measurements were recorded on a single card. Anthropometry was soon adopted around the world, including in Canada. As a system, Bertillonage (as it was called) had serious flaws. Those taking the measurements had varying levels of skill, and this led to unreliable results. In the United States in the famous 1903 case of the two Will Wests, two men with the same name and similar anthropometric measurements were mistaken for each other.[1] Also, the system was really only useful after a crime was solved. Criminals rarely leave records of head length at a crime scene.

The real revolution in crime detection through bodily traces was the development of fingerprinting, or dactyloscopy. Fingerprinting was not a new practice. For centuries in Asia, people had been signing contracts with palm-prints or fingerprints, and works of art had been identified with fingerprints for just as long. This came to the attention of European colonial agents in the nineteenth century, most notably William Herschel, an employee of the East India Company. Herschel studied the uses of fingerprinting extensively and in 1877 recommended to the British Inspector General of Indian Prisons that it be adopted to stop widespread local practices such as the impersonation of dead pensioners or the hiring of others to serve prison sentences (Wright Mercer, 1995: 25). His idea was rejected. Not until 1895, when noted eugenicist Sir Francis Galton published a scientific study of fingerprinting titled *Fingerprint Directories* did police authorities begin to grant credence to the new science. Galton was the first to calculate that no two people's fingerprints were alike, and he devoted a number of years to promoting this system of criminal identification. Yet, the first murder trial using fingerprint evidence did not take place in England, but rather in Argentina in 1892. Five years later, Sir Edward Henry, Inspector General of Police in Nepal and India, developed a system for filing and retrieving large numbers of fingerprints. A system now existed for recording and filing fingerprints, and in 1901, Scotland Yard established its Fingerprint Branch.

Canada moved fairly quickly to embrace fingerprinting for criminal identification. It was pioneered in this country by Inspector Edward Foster of the Dominion Police.[2] Sent to guard an exhibit of Canadian gold at the 1904 Saint Louis World Fair, he attended a talk by Detective John Ferrier of Scotland Yard, a fingerprint expert. Foster studied under Ferrier, but when he returned to Canada he found that politicians, judges, and lawyers were ambivalent about the new technology. With the support of the Commissioner of Police, Sir Percy Sherwood, Foster convinced the government in 1908 to pass an order-in-council, allowing for the use of fingerprinting under the Identification of Criminals Act of 1898. Yet little was done to support the new technology until 1910, when a fugitive who had killed a constable six years earlier was finally captured. The public was outraged that he had never been fingerprinted or photographed, and the justice minister hastily established the Canadian Criminal Identification Bureau with Foster as its head.

The shift from anthropometry to fingerprinting was more than an enhancement of technology; it also marked a shift in notions of evidence. Anthropometry determined identity as a product of the whole – as a series of measurements from which a human body could be reconstructed. Fingerprinting promised a more precise identification from a small part that had no role in the individual's overall physical or moral character. Fingerprints are unique, and that is their strength. Dactylography marked the beginning of the culture of the trace, the idea that unconscious detectable traces surround people and can be used to construct narratives explaining past events and the nature of an individual. From this perspective, truth can be determined provided that two requirements are met: first, involuntary evidence has been deposited, and second, this evidence can be tied uniquely to a certain individual or crime (Joseph and Winter, 1996: 200). The linking of evidence to the individual can take two forms. First, there is a unique connection between a clue and a certain individual or crime, as in fingerprinting. Second, the unconscious trace carries an essential aspect of the individual who produced it. The goal of forensic science has been to find an ideal basis for establishing the second type of link.

Since the turn of the last century a number of attempts have been made to develop biometric forms of identification. Fingerprinting was the first, but research continues into a host of others. For example, identification based on the iris of the eye is currently popular. No two iris patterns are the same (also, no individual's left and right irises are the same). The iris has 266 measurable characteristics; fingerprints have only 40. Face recognition technology is already in use. The Mr Payroll cash machines in the southern United States utilize face recognition to verify customer identity. Face recognition systems measure fifty points around the nose, mouth, eyebrows, jaw, and other facial areas, and computers have been programmed to allow for shifts in facial expression. Voice recognition technology is the least accurate biometric system because it has a behavioural component – that is, voices change with shifts in mood as well as physical condition. Voice recognition operates on the principle of plotting a voice's frequencies every hundredth of a second and producing a graph of the sound. Hand technology, as distinct from fingerprinting, is the last of the major biometric systems; this measures the size and shape of individual fingers and knuckles as well as the overall size of the hand in three dimensions. When one presses one's hand against a scanner, the image is compared to a database of qualified users. Although less accurate than fingerprinting, iris identification, or face recognition, border crossing agencies are developing this technology for detecting undesirable visitors (Schlesinger, 1999: 58).

All of these forms of biometric identification are still in use and still being researched. However, they are being threatened with obsolescence by DNA identification. Although often referred to as DNA 'fingerprinting,' this new technology is not simply another form of biometric identification – rather, it is a new forensic paradigm with tremendous authority. Other forms of identification are powerful insofar as they involve something unique to the individual, but they do not contain a person's essence. DNA identification accomplishes the ultimate goal of the culture of the trace – it traps an essential aspect of the individual who produced it, a map of a person's fundamental characteristics.

DNA Identification

Alec Jeffreys, who invented DNA forensic testing, first spoke publicly about his discovery in late 1984, after a series of tests he and his team conducted at the University of Leicester. Their experiments involved members of a family, from whom tissue, blood, and semen samples were taken to test simple inheritance, the constancy of the genetic map in different types of cells from the same person, and the sensitivity of the procedure. They also tested three-year-old blood and semen samples from police storage to determine the effects of sample degradation on DNA. Next, they tested a variety of animals and fish. In each of these tests, the procedure succeeded in producing an identifying code. Jeffreys delayed publishing his results until he had received patents on his techniques. When he published the results in 1985, he claimed that the likelihood of two people, even siblings (with the exception of identical twins), having the same DNA pattern was unimaginably remote. He went on to state that the procedure would prove highly effective in crime detection, since it required only a minute sample of biological material from the crime scene.

That claim was soon tested in Jeffreys's own backyard. As noted earlier, in 1983 a teenage girl had been sexually assaulted and murdered near Leicester. In 1986 a very similar crime took place in a nearby village. The police decided to utilize the new technology by asking all males between seventeen and thirty-four in three neighbouring villages to submit blood samples for DNA testing. Although the DNA dragnet did not capture the killer, his guilt was verified by Jeffreys's technique.

The DNA matching technique developed by Jeffreys is referred to as the restriction fragment length polymorphism (RFLP) method. It involves chemically extracting DNA from a sample and then employing enzymes called restriction endonucleases to cut the DNA into fragments. These fragments are placed in a sieving gel and separated according to size through electrophoresis (i.e., the application of an electric current that causes pieces of different molecular weight and electrical charge to move at different rates). The charged molecules move to different points in the gel and stop. Once separated, the fragments are blotted onto a nylon membrane. There, they are combined with DNA probes. These probes are single-stranded pieces of DNA that have been separated into fragments and made radioactive. When placed on the membrane, they combine with complementary bases in the target DNA. X-ray film is then placed on the membrane to record the radioactive probe pattern. The result is an image similar to a bar code, referred to by Jeffreys as a DNA 'fingerprint.' This image can be analysed visually by an expert examiner or by computer imaging analysis. In this way, DNA fragments are rendered visible to scientists and can be compared to other DNA samples to see how well the 'bar codes' match. RFLP analysis can be applied to any substance containing genetic material and has a high degree of individual discrimination. It has some drawbacks, however, including the need for relatively large quantities of genetic material (as compared to later developments). Also, various things such as fungal or bacterial decay can destroy the long sections of DNA needed for RFLP analysis.

These types of problems have been solved in part by another development in DNA testing technology known as polymerase chain reaction (PCR). PCR involves placing DNA in a small machine resembling a microwave oven, heating the DNA until it begins to melt and the two strands separate, cooling it to enable each strand to build complementary pairs, then repeating the heating and cooling cycle to double the amount of DNA each time. Polymerases are a class of enzymes involved in building new strands of DNA. The polymerase used in the PCR machine is from bacteria that live in hot-water springs; this means it can function at the near–boiling point temperatures required to split DNA molecules. Polymerases act as primers to initiate the building of new genes. The inventor of the PCR process, Kerry Mullis, won a Nobel prize for his research in 1993.[3] PCR can produce millions of copies of a DNA molecule within hours, so its usefulness in criminal identification is obvious – only a very small sample of DNA is required for matching because it can be copied as much as necessary.

A third key development in DNA matching technology is short tandem repeat (STR) analysis. STR differs fundamentally from RFLP in that it uses an idiosyncrasy of DNA for identification. DNA contains repeating blocks called short tandem repeats. Their biological function is unknown. In forensic science, they are very useful because different repeats occur in differing lengths and the same repeats vary in length between individuals. Furthermore, the frequency of different STR lengths varies among different ethnic groups. Thus, some lengths will be common in some groups and rare in others. When PCR is used to amplify lengths of DNA that contain STRs, a profile can be created based on the differences among individuals relating to repetitions of some sequences. The strength of STR analysis is that it can be performed on very small samples – far smaller than with the RFLP method. Also, it works better on old fragments, even DNA attacked by bacteria and fungi. However, it is extremely sensitive, which means that contamination can be a problem. This was an important factor in the O.J. Simpson murder trial, during which defence lawyers pointed out the sloppy handling of crime scene DNA evidence. Nevertheless, the STR method is now the standard in forensic DNA testing.

Very briefly, these are the technological tools available to forensic scientists in the investigation of crime. For both scientific and cultural reasons, they are extremely powerful identifiers. Consequently, DNA identification methods have been controversial from the very beginning, not just for social and legal reasons but also for scientific ones. As DNA testing spread from England in 1986 to the United States in 1987 to Canada in 1988 and elsewhere, a series of controversies accompanied it within the scientific community. Interestingly not one of the controversies specifically questioned the science and technology. Rather, they all centred on how to properly present DNA evidence in the courtroom to avoid prejudicing judges and juries.

Population Genetics

The first and most significant controversy in the scientific community involved population genetics. DNA matching is only the first part of the process of identifying a criminal. The second involves applying population genetics statistics to consider the probability that someone other than the suspect could match the DNA profile found at the crime scene. In the United States, controversies over how to interpret a DNA match led the National Academy of Sciences to form a National Research Council Committee, chaired by a prominent geneticist, Eric Lander. In 1992 this committee produced a report, *DNA Technology in Forensic Science*, which made several recommendations regarding the need to define standards for laboratory work as well as standards for calculating the odds that an apparent match between a suspect's DNA and crime scene DNA is the result of chance.

Three main methods for calculating the probability of a chance match have been used. Before the NRC report in 1992, the most common method was the 'product rule.' Under this rule, scientists simply calculate the frequency with which each allele from a matching pair of DNA samples occurs in a reference database, which usually contains the profiles of individuals from the same racial group as the suspect. They multiply these individual frequencies together to calculate the frequency with which the suspect's profile as a whole is likely to be present in the general population. The answer is usually an extremely small number – one chance out of millions or billions.

A number of prominent biologists have questioned the assumptions of the product rule in their court testimony, arguing that it ignores the possibility that particular combinations of alleles may be more frequent in certain subpopulations than in the racial group as a whole.

For example, ethnic Swedes may share a common combination of alleles that is not characteristic of ethnic Russians even though Swedes and Russians are classified within the same racial group. Before probabilities of chance matches can be calculated accurately, detailed knowledge of subpopulations is required, because the inheritance of traits within subpopulations is not completely random. Influenced by this argument, the NRC panel called for use of the 'ceiling principle.' This would involve creating a database consisting of DNA profiles from one hundred randomly selected individuals from as many as twenty ethnic, genetically homogenous reference populations. Crime laboratories would determine the highest frequency with which each allele in a suspect's DNA profile occurs in any of these reference populations. These ceiling frequencies would then be multiplied together to give the matching probability of the profile as a whole. The 1992 report recommended that the minimum figure used to calculate for any individual allele should be 5 per cent. While the database is being collected, scientists should use maximum allele frequencies found in each of the four major American racial groups – Caucasian, African American, Hispanic, and Native American – or 10 per cent, whichever is higher.

The NRC report, especially its endorsement of the ceiling principle, unleashed an assault on the committee of unprecedented hostility. Geneticists from around the world convened to discuss and condemn the NRC's recommendations. Prominent scientists published articles that systematically critiqued the committee's assertions. Lander bravely defended the ceiling principle; he publicly argued that it met court requirements for a generally accepted scientific principle and also that it was conservative enough to win over most critics of the product rule while still generating high enough odds to allow convictions.

Lander's defence notwithstanding, a number of scientists and law enforcement agencies – including the FBI and the Institute of Justice – called for a second NRC committee to reconsider the 1992 recommendations. This new committee was established, chaired by geneticist James Crow. In 1996 it published its report, which concluded that the 1992 committee had made certain arbitrary assumptions and that the ceiling principle was too conservative and no longer valid. It called for a more flexible approach to population genetics. It based its conclusion in part on the fact that since the early 1990s, the FBI and other agencies had tested thousands of DNA samples from the main ethnic groups in the United States and had developed a much more thorough knowledge of DNA marker inheritance within ethnic and racial groups. The data suggested that the assumptions behind the ceiling principle – that there is broader variation in combinations of alleles within subpopulations of an ethnic group than between ethnic groups – is false. This suggests that it is best to use data for a single racial group taken as a whole rather than an average or a mix of values from various subpopulations. Thus, when the race of the person leaving evidence at the crime scene is known, the court should use the appropriate ethnic database to calculate the odds of a DNA match occurring by chance. If the race of the perpetrator is not known, the odds should be calculated using several different population profiles and the court should decide which is the best to use. Although this approach also has its critics, it has been generally accepted and has come to define the standards followed in courts in the United States and Canada.

Laboratory Techniques

A second debate over DNA evidence focused on the reliability of the laboratory techniques employed to produce the evidence. The classic case on this issue is *New York v. Castro* (1989). A woman and her two-year-old daughter were brutally murdered in their apartment in the Bronx. Suspicion fell on the building's janitor, José Castro, who had a small bloodstain on his watch. The watch was sent to Lifecodes Corporation, a private forensic testing company, whose scientists declared that the blood on the watch matched that of the mother. In a pre-trial hearing concerning the admissibility of the DNA evidence, it became obvious that there were a number of problems with the tests. There were two extra bands in the DNA bar code sample from the watch that did not match either of the victims' DNA. Lifecodes scientists argued that these were due to non-human contaminants; forensic experts countered that this could not be determined simply by looking at the pattern. Also, the bands fell outside of Lifecodes's own matching rule – the rule about how far away bands may be from the same locus and still be considered a match. On further questioning, it became clear that the Lifecodes technicians had not even measured the distances between bands in each sample. They simply 'eyeballed' it. Even so, and despite other problems, Lifecodes had declared the samples a match. Faced with these criticisms, the judge ruled that although DNA evidence is generally admissible in court, the evidence in this case was not admissible. As it turned out, the point was moot – Castro pleaded guilty to the murders.

A more famous example of questionable DNA forensic practices was the O.J. Simpson case. In 1994, Simpson, a retired professional football player and Hollywood actor, was accused of murdering his estranged wife, Nicole Brown Simpson, and her friend, Ronald Goldman. In a trial lasting several months, the prosecution built its case largely around a trail of blood leading from bloody footprints at the scene of the murder to the door and floor of Simpson's white Bronco, to blood-stained gloves and socks, to drops of blood in the accused's bedroom. According to the prosecution's forensics expert, DNA from a blood sample found at the crime scene matched Simpson's DNA with a 1 in 170 million chance that it was a random match. A blood sample on a sock found near Simpson's bed contained DNA that matched that of Nicole Brown Simpson with an astronomical 1 in 9.7 billion chance of a random match. Yet, in the end, the jury, after only four hours of deliberation, found Simpson not guilty. The DNA evidence did not determine the nature of the case. Rather, the defence succeeded brilliantly in diverting the jury's attention away from the evidence itself to the people who gathered it and the sloppy methods they used to analyse it. The implication was that the Los Angeles Police Department had arrested Simpson only because he was black.

The *Castro* and *Simpson* cases were tried during a period in forensic DNA identification technology when the 'black box' of DNA testing was still open. Other forms of expertise could still intervene in its interpretation and propose alternative forms of seeing based on traditional social and legal categories of knowing. I suggest that this era has ended. The courts have established rules under which biological expertise may claim clear authority to address issues of guilt or innocence. The Canadian government has centralized control of laboratory protocols within the RCMP; in the United States, both public and private forensic laboratories can acquire accreditation by following the protocols established by the American Society of Crime Laboratory Directors. The veracity of the science is much harder to question today than it was in the early 1990s, and the practices are much more tightly regulated and controlled. If O.J. Simpson were tried today on the basis of DNA evidence, he would probably be convicted.

Impact on Juries

A third debate within the scientific community concerns the impact on judges and juries when experts report odds of chance DNA matches as low as one in several billion. At the 1998 meetings of the American Association for the Advancement of Science, Jonathan Koehler, a professor of behavioural decision making at the University of Texas at Austin and a member of the O.J. Simpson defence team, reported that the precise words used to describe the validity of DNA analysis can have a profound impact on the jury's sense of guilt or innocence. In two experiments to evaluate the efficacy of DNA evidence, Koehler asked university students to serve as mock jurors. In the first experiment, 249 students were divided into two groups. One group was told that there was only a 0.1 per cent chance that the accused would match the crime scene sample if he were not the perpetrator. The other group was told that there was a 1 in 1,000 chance that another person had the same genetic fingerprint. Of the students in the first group, 82 per cent found that the defendant was definitely the source and 75 per cent concluded that the defendant should be found guilty. Of the students in the second group, only 43 per cent viewed the defendant as definitely the source and 45 per cent concluded the defendant should be found guilty.

In the second experiment, 147 students were asked to make a decision on the then current matter of the alleged affair between White House intern Monica Lewinsky and President Bill Clinton. The students were told that the infamous semen stain found on Lewinsky's dress had been matched to the DNA pattern of the president. When the statement read: 'The probability that Mr. Clinton would match the semen stain if he were not its source is 0.1 percent,' 28 per cent believed there was a 99 per cent likelihood that it was from him. When the statement read: 'One in one-thousand people in Washington would also match the semen stain,' only 8 per cent said they were almost absolutely sure it was from the president (Strauss, 1998: A9). A third study found that when juries hear both ways of presenting the statistics, the levels of certainly fall between the two extremes.

The implication is that how DNA evidence is presented has a huge impact on the jury's perceptions. When jury members are told how unlikely it is that a suspect could match and still not be guilty, they tend to convict; the focus is on the defendant. When they are told how likely it is that someone else could also match, they tend to acquit; the focus is on those who are not suspects. Koehler notes that defence lawyers in the United States have been arguing for the 1 in 1,000 approach as the standard for presenting of evidence to ensure that the presumption of innocence is maintained. Therefore, DNA evidence is not simply a matter of the pure application of science; people's perceptions and misunderstandings of the actual meanings of the science come into play and must be accounted for.

The Prosecutor's Fallacy

Misperception by non-scientists is also the subject of the fourth scientific controversy around DNA evidence in the courtroom. Judges and lawyers, and even scientists, are all too easily misled regarding the sorts of conclusions a DNA match allows them to make about the defendant's guilt or innocence. I am referring here specifically to what has been termed the 'prosecutor's fallacy.' Faulty legal reasoning has arisen in a number of cases involving DNA evidence in such a way as to favour the prosecution. Two questions can be asked of a probability calculation for a random DNA match. First, what is the probability that the defendant's DNA profile will match the profile from the crime sample if he or she is innocent? Second, what is the probability that the defendant is innocent, given that his or her DNA profile matches the profile from the crime sample? The first question assumes that the defendant is innocent and asks about the chances of getting a match. The second question assumes a match and asks about the defendant's innocence. The probability in the first question is usually low and can generally be accurately ascertained by experts. However, this does not mean that the probability in the second question is low, and it is this question that is ultimately of interest to the courts. The prosecutor's fallacy consists of giving the answer to the first question as the answer to the second and thereby equating the probability of a random match with the probability of the defendant's innocence.

Richard Overstall (1999: 31) asserts that to address this fallacy, courts must weigh two alternative scenarios:

1(a)   The defendant is the culprit *and*
 (b)   the crime scene DNA profile matches that of the defendant.
2(a)   Someone other than the defendant is the culprit *and*
 (b)   that person's DNA profile matches that of the defendant.

Assessment of the probabilities of 1(a) and 2(a) should be made on the basis of evidence other than DNA evidence. If the jury assesses the probability of this evidence as low (i.e., if that evidence tends to exonerate the defendant), then the DNA evidence may not be sufficient to establish the defendant's guilt beyond a reasonable doubt. Consequently, it is not possible to say that a defendant is the source of the crime sample solely on the basis of DNA evidence. It is also not appropriate for an expert witness to assess other evidence. Forensic experts cannot give an opinion on whether or not a defendant is the source of the crime sample. That inference is strictly a matter for the judge or jury.

Canadian courts have varied widely in the attention they have paid to the prosecutor's fallacy. For example, in the appeal case *R. v. Legere* (1994), the appellant was an aboriginal man appealing a conviction for murder while committing a sexual assault. His appeal was centred on 'whether or not the frequencies of genetic patterns might be different because of ethnic ancestry, regional variations or the fact that interbreeding has occurred in a particular geographic area' (18 C.R.). The New Brunswick Court of Appeal accepted the Crown's evidence on the scientific and statistical issues raised by the accused and committed the prosecutor's fallacy by equating the probability of a random match with the probability of the defendant's innocence. A statement by the trial judge in this case provides some worrying clues as to why this sort of mistake can occur: 'Forget about discrete alleles, forget about Hardy-Weinberg theory equilibrium, forget about polyzygotes, monozygotes even. I don't understand those things and you don't either and we're not expected to understand them, we're not scientists ... You may have understood Dr. Carmody's new equation that he devised when I didn't' (21 C.R.).

This is a problematic statement in terms of the new mode of justice in cases of violent crime. The language of science is distinct from the language of law and there is a danger that courts may mechanically reach verdicts on the basis of scientific evidence the terms and the implications of which they do not understand. Furthermore, this raises the question of what is happening in terms of the type of expertise privileged to speak on issues of guilt and innocence in the quest for ever greater objectivity (see chapter 6). In other cases, such as *R. v. Terceira* (1998), appeal courts have taken more care in considering DNA matching evidence. In that case the Ontario Court of Appeal ruled that 'in the absence of other qualification, a match is no more than a failure to exclude a suspect's DNA from the crime scene' (184). However, the court also stated that when a match is found, probability statistics must be applied to determine its significance. The court recognized the danger of the prosecutor's fallacy, but it also found that the trial judge had properly instructed the jury and that there was no basis for assuming that the jury would use probability statistics to predict the likelihood of guilt (200). Leave was granted to appeal to the Supreme Court of Canada. That appeal is still pending.

Almost from the beginning, there was little controversy about the veracity of RFLP, PCR, and STR methods of DNA matching. Instead, debates
centred on how to manage processes of DNA evidence production and
how to control the impacts of DNA evidence on judicial decision makers. In terms of the former, questions about laboratory standards and
the control of human error in the production of DNA evidence spoke to
the need to ensure reliability of DNA evidence. The population genetics
controversy addressed the issue of how to measure the uniqueness of
DNA samples. Both of these issues were about defining the boundaries
of the culture of the trace. Now that we can take the microscopic traces
left behind at crime scenes and link them to the inescapable essence of
perpetrators, we must be sure that our methods are correct. There are
still some questions about how accurate we can be, but those questions
have been largely resolved through agreed-upon scientific practices
and standardized calculations of odds. These laboratory practices and
statistical calculations, which constitute the new methodology of the
culture of the trace, are increasingly beyond question.

Controversies over the impact of population genetics on judges and
juries and the problem of the prosecutor's fallacy point to the need to
control the impact of DNA evidence. This relates to questions about the
charisma of genetic science. Given the authority that genetics enjoys in
our society, how should DNA evidence enter into the courtroom to
ensure a minimum of prejudice to the accused? How can we avoid
equating population genetics calculations with the probability of an
accused's innocence? In other words, how do we avoid substituting a
scientific finding for the Reason of judges and juries? This has become a
significant problem not only because of the authority accorded to
genetic science but also because of its complexity and the limited ability
of laypeople to completely understand the issues of knowledge production involved in DNA evidence. Not surprisingly, since the introduction
of DNA identification in the late 1980s, the tendency has been to
empower genetic science and scientists in the courtroom. In this sense,
a genetic justice system seems to be on the ascendence.

The Social Context

In technical and scientific terms, DNA testing and banking became
practical in the mid-1980s. In social terms, societies were ready for it
long before that. To understand why, we must consider how risk society came to be formed. Two interrelated social factors were especially

significant in opening society to biotechnological intervention in criminal justice as an element of biogovernance: fear of crime, and growing comfort with the surveillance of public and private spaces. These two factors provide us with narrative frames and legitimating language for constructing biogovernance in the Canadian criminal justice system and for discussing the legal and scientific controversies surrounding the technology.

Fear of Crime

It is a truism among criminologists that although crime rates systematically declined in Canada in the 1990s, fear of crime increased or at best remained steady (Statistics Canada, 2001). In the 1999 General Social Survey (GSS), 73 per cent of Canadians felt reasonably safe or very safe walking alone in their neighbourhoods at night -- the same percentage as in the international Crime Victimization Survey of 1996. In that survey, Canada had the third-lowest rate of feelings of safety among the eleven participating countries (Canadian Centre for Justice Statistics [CCJS], 1999: 111). The aggregate average for the eleven nations was 77 per cent. The same survey was conducted in 1992 among five participating countries, including Canada. Among the other four – England and Wales, Finland, the Netherlands, and Sweden – there was no significant change between 1992 and 1996. Yet, the percentage of Canadians who felt fairly safe or very safe dropped by 5 per cent over the same period (CCJS, 1999: 111).

Although most Canadian citizens feel safe in their neighbourhoods, many do not, despite a 3 per cent decline in victimization rates in Canada during the 1990s (CCJS, 1999: 103). That drop has not translated into public perceptions of declining crime rates. Criminologists disagree over why this is happening, though most focus their attention on media representations of crime and their possible effects on public perceptions of security and risk. The classic research is that of George Gerbner and his colleagues (1980), who argued that over time, the themes and content of the mass media – especially television – 'cultivate' a common social reality for the audience. After measuring the large amount of violent content on television, Gerbner argued that a 'heavy viewer' of television would overestimate the occurrence of violence in society and develop a 'mean world view.' People develop a mean world view as a result of 'mainstreaming,' which involves the elimination of divergent opinions of reality based on differing social circumstances and a homogenization of views on violence. 'Resonance' – that is, the intensification of issues of particular salience to a particular group – explains differences in opinion among different categories of heavy viewers. For example, women may express higher levels of fear of violence than men, given the different pressures they face in society. With this research, Gerbner set the terms of much of the debate over fear of crime and the impact of media consumption. Research in this 'media effects' tradition continues; scholars are now examining media representations of offenders, victims, and crime statistics and the impact of these representations on public perceptions (Chiricos et al., 1997; Ericson et al., 1989; Valkenburg and Patiwael, 1998).

Media effects research has been strongly criticized for a number of reasons. Some have pointed out flaws in Gerbner's methodology and findings (Graber, 1980; Sacco, 1982; Sparks, 1992). The notion of resonance has not been widely supported by others who have replicated Gerbner's studies. Mainstreaming has been a more important focus of subsequent research, but Sparks (1992) criticizes it for being based on circular reasoning and for lacking definitional precision. He also points out that cultivation analysis is undermined by what it ignores – the reflexive aspects of media consumption. That is, mainstreaming assumes a simple stimulus response model of media consumption and fails to account for the agency of viewers as they interact with media texts to produce their own meanings and narratives.

A more profound critique of media effects research is paradigmatic rather than methodological. There is a growing body of work attempting to understand fear of crime as a multidimensional phenomenon of late modernity. Few would deny that the media play a significant role in perceptions of crime. But how much are the media responsible for fear of crime? And what role do other factors play? Questions like these are often framed as challenges to the implicit assumptions of the media effects tradition as it relates to the truth or falsity of perceptions of crime and the rationality or irrationality of fear of crime. It may not be enough simply to free oneself from 'false' media representations and to embrace 'true' information about victimization as revealed by official statistical data.

Lupton and Tulloch (1999) contend that information about crime can be obtained through other channels of communication besides the media. People are rational subjects who engage in self-monitoring, but they also engage in non-rational self-interpretation based on cultural signs and symbols and personal experience. Intuition, emotion, and spiritual assumptions are as important as rationality. Thus, fear of crime is not simply a stimulus response reaction to the environment; it is also a product of subjectivity-forming life experience and cultural expectations. Distinctions such as true and false, and rational and irrational, are not salient to understanding fear of crime. Media exposure is not the only basis for fear of crime, and neither are crime data. Sparks (1992) makes a similar argument in his textual analysis of crime dramas on television. People's responses to crime are rarely grounded in rational calculations of probability based on official information. Rather, they are part of a hermeneutic response proceeding from a summary of diffuse anxieties about one's social position and identity.

Fear of crime arises from life experiences, interpersonal modes of communication, and generalized anxieties about identity and social position. That said, media impacts still must be granted a significant place. Osborne (1995) makes this point when he draws from Baudrillard's notion of the hyperreal to explain the experience of crime in postmodernity. He begins by pointing out that popular culture is obsessed with crime. This is apparent even from a casual glance at film offerings, bookstore selections, television dramas, and news coverage. An Internet search on Yahoo Canada using the keyword 'crime' turns up 246 separate categories devoted to the subject. The tremendous amount of time and space devoted to crime in popular culture has contributed to a hyperreality in which the sign and the referent have imploded within a highly mediated environment. In this way, the hyperreal contributes to the formation of risk society by producing public anxieties that must be addressed even though actual crime statistics indicate that the risk of crime is less immediate. Statistical information is only part of the environment – it is not a statement of definitive fact. It adds to the matrix but does not determine it.

Feminist scholars point out another aspect of fear of crime, specifically in relation to women's experiences of crime and fear of crime. From this perspective, fear of crime emanates from a fear of sexual danger (Walklate, 1998: 408). Radical feminists argue that women must structure their daily lives in order to manage their relationships with male family members, acquaintances, and colleagues in both public and private domains. At some level, this becomes a question of trust or lack of trust – a question of ontological security, which according to some feminists is lacking for women in all spheres of life.

This research points the way to a more general perspective on fear of crime. Women's experiences and fears of crime are specific to their sex;

in a more general sense, ontological security may provide the clearest lens through which to view fear of crime. In the context of crime management, Giddens's concept of ontological security suggests that the increase in fear of crime is an emotional response to perceived threats to the self and to the social and material environments. The growing sense of risk from crime is the opposite of a feeling of trust in the stability of the social environment. As Osborne points out, rapid shifts in the postmodern conditions of the production of self and society may lead to this. Popular culture's obsession with crime can thus be understood as an outward manifestation of this insecurity. The politicization of crime management can be understood in the same way.

David Garland (1996) explains the growing sense of unease about crime by asserting that two discursive shifts have occurred in recent crime management. First, high crime rates have become a normal social fact; this is reflected in fear of crime and in media representations of crime. Crime is no longer unexpected or abnormal; rather, it is a routine part of modern life, an everyday risk to be assessed and managed. Second, government discourse has moved away from asserting confidently that the state is capable of providing security, law and order, and crime control. Having taken over many of the social control functions that used to belong to civil society, the state is now faced with its own inability to provide the promised levels of crime control. As a result, processes of responsibilization are beginning to penetrate crime policy, with citizens being called on to manage their own crime risks by adopting everyday routines that reduce opportunities for victimization – a 'criminology of the self.'[4] At the same time, governments periodically engage in 'get tough' policies aimed at controlling the criminal population through more punitive sentencing – a 'criminology of the other.' This contradiction between self-responsibility and periodic bursts of government 'get tough' policies reinforces the sense that governments do not know how to control crime and are withdrawing from the responsibility for doing so. As criminality is increasingly redefined as ubiquitous and simply a normal fact of everyday life, members of the public lose their trust in crime control experts. The resulting ontological insecurity generates a need to find other forms of expertise that can promise to act on crime.

Surveillance Society

Intimately linked to fear of crime is a second social enabling condition of DNA banking and testing – the development of surveillance society.

Giddens (1985) asserts that surveillance is one of the central institutions of modernity (others include capitalism, industrialism, and military power). DNA identification and banking technologies intervene at the level of the social body through the surveillance and coding of individual bodies. They enter into society through pre-existing relationships between citizens and surveillance technologies. Over the past twenty years, social scientists have been paying more and more attention to questions of surveillance and its converse, privacy, as a result of the deployment of new surveillance technologies, initially in workplaces and more recently in the sphere of consumer activities.

Earlier sociological analyses of surveillance techniques tended to follow Marxist and Weberian theoretical lines. Simply stated, Marxists approach surveillance as a function of the capitalist quest for greater profit through increased efficiency and productivity. The Weberian approach views surveillance as a means of further rationalizing organizational functioning. From this perspective, there may be other logics at work besides profit enhancement, and each situation must be examined in its own particular context. Beginning in the 1980s, another perspective became important in this field of study – the Foucauldian approach, which has altered the other two perspectives quite dramatically. Foucault focused on the 'disciplinary practices' that have become a part of modern institutional functioning in general, arguing that power is a ubiquitous social field that permeates all social relationships for both good and ill. Within modernity, surveillance has had the effect of bringing people under stricter regimes of social control.

In *Discipline and Punish* (1979), his well-known study of the history of prisons, Foucault employs the architectural notion of the 'panopticon' to explain not only the development of control within prisons, but also the development of a generalized form of power in society as a whole. The panopticon was a building design featuring a central observation tower surrounded by cells arranged in a circular fashion; this allowed the watcher in the tower to observe any cell at any time. Ideally, the watcher would be invisible to the cell occupants; thus, they would never know if they were being watched and would always have to assume that they were. In this way, they would internalize their discipline. The panopticon was designed in the late eighteenth century for use in workplaces and prisons, but Foucault suggests it is a model for surveillance in the modern world. Modern institutions are organized in space and time to render populations and their processes observable. Put another way, we are a surveillance society.

Foucault's analysis was directed at practices in early modernity.

Others have extended his discussion to late modernity, arguing that electronic surveillance in the late twentieth and early twenty-first centuries is panoptic in nature, albeit in different ways than in the past. For example, Castel (1991) suggests that in the present day, virtual selves develop through processes of coding and are circulated and managed independently of the bodies to which they refer. Poster (1996) goes even farther, pointing out that databases are configurations of language – that is, they are texts within a discourse of surveillance. Drawing from Foucault, he defines discourse as a means of linking knowledge to the subject and as the process by which subjects are constituted through power. Discourse positions the subject in relation to structures of domination in such a way that those structures can act upon him or her. The panopticon is more than simply a guard tower – it is a discourse that constitutes the modern subject in a particular way and that normalizes him or her to a process of surveillance.

Databases form a 'superpanopticon' (Poster, 1996: 182). They constitute subjects through a process of textual production. However, the database has certain new properties that make it especially effective. It is electronic and digital and therefore easily transferable in time and space. It has no particular identifiable authors; rather, it is authored by whoever or whatever enters data, including machines automatically recording information. Nevertheless, it belongs to someone – the corporation, the state, the military, the hospital, the university – and amplifies the power of its owner (183). Finally, everyone knows about these databases and accepts their operation with a curious mixture of unease and acceptance.

Civil liberties groups, privacy watchdogs, and the media are warning with ever increasing alarm that a 'Big Brother' mentality is taking root among governments and corporations. For example, a 1998 American Civil Liberties Union report contended that the U.S. government was 'using scare tactics to acquire vast new powers to spy on all Americans' (Bovard, 2000: 68). This reported cited a number of examples. In 1993, the U.S. government revealed that the National Security Agency (NSA) had developed a new microchip, the 'Clipper Chip,' with the capacity to locate anyone who was using encryption software. Furthermore, the NSA was proposing that anyone using encryption software be required to hand over their decryption keys to the government. This would allow government authorities to access their databases and monitor and record their communications. The Clipper Chip proposal was eventually abandoned, but the following year the U.S. administration convinced Congress to pass a bill requiring the telecommunications industry to 'dumb down' telephone technology to facilitate wiretapping. As a result of this bill, all cellular telephones will be required to contain homing devices so that the precise location of anyone using them will be determinable; the users will not be able to turn off these devices. In 1999, members of the international Internet Engineering Task Force announced that the FBI was pressuring them to create a surveillance-friendly architecture for Internet communications. Specifically, the FBI wanted to be able to access all e-mail communications. The task force succeeded in resisting this pressure, but civil liberties groups consider it worrisome that the bureau would even attempt to do this. In autumn of 1999, news broke about the existence of the Echelon spy satellite system, a joint project of the NSA and sister agencies in Canada, the United Kingdom, Australia, and New Zealand. Echelon scans millions of telephone calls, e-mail messages, and faxes every hour, searching for key words. It has been used to tap into telecommunications in countries and corporations around the world. Since September 11th, the process has greatly intensified.

Surveillance has also penetrated deeply into workplaces and commercial transactions. Shoshana Zuboff (1988) refers to this form of surveillance as 'informating' – the use of information technology to automatically record transactions for the purpose of creating an electronic information environment. In this way, managers and decision makers have an immediately available window onto the workplace or marketplace in terms of what is being done, how productive individual employees are, what is selling, and so on. Informating describes the more generalized process of the superpanopticon. The one who is being surveilled provides the necessary information. There is no need for a carefully designed architecture of power based on a complex bureaucratic organization manned by experts in labour and marketing. Voluntary transactions are recorded automatically and converted into texts through the cables and circuits that form the capillaries of power and knowledge. These texts form the discourse of surveillance; they constitute their own object by producing a collective account of a multitude of private actions.

Perhaps the greatest danger in all this relates to how easily the public can be socialized into accepting the workings of panoptic power as simply a background element of the everyday environment. All of us have long been conditioned to use and accept social insurance numbers, bank machine codes, employee numbers, credit card numbers, and so on. As a result, continued developments in surveillance and coding may appear to us as simply one more layer of enumeration with no direct impact on our lives. Gary Marx (1988) makes this point in his analysis of the 'new surveillance,' which he characterizes as invisible, involuntary, capital rather than labour intensive, involving decentralized policing, and introducing suspicion of entire categories of people and not just specific individuals. The result is that new forms of control develop based on manipulation rather than coercion, computer chips rather than prison bars, and remote and invisible tethers rather than handcuffs and straitjackets. In other words, panopticism in the public sphere does not proceed through the prisonlike atmosphere of surveillance, as in George Orwell's *Nineteen Eighty-Four*. Rather, it operates through the embedded nature of surveillance technologies. As our everyday transactions are silently and unobtrusively entered into databases, we lose sight of the fact that we are constantly under surveillance. We are not watched by people, we are recorded in databases. DNA surveillance technologies have entered criminal justice as simply another form of database. This is an enhancement of what Max Weber identified as a central characteristic of a rational-legal form of authority. Within Western modernity we do not submit ourselves to the will of other individuals, but rather to institutional processes and abstract rules. Thus we do not notice that we are losing our sovereignty.

Fear and surveillance are in many ways, the opposites of trust and privacy. It is interesting to speculate on what a society premised upon trust and privacy would be like, but it is a utopian fantasy or a nostalgic vision of a past that probably never was. In the risk society, our sense of the social is very different. It is characterized by ontological insecurity brought about by rapidly transforming experiences of subjectivity formation and social positioning. The resulting anxiety manifests itself in part through a fear of crime and victimization – a fear that is deepened by our interaction with a hyperreal media environment obsessed with crime and by mixed messages from the state authorities, who simultaneously 'get tough' on crime while calling on citizens to take responsibility for crime control. In this environment, surveillance takes on different meanings than in the past. Although the state still has Big Brother tendencies, surveillance is increasingly either accepted or ignored as a part of society's background noise. Vigilant surveillance may even contribute to ontological security by promising to contain risks before they can become full-blown dangers. In this sense, surveillance is welcomed and we take the final step in becoming a surveillance society.

The Legal Context

The third context in which DNA technologies are entering Canadian criminal justice is that of the law. In tandem with technological and social developments during the 1980s and early 1990s, Canadian law grappled with developments in biological identification technology and its implications for the relationship between the citizen and the state. DNA testing and banking promised better criminal identification, but questions arose over whether the seizure of biological samples from suspects violated the Charter of Rights and Freedoms as well as the common law right to bodily integrity. Conflicting court decisions rendered the law confusing. Police did not know whether they had the right to seize and store DNA samples. In 1994, the first Supreme Court decision regarding the seizure of DNA samples made it clear that the state has no common law right to seize bodily materials. However, the government by then was already preparing to revise the Criminal Code to empower the police to obtain biological samples from suspects. This set a course that would quickly lead to the DNA warrant and banking system.

Bodily Integrity

Legal debates over DNA testing and the seizure of DNA samples came to focus on the question of bodily integrity and its relationship to the police power of search and seizure. The concept of bodily integrity is recognized in the common law and is also generally taken as implicit in section 7 of the Charter, which states: 'Everyone has the right to life, liberty and security of the person and the right not to be deprived thereof except in accordance with the principles of fundamental justice.' Arguably, bodily integrity also has relevance in the application of section 8, which states: 'Everyone has the right to be secure from unreasonable search or seizure.' The problem, of course, is that the principle of bodily integrity is not clearly defined in the common law; its definition has been context-driven and has mutated in different directions. In a legal analysis of bodily integrity, Renee Pomerance (1995) identifies three categories in which the term is employed. One of these categories is the right to access or refuse medical treatment. This particular category helps us define the components of certain criminal offences with reference to the bodily integrity of victims and to police seizures of hospital medical samples as evidence.

In terms of the right to access or refuse medical treatment, protecting bodily integrity means recognizing the right of a patient to control his or her own body and to make voluntary and informed choices about invasive medical procedures. In *Fleming v. Reid* (1991), psychiatric patients were treated with neuroleptic drugs without their consent. The court stated:

> The common law right to bodily integrity and personal autonomy is so entrenched in the traditions of our law as to be ranked as fundamental and deserving of the highest order of protection. This right forms an essential part of an individual's security of the person and must be included in the liberty interests protected by s.7. Indeed, in my view, the common law right to determine what shall be done with one's own body and the constitutional right to security of the person, both of which are founded on the belief in the dignity and autonomy of each individual, can be treated as co-extensive. (88)

This case dealt with a civil context. Arguably, however, the focus on consent, autonomy, and dignity also applies to the criminal context.

Bodily integrity has been especially important in certain Canadian cases that reflect significant social issues. For example, in *R. v. Morgentaler* (1988) the Supreme Court struck down section 251 of the Criminal Code, which prevented therapeutic abortions outside an administrative regime, as unconstitutional under section 7 of the Charter. Chief Justice Dickson stated:

> The case-law leads me to the conclusion that state interference with bodily integrity and serious state-imposed psychological stress, at least in the criminal law context, constitute a breach of security of the person ... Not only does the removal of the decision making power threaten women in a physical sense; the indecision of knowing whether an abortion will be granted inflicts emotional stress. Section 251 clearly interferes with a woman's bodily integrity in both a physical and emotional sense. Forcing a woman, by threat of criminal sanction, to carry a foetus to term unless she meets certain criteria unrelated to her own priorities and aspirations, is a profound interference with a woman's body and thus a violation of security of the person. (466–7 C.C.C.)

The court concluded that section 251 was not in accordance with the principles of fundamental justice and could not be saved by section 1 of the Charter, which states: 'The Canadian Charter of Rights and Freedoms guarantees the rights and freedoms set out in it subject only to such reasonable limits prescribed by law as can be demonstrably justified in a free and democratic society.' The court did not view section 251 as a reasonable limit on the bodily integrity of women.

A second landmark case was *Rodriguez v. British Columbia (Attorney General)* (1993), in which a terminally ill patient challenged section 241(b) of the Criminal Code, which criminalizes the aiding or abetting of suicide. Rodriguez argued that this section infringed section 7 of the Charter by inhibiting her right to control what happens to her body. The majority of the Supreme Court held that there was a violation of the security of the person. Justice Sopinka wrote:

> In my view, then, the judgements of this court in *Morgentaler* can be seen to encompass a notion of personal autonomy involving, at the very least, control over one's bodily integrity, free from state interference, and freedom from state-imposed psychological and emotional stress ... There is no question, then, that personal autonomy, at least with respect to the right to make choices concerning one's own body, control over one's physical and psychological integrity, and basic human dignity are encompassed within security of the person, at least to the extent of freedom from criminal prohibitions which interfere with these. (63 C.C.C.)

However, the court went on to find that although Rodriguez's bodily integrity was violated, this deprivation was in accordance with the principles of fundamental justice and did not infringe upon section 7. The criminalization of assisted suicide was justified by the principle of the sanctity of life, which takes precedence. Bodily integrity, therefore, is not an absolute principle and must be weighed against equally important interests in society.

Regarding medical treatment, bodily integrity involves notions of self-determination and the right of the individual to make choices about the disposition of his or her own body; the central issue is the freedom to control one's own body. This raises difficult questions in the criminal context, since search warrants may interfere with the person very directly. In criminal investigations, judicial officers can limit the section 7 right to self-determination if they determine that the social interest outweighs the individual interest of bodily integrity.

The second context in which bodily integrity has been invoked is that of the bodily integrity of victims of crime. Crimes of violence, by definition, are an interference with the bodily integrity of the victim. For example, in R. v. McCraw (1991) the Supreme Court defined rape as the 'violation of the bodily integrity of a woman' (527–8 C.C.C.). In R. v. Creighton (1993) the Supreme Court stated that the offence of manslaughter requires 'proof that the unlawful act was likely to injure another person, or in other words, put the bodily integrity of others at risk' (3 S.C.R.). In both cases the infliction of injury was considered an interference with bodily integrity. Once again, use of this definition in the context of a police search may not be applicable due to the generally non-injurious nature of the physical invasion.

The third context in which bodily integrity has been an important consideration relates to police seizure of medical samples. This arises most often in impaired driving cases where the suspect is injured and has given blood and urine samples to medical personnel. These samples are a potential source of evidence of blood alcohol levels and are often seized by the police. In R. v. Dyment (1988) the Supreme Court held that in the absence of a warrant, the seizure of a medical sample by the police violated the suspect's rights under section 8 of the Charter. The police seizure was held to constitute a 'gross violation of the sanctity, integrity and privacy of the appellant's bodily substances and medical records' (263 C.C.C.). In this and other cases, the Supreme Court has used bodily integrity in a broad sense, to include not only the physical body but also the privacy of information about the body. In this way the Court has linked the right of privacy to doctor/patient confidentiality.

Search and Seizure

The obverse of bodily integrity is the police power of search and seizure. Before 1993 that power was generally restricted to the search for tangible physical evidence in a building, a receptacle, or a place. Entering a citizen's body to seize biological material would have constituted an assault except in extreme cases. With the passage of the Constitution Act in 1982, which contained the Charter of Rights and Freedoms, the right to protection against unreasonable search and seizure was enshrined in section 8 of the Charter. Over the course of the 1980s and early 1990s, the Supreme Court through its rulings placed restrictions on this police power.

The leading case on section 8 is *Hunter v. Southam* (1984). Here, the

Supreme Court held that privacy was the rationale underlying the guarantee against unreasonable search and seizure. Section 8 is intended to protect a person's reasonable expectation of privacy. Therefore, government intrusion into a citizen's privacy rights will only be condoned if it is reasonable. What constitutes reasonableness in the context of search and seizure? The court decided that reasonableness has three requirements: (1) issuance of a warrant (2) by an impartial arbiter (3) based on reasonable and probable grounds sworn under oath. But even if these requirements are met, a search may still violate section 8. Justice Dickson stated: 'Where the state's interest is not simply law enforcement, as for instance, where state security is involved, or where the individual's interest is not simply the expectation of privacy as, for instance, when the search threatens his bodily integrity, the relevant standard might well be a different one' (168). In other words, the context of the search is relevant in determining what is reasonable. *Hunter v. Southam* involved a search of a place rather than a person or a body; however, the basic principles set out in that decision have formed the basis for subsequent constitutional discussions about the seizure of DNA material. Once again, this raises the issue of bodily integrity.

The matter was further considered in *R. v. Colarusso* (1994). Justice La Forest addressed the matter of section 8 in the context of the body: 'The need for privacy can vary with the nature of the matter sought to be protected, the circumstances in which and the place where state intrusion occurs, and the purposes of the intrusion. That physical integrity, including bodily fluids, ranks high among the matters receiving constitutional protection, there is no doubt' (53). From these decisions, it is clear that the Supreme Court was actively engaged in limiting the expansion of police powers of search and seizure. However, countervailing forces were at work in the legal community – forces operating to expand those powers.

Legal Developments in Bodily Searches

Prior to the 1995 passage of Bill C-104, the DNA warrant legislation, two reviews of the common law on bodily searches summarized the state of the law at that time. The first was *Investigative Tests* (1984), a research paper by the Law Reform Commission of Canada. It concluded: 'As to obtaining bodily samples, there is at common law no power to compel either a suspect who has not yet been arrested or a person who has and is already in custody to provide a sample of his blood, hair, saliva, or other bodily matter. Any use of physical force to obtain such a sample whether by the police or by a doctor at their behest, would constitute an assault' (45).

The following year, the commission published another report, *Obtaining Forensic Evidence* (1985), which made a number of recommendations for regulating investigative procedures involving the person. First, after reviewing case law, the commission concluded that in considering the application of section 8 of the Charter, five factors should be considered in assessing the reasonableness of bodily search and seizure: (a) the seriousness of the offence, (b) the grounds and authority for conducting the procedure, (c) the manner in which the procedure is carried out, (d) the inherent intrusiveness of the procedure, and (e) the probative value of the procedure.

The commission then proceeded to outline a legislative regime for obtaining warrants for removal of certain bodily substances (38).[5] None of the procedures in Bill C-104 were specifically recommended in this regime, although one might argue that 'hair clippings' include hair root samples and that 'saliva samples' include mouth swabs. Blood samples were not included on the list. However, in the list of procedures that should be expressly forbidden, 'surgical procedure that involves the puncturing of human skin or tissue' specifically excluded blood samples, which were classified as less intrusive and only 'quasi-surgical' (36–7).

By the early 1990s, after further consultation, the Law Reform Commission had changed its position quite radically. In a new report, *Recodifying Criminal Procedure* (1991), the commission summarized its new position: 'The only procedure that we continue to recommend be prohibited is the administration of drugs known or designed to affect mood, inhibitions, judgement or thinking ... However, one procedure which we formerly recommended be prohibited – radiographic or ultrasonic examination (paragraph 56(j)) – may now be judicially authorized, subject to considerations of health and safety' (62). Clearly, the commission's thoughts on bodily searches and seizures were evolving in parallel with social developments in the same period. Although the commission's recommendations were not binding on the government, they did represent the considered views of legal experts regarding the state of the law and normative prescriptions of what the law should be. As such, they carried significant weight.

A second review of the common law on search and seizure was conducted by the Supreme Court in *Cloutier v. Langlois* (1990). Here, the

Supreme Court found three general rules for governing the power of the police to search a person upon a lawful arrest: (a) the search must be for a valid objective in pursuit of the ends of criminal justice, (b) the purpose of the search must not be unrelated to the objectives of the proper administration of justice, and (c) the search must not be conducted in an abusive manner. In Supreme Court findings as well as in the Law Reform Commission's reviews, the level of physical intrusion is an important measure in determining whether searches are justified at common law. A brief review of a number of relevant cases shows that the common law does not allow the following: forcible removal of a hair sample (*R. v. Legere*, 1994); taking of teeth impressions (*R. v. Stillman*, 1995); and the use of surgical or quasi-surgical procedures (*Laporte v. Laganière*, 1972, and *R. v. Greffe*, 1990). On the other hand, the common law does permit compelling a suspect to participate in police line-ups (*Marcoux and Solomon v. R.*, 1975) and compelling a person in police custody to give fingerprints (*R. v. Beare*, 1988). However, these last two instances do not involve the removal of bodily substances. That question remained unclear in the common law. Then in the early 1990s the Canadian government began taking legislative steps to clarify the law by authorizing greater powers of search and seizure.

Developments in the Criminal Code

The context for seizing DNA material in criminal investigations was set only two years before Bill C-104 was passed. In 1993, Bill C-109 was proclaimed into force, with significant amendments to the warrant provisions in the Criminal Code. Under sections 487.01, 492.1, and 492.2 there were four new types of warrants: the general warrant, the video warrant, the tracking warrant, and the number recorder warrant. The same bill also amended wiretapping provisions. Obviously this bill was intended to clarify police powers regarding electronic surveillance. Prior to 1993, in cases such as *R. v. Wong* (1990) and *R. v. Wise* (1992), the Supreme Court had ruled that the use of electronic surveillance devices without prior judicial authorization was a violation of section 8 of the Charter where the subject had a reasonable expectation of privacy. Yet, there was no statutory mechanism by which the police could obtain prior authorization.

Bill C-109 was the government's attempt to address this gap in the law and also to enact a general warrant provision that could be utilized in situations where a proposed surveillance, search, or seizure technique was not specifically addressed by legislation. The general warrant was intended as a catchall category; its purpose was to eliminate the need for Parliament to legislate on every specific device as it was developed and became pertinent to police investigations. The general warrant, however, extends beyond the realm of electronic surveillance. Section 487.01 is very broad; it seems to allow police to obtain a warrant authorizing the use of any device or procedure that would otherwise constitute an unreasonable search or seizure of a person or a person's property. Arguably, the general warrant provision is a significant step toward raising community security over individual privacy rights. The legislation apparently recognizes this, and thus requires that such a warrant be issued by a provincial court judge or a judge of the superior court rather than by a justice of the peace. As well, section 487.01, subsection (2), states that a general warrant cannot be obtained to authorize a technique, procedure, or device, or the doing of a thing, that would interfere with the bodily integrity of any person. Unfortunately, Parliament did not define bodily integrity in Bill C-109, nor did it mention the concept in the Parliamentary debates that resulted in the bill's passage.

A propos to all this is the law regarding drinking and driving offences and the seizure of bodily substances. Under section 254(2) of the Criminal Code, police may demand a breath sample from a person operating a motor vehicle and suspected of having alcohol in his or her body. The demand is made for the purpose of providing a sample for analysis by an approved screening device. Under section 254(3), police officers may demand a blood sample, without a warrant, from a person suspected of committing an impaired driving offence, in order to determine the concentration of alcohol in the suspect's body. There are strict conditions around obtaining these samples. It is necessary that the person 'is committing, or at any time within the preceding two hours has committed,' the impaired driving offence (s. 254(3)). Also, a demand for a blood sample can be made only if the officer has reasonable grounds to believe that the suspect 'may be incapable of providing a sample of his breath' (s.254(3)(b)(i)) or 'it would be impracticable to obtain a sample of his breath' (s.254(3)(b)(ii)). As well, blood samples may only be taken under the direction of a qualified medical practitioner who is satisfied that the taking of samples will not endanger the life or health of the suspect (s. 254(4)). Refusal to comply with the police officer's demand is an offence (s.254(4)).

Furthermore, under s. 256 of the Criminal Code, a warrant may be issued to obtain blood samples in cases of impaired driving. The circumstances are very restricted. The judge must be satisfied that within the preceding two hours the person has committed an impaired driving offence that has resulted in bodily harm or death to another. A medical practitioner must be of the opinion that the person is medically unable to consent to the taking of blood and that there is no threat to the life or health of the person. Only a qualified medical practitioner or a technician under his or her direction may take the blood sample.

Section 254 has been challenged in the courts, but has withstood these challenges. In *R. v. Pelletier* (1989) the seizure of blood samples was challenged as a violation of section 8 of the Charter. The court agreed that it was, but concluded that such a violation was justified under section 1. In *R. v. Metcalfe* (1993) the breath demand provision was challenged under section 8. The court found that this provision did not violate section 8 and that in the interests of public safety, it is not unreasonable for the state to attach certain conditions to the privilege of operating a motor vehicle.

The general warrant provision and the impaired driving provisions established a legal basis for enhancing the state's power to search and seize materials from a citizen's body. These provisions have strengthened police powers to interfere with citizens' privacy rights, in a social context marked by increased fear of crime and an acceptance of the fact of surveillance.

Before the passage of Bill C-104 (i.e., the DNA warrant provisions of the Criminal Code), the law governing seizure of DNA samples was uncertain. With the general warrant provision and the authorization of blood samples in impaired driving cases, criminal legislation seemed to be tending toward enhancing police power over citizens' bodies to an unprecedented level even while incorporating the concept of bodily integrity as a limit on police authority. The Law Reform Commission recommendations in the late 1980s and early 1990s busttressed this trend. In terms of the case law around sections 7 and 8 of the Charter, the Supreme Court repeatedly upheld the principle of bodily integrity in a number of cases; this signalled an inclination toward curbing police powers of search and seizure. However, there were no decisions involving the seizure of DNA material at the Supreme Court level, nor was there any legislation addressing the issue before 1995. There was no statutory law governing the use of DNA testing in crime investigations. A number of courts granted warrants for seizing DNA samples under the general warrant provision; others did not, on the basis of section 8 of the Charter. Also, there were a number of cases involving DNA evidence in which criminal defence lawyers sought to challenge the constitutionality and scientific veracity of this new form of evidence (see chapter 6).

This was the legal context in which DNA testing and banking entered the criminal justice system in Canada. Even before Bill C-104 was passed in 1995, means were being developed to utilize the law as a technique for objectifying the criminal body. Legislation and government policy were moving toward an ever greater acceptance of limiting the doctrine of bodily integrity in favour of granting police new powers to enter the citizen's body. There, they would be able to objectively confirm the origin of traces found at crime scenes. Given the charisma of genetic science and the public's fear of crime, it seemed unlikely that voices favouring a strong doctrine of bodily integrity would be able to make themselves heard in the domain of DNA testing in criminal cases. The technological, social, and legal climate in Canada and elsewhere seemed highly conducive to the development of a genetic justice system.

3 Framing DNA: Negotiating the DNA Warrant and Data Bank System in the Public Sphere

In 1994 the Supreme Court of Canada rendered its first decision on the gathering and use of DNA evidence. In this crucial case, *R. v. Borden*, the accused had been identified and arrested as the perpetrator of a sexual assault in 1989. The police asked him to provide a DNA sample for that offence, which he agreed to do. DNA from the sample matched that from a semen sample found at the crime scene. However, the police also suspected Borden of a previous sexual assault on an elderly woman in a nursing home. She had been unable to identify her attacker because he had held a pillow over her face. Police forensics experts compared the DNA from Borden's sample with that taken from a semen sample at that crime scene. It also matched, and Borden was charged with both sexual assaults. At trial he was convicted of both crimes; however, on appeal the court overturned the conviction for the earlier assault. Borden had not been asked to provide a sample for that crime. In 1994 the Supreme Court upheld the appeal court's decision. Borden had volunteered a blood sample relating to a specific charge of sexual assault; the police were obligated to inform the accused that they intended to use the sample to investigate an earlier crime. There was no consent to this, and thus the evidence was inadmissible. Borden's acquittal for the first assault was upheld, and he was sentenced to only four years in prison for the second assault.

This was exactly the kind of situation the government feared – a contradiction between court interpretations of common law principles and Charter rights on the one hand and legislative trends and public opinion on the other. Although the social context was conducive to the implementation of a DNA testing regime in the criminal justice system, and although legislative developments for general warrants and for seizure of blood samples in impaired driving cases had opened the door to police seizure of DNA samples, the courts had a different view. The Supreme Court interpreted section 8 of the Charter and the common law doctrine of bodily integrity as requiring the suspect's consent for any use of substances seized from his or her body. Clearly, the law was in an uncertain state. Associations such as the Canadian Police Association, the Canadian Association of Chiefs of Police, and victims' rights groups began lobbying the government to clarify the situation through legislation.

Borden highlighted a fundamental debate that surrounds many criminal justice issues – how to balance individual rights with public safety. This debate has been one of the dominant themes of modernity and has been central to criminal justice in particular since the early nineteenth century, when foundational liberal theorists such as Jeremy Bentham and John Stuart Mill considered the degree to which society should be empowered to curtail individual rights through criminal sanctions. Regarding DNA policy, stakeholders in the policymaking process debated this distinction in terms of two kinds of risks: the risk of oversurveillance by the state through DNA testing and banking, and the risk of victimization by criminals.

The debates among policy stakeholders led to a particular, official framing of biotechnology in criminal justice that locates its meaning along a continuum between individual rights and public safety. Generally speaking, the Canadian public was not politicized over DNA testing and banking; that said, policy framers were careful to address the general public's ontological insecurity and to identify areas where the public might challenge the implementation of yet another surveillance technology. Thus the issue was cast as a technical one: How could information stored in the DNA data bank be protected from abuses? Even more important than this, policymakers succeeded in normalizing the idea of genetic justice by capturing it within pre-existing frames of reference; in this way they rendered the new technology trustworthy and unthreatening. In this chapter I outline the policymaking process and the main features of the resulting DNA warrant and data bank legislation. I then explore the ways in which the technology was framed as a particular system of meaning designed to address the risks posed by the intersection of state power and technologies of genetic surveillance. I argue that in the policy process, DNA warrant and data bank legislation was framed in ways that constituted a shift in criminal justice policy toward greater emphasis on public safety and away from individual rights.

Individual Rights versus Public Safety: Constructing the DNA Justice System

After *Borden*, then Justice Minister Allan Rock decided to move quickly. On 20 September, 1994 the Department of Justice released a discussion paper on the question of police powers in DNA testing and banking. After briefly describing the science involved in DNA testing as well as the benefits it provides to police, the consultation paper presented three broad issues for public discussion: methods for obtaining DNA evidence, methods for banking that evidence, and laboratory regulation.

On the issue of obtaining DNA evidence, the document noted that the simplest ways to obtain cells are through hair roots, saliva and mouth swabs, and blood samples. It described how police had been turning to the general warrant provision of the Criminal Code to obtain warrants but pointed out that this warrant did not permit interference with the bodily integrity of a person. Therefore, a number of questions needed to be addressed, including whether to legislate a separate warrant for seizure of biological samples, what kinds of biological samples such a warrant should cover, and what justifications and conditions would be necessary (Department of Justice, 1994: 10).

On the issue of DNA data banking, the document pointed out that this was already being done in twenty-one American states as well as federally through the FBI. Also, the British were considering establishing a national data bank. The consultation paper framed the main problem with this technology as one of privacy. DNA samples might reveal more about a person than his or her identity, such as genetic traits and inherited diseases. If this information fell into the wrong hands, it could be used to discriminate against people. There was also the question of how long samples should be retained. Should they be destroyed once the digital profile had been created, or should they be kept for later analysis by improved techniques of DNA testing? Having considered all this, the consultation paper asked whether Parliament should legislate a DNA data bank, what biological samples should be included in it, what kinds of offences should be involved, and what privacy safeguards should be provided.

Regarding laboratory regulation, the document noted that Canada had only a few public forensic laboratories; in contrast, the United States had many private and public laboratories throughout the country, but without any common standards of testing and without any accreditation procedures. So the consultation paper asked whether Parliament should legislate accreditation or licensing requirements for laboratories and what these requirements would be.

This Department of Justice discussion paper was presented to the public in September 1994. It was framed carefully to explain the benefits of DNA testing, and in articulating potential problems, it limited itself to questions of privacy. It raised questions about DNA warrants and DNA data banking together, and it suggested that the minister intended to bring in legislation that would encompass both technologies. In terms of the reaction it received, a number of submissions were made by interested agencies and individuals. One of these perhaps best summarizes the debate that was now beginning to form around the use of DNA technologies in criminal justice. This one came from then Privacy Commissioner, Bruce Phillips. Much of the discussion in the consultation paper was a response to the Privacy Commission's 1992 report, *Genetic Testing and Privacy*. In that report the commissioner had addressed the question of forensic uses of genetic tests and had formulated a set of recommendations about them, most notably these: suspects should be forced to provide genetic samples only if there is specific statutory authority to collect them; DNA analysis should be restricted to questions of identity and should not be used to assess psychological characteristics of the suspect; and a DNA databank for criminal offenders or the general public should not be established, and if it is, its use should be restricted to identification (45).

The Privacy Commissioner's response to the Department of Justice discussion paper echoed these general principles. It pointed out that taking a genetic sample from a person is a violation of 'physical integrity' (Privacy Commissioner, 1995: 2). Thus, if it is to be done, the procedure should only be performed by a competent health care professional. Suspects should be able to specify the method of sampling as long as that method produces a reliable sample. Designated offences should be restricted to crimes of violence. In terms of conditions for granting warrants, there must be reasonable grounds for suspecting the person, a DNA sample must be relevant to proving the offence, and a judge (i.e., rather than a justice of the peace) must authorize collection. The Privacy Commissioner also recommended against keeping biological samples. Once the information is recorded, the actual sample should be destroyed; otherwise there would be too much temptation to use it for purposes other than identification. At the end of the response is a list of Criminal Code offences properly falling under a DNA testing and banking regime; these are strictly violent and sexual offences. In other words, the Privacy Commissioner was not suggesting that there be no DNA testing and banking; rather, he was recommending that its scope and uses be restricted. He was putting forward an alternative approach to the one implicitly advocated by the Minister of Justice – one that was more closely in step with the spirit of the Privacy Act.

Other responses to the justice minister's discussion paper were generally favourable, and progress continued toward a Parliamentary bill. The minister intended to table a comprehensive bill in the fall of 1995, one that would address all three of the issues set out in the consultation document. However, a number of factors resulted in a more restricted bill. The *Borden* decision of 1994 indicated the need for haste. That same year, a young girl, Tara Manning, had been sexually assaulted and murdered near Montreal. Her family began a public campaign for the enacting of DNA legislation to assist in capturing dangerous offenders of this sort. As well, during the consultation process it became evident that the most controversial part of the proposal would be the DNA data bank, which had greater implications for invasion of privacy. Therefore, the government decided to put forward a bill dealing with DNA warrants alone. The data bank would wait for another round of legislation. On 22 June 1995, the day before the summer adjournment of Parliament, the House of Commons passed Bill C-104, An Act to amend the Criminal Code and the Young Offenders Act (forensic DNA analysis). It passed after only one day of debate, having received support from all parties. One justice department official commented: 'It was so fast that I got a speeding ticket leaving the House of Commons for taking a Bill through the House too fast' (in Schmitz, 1995).

From there, the bill went to the Senate, where it was referred to the Senate Standing Committee on Legal and Constitutional Affairs. This committee held two public meetings in which various witnesses spoke in favour of the bill, with the exception of the Privacy Commissioner. He pointed out that the list of designated offences was too broad, that the hearings for such a warrant would be conducted without the accused, and that the bill provided no right for adult offenders to have counsel present when a sample was taken. On 11 July the committee referred the bill back to the Senate without revision, with the recommendation that the Minister of Justice consider giving adult offenders the right to have counsel present at the execution of the warrant. This provision was added to the bill. On 13 July 1995, Bill C-104 was proclaimed into force. The uncharacteristically smooth process reminds us just how charismatic genetic science had become and how intent the government was on crime control.

But there were some critics of the bill and of the process by which it had been passed. Senator Noel Kinsella, the Conservative Party's critic on Bill C-104 in the Senate, commented:

> We are not going to have good law in Canada if the legislators who represent the people in both Houses don't do their job – if they just rubber stamp things. It's not that any given group of legislators in the House or the Senate have any special wisdom – that's why we bring in witnesses from outside who have expert knowledge and they share that with us and it's through the vehicle of committees that the good of the country in terms of good law happens ... When you allow the state to have special powers, in this instance to intrude into the very body of the citizen, you have to have safeguards. It can become quite Orwellian if you don't and I'm not sure we have that here. (in Schmitz, 1995)

A number of legal experts also commented on the continuing ambiguity regarding use of seized DNA samples for offences other than those for which they are collected. This had been the issue in *Borden*, and the law was still unclear about it.

Despite these criticisms, the minister was pleased with the bill. In a number of public statements he noted that Bill C-104 was part of the government's broader 'Safe Homes, Safe Streets' agenda – a 'get tough' approach to crime that the Liberals had promised in 1993 in their election 'Red Book.' As a part of this strategy, other laws had been passed or proposed during this session of Parliament, included the following: Bill C-37, which doubled to ten years the maximum penalty for first-degree murder committed by young offenders; Bill C-72, which restricted use of the defence of extreme drunkenness in criminal proceedings; and the proposed gun registry law, which would require gun owners to register their firearms in a central government registry and pay a registration fee. Bill C-104 was only the first step in incorporating genetic science into criminal justice. The next step would involve the much more contentious issue of DNA banking. This would have to wait for the next session of Parliament.

Highlights of Bill C-104

Bill C-104 details the procedures and limitations involved in obtaining DNA samples from suspects. In section 487.05(1), provincial court judges are authorized to issue DNA warrants if there are reasonable grounds to believe the following: first, that one of the designated offences has been committed; second, that a bodily substance has been found at the place where the offence was committed, on or in the body of the victim, or on anything the victim was wearing or carrying when the offence was committed, or, on or within the body of anyone or thing at the place associated with the offence; third, that a person was a party to the offence; and fourth, that a DNA analysis from the suspect will provide evidence about whether that person was involved.

The sampling procedures allowed by the act are the same as those proposed in the discussion paper – the plucking of hair roots; buccal swabs of the lips, tongue, and inside cheeks; and use of a lancet to take a blood sample. According to section 487.08(1), the sample can be used only 'in the course of an investigation of the designated offence for the purposes of forensic DNA analysis.' Section 487.08(3) states that anyone violating this restriction is 'guilty of an offence punishable on summary conviction.' This provision is meant to address concerns about the potential use of DNA testing results outside of the criminal context. Privacy concerns are further addressed in section 487.07(3), which states: 'A peace officer who executes a warrant against a person or a person who obtains a bodily substance from the person under the direction of a peace officer shall ensure that the privacy of that person is respected in a manner that is reasonable in the circumstances.'

Besides requiring respect for the privacy of the suspect, Bill C-104 requires that DNA samples be destroyed if the suspect is cleared by DNA testing, if the suspect is acquitted of the offence, or if one year has passed since certain types of proceedings have occurred. In some circumstances, however, the judge can defer the destruction of the sample and the information obtained from it for any period he or she considers appropriate. Generally, this is meant to permit the police to investigate the same suspect for other designated offences; in this way, the scope of the DNA warrant has been broadened beyond the immediate offence.

There are certain absences in the act that are as striking as what is present. Because the issue is not specifically mentioned, there seems to be a presumption that if a person consents to the removal of bodily substances, there is no need for a warrant. Yet, the act does not define proper consent. The warrant itself can be executed without any requirement of consent on the part of the suspect, and according to section 487.07(1)(e), an officer may use 'as much force as is necessary for the purpose of executing the warrant.' This provision is especially noteworthy because nowhere in the act is the concept of bodily integrity mentioned. In fact, it seems to have been replaced with a police power to use as much force as necessary in taking bodily samples – an escalation in police powers beyond what is available in the impaired driving provisions of the Criminal Code as well as in regular warrants for property. This being so, the next question is whether section 7 of the Charter can be read as protecting bodily integrity, thereby placing limits on how police may carry out DNA testing. A final point worth noting about Bill C-104 is that the list of designated offences encompasses everything from piracy and hijacking to violent and sexual offences to arson and breaking and entering. Attempts to commit these offences are also designated. The list is generally limited to those offences in which bodily substances may be expected to be left at crime scenes; even so, it is considerably more extensive than the one recommended by the Privacy Commissioner.[1]

Reaction to the new legislation was generally positive. Police and victims' groups praised the act as a first step in the right direction. Negative responses came mainly from the Privacy Commissioner and certain legal analysts. In his 1996 annual report, the Privacy Commissioner raised concerns about the ambiguity regarding how long samples and information could be stored, as well as the absence of provisions relating to volunteered samples (1997: 26). Legal scholars were concerned that this legislation would enhance the state's power over citizens' bodies in ways not yet foreseen. Their consensus was that Bill C-104 would not withstand Charter challenges. However, in a number of landmark cases they were proven wrong.

The DNA Data Bank

Passage of the DNA warrant provisions in Bill C-104 was relatively smooth. There was little debate at the policy and legislative levels. Instead, the bill's passage seemed to serve as the catalyst for opening up debate about the meaning of genetic technology in criminal justice. Contestation over DNA testing and banking occurred at two different sites after Bill C-104: in the courts, and within the policy process around the next step in the DNA system – a DNA data bank. It was in the latter that the frames for producing the official meaning of this technology were worked out among stakeholders.

Immediately after Bill C-104 was implemented, a number of cases were heard in appeal courts across the country. Most of these cases challenged the constitutionality of DNA warrants. The first statement on the matter by the Supreme Court was in *R. v. Stillman* (1997). Although this case involved a murder and a trial that occurred before Bill C-104 was passed and therefore was not affected by the new legislation, in an *obiter dictum*, Justice Cory commented on the new legislation:

> Although the issue was not raised it would seem that the recent provisions of the *Code* permitting DNA testing might well meet all constitutional requirements. The procedure is judicially supervised, it must be based upon reasonable and probable grounds and the authorizing judge must be satisfied that it is minimally intrusive ... It seems to me that the requirement of justification is a reasonable safeguard, which is necessary to control police powers to intrude upon the body. This is the approach I would favour.[2]

Cases directly involving the DNA warrant provisions involved challenges on a number of bases. In *R. v. Brighteyes (P.J.)* (1997) the accused was charged with first-degree murder and was compelled to provide a DNA sample. He sought to have the DNA evidence excluded from trial, arguing that the entire DNA warrant scheme violated sections 7 and 8 of the Charter. The Alberta Court of Queen's Bench found that the warrant had in fact violated the section 7 right to security of the person because the warrant had permitted the state to force a suspect to provide self-incriminating evidence. However, this violation was found to be reasonable in terms of section 1 of the Charter. The court also found that the seizure of DNA samples did not constitute an unreasonable search and seizure under section 8 of the Charter.

In *F(S) v. Canada (Attorney General)* (1998) the accused challenged the constitutionality of the entire scheme, including the *ex parte* hearing process whereby the accused is not present to make counter-arguments against the warrant. He argued that the suspect should be notified of an application for a DNA warrant and be given the opportunity to appear before the judge prior to the warrant being issued. The court rejected this challenge: 'While the subject matter of the seizure cannot be altered or destroyed, the person to be searched can, nevertheless, evade execution of the process if charged with pre-notification of the potential for seizure ... On balance, the interests in preserving the element of surprise in the execution of the warrant surmount the gains to be derived from an adversarial hearing as to whether the warrant should issue' (286). The accused in this same case also argued that the legislation infringed on section 7 of the Charter in terms of procedural fairness, because it failed to legislate national laboratory standards. The court rejected this argument and, in contrast to the *Brighteyes* decision, found that the DNA warrant legislation does not violate the principle against self-incrimination guaranteed by section 7. In considering whether the provisions violate section 8, the court concluded that the provision for removing hair roots does violate the right against unnecessary seizures because 5 to 10 per cent of the population does not give a root sheath when hair is plucked from the scalp. This could lead to successive seizures and an increase in detention time. The court considered this not justifiable under section 1 and struck down the hair root provision. The Attorney General of Canada and the Attorney General of Ontario appealed the decision and it was subsequently overturned.[3]

When tabling Bill C-104, the justice minister stated that he intended to introduce a second bill in the next Parliamentary session to regulate the banking of DNA samples and information collected in criminal investigations. On 18 January 1996 the Solicitor General of Canada distributed a consultation document, *Establishing a National DNA Data Bank*, thereby initiating the final stage of the process of incorporating biotechnology into the criminal justice system. Like the previous consultation document on DNA warrants, this one began with a discussion of what DNA is and how it can assist the police and the courts. It described the DNA data bank as potentially consisting of three indexes: a crime scene index storing information and samples from the scenes of unsolved crimes; a convicted offender index of samples and information taken from offenders convicted of designated offences; and a missing person index containing genetic profiles of unidentified bodies or body parts. It also raised the point of potential privacy issues around the data bank, characterizing those issues as 'less about using the technology for identification purposes in crime detection, than about using this information for more than crime detection or using the technology for purposes other than identification' (4).

The consultations focused on a number of questions. First, what should be included in the data bank – that is what types of offences should result in sampling and banking, who should collect the samples, at what stage of processing convicted offenders should those samples be collected, and what should be the involvement of health care professionals, if any? Second, should biological samples be retained or only the digitized data taken from those samples? The remaining questions related to options for funding local laboratories and the proposed national DNA data bank. After the consultations were completed in early 1996, the Canadian government produced a bill to create a national DNA data bank. The bill was introduced to the House of Commons on 10 April 1997, but died when an election was called for 2 June of that year. However, the re-elected Liberal government demonstrated its determination to pass the bill into legislation by reintroducing it as one of the first bills of the new Parliamentary session in 1997. In December 1998, Bill C-3, The DNA Identification Act, was passed.

Highlights of Bill C-3

The DNA Identification Act established the National DNA Data Bank (NDDB) under the jurisdiction of the RCMP. It was to be located in Ottawa, and it would consist of two indexes: a crime scene index of DNA profiles found at crime scenes or on any person, place, or thing associated with the offence; and a convicted offenders' index of profiles taken from people convicted of the designated offences. Safeguards would be included to protect the privacy of individuals. Only authorized law enforcement personnel would be authorized to inquire as to whether a suspect's DNA profile was present in the Convicted Offenders Index. The RCMP Commissioner would be permitted to communicate that same information to foreign law enforcement agencies and to allow access to anyone assisting in the data bank's operations or being trained to work there. Criminal penalties would apply to anyone who violated the conditions of privacy contained in the act. Besides information profiles, the NDDB would also store bodily substances for future analysis. Generally, the information and the biological samples would be stored indefinitely, although the information would be destroyed if the offender was acquitted. In the case of young offenders, the information would be destroyed after ten years, five years, or three years, depending on the severity of the offence.

The list of designated offences was longer than in Bill C-104 and was divided into two types: primary designated offences and secondary designated offences. In this list, primary offences were generally the most serious violent and sexual offences in which DNA evidence was likely to be useful in investigating the crimes. It was presumed that an offender convicted of a primary designated offence would be required to submit a sample to the NDDB unless he or she could demonstrate a substantial harm. Secondary offences were less serious offences for which the Crown would have to apply to the courts for retention of a sample from a convicted offender. In these cases the courts could have more discretion in determining whether DNA sampling was appropriate. The legislation was retroactive – that is, people convicted of designated offences before the passage of the act could be sampled if they had been declared 'dangerous offenders,' if they had been convicted of more than one sexual offence, or if they had been convicted of two or more murders committed at different times.

In 1999 a further addition was made to the NDDB provisions through Bill S-10, a Senate bill, which added certain military offences to the list of designated offences and provided for a Senate review of the legislation after five years. In July 2000 the the NDDB was officially launched in Ottawa.

Overall, the provisions of the new laws were the result of a series of debates during the policymaking process and were carefully crafted to survive the inevitable Charter challenges. These debates uncovered sets of competing assumptions, all of which crossed at the point where genetics intersects with crime control and individual rights with public safety.

Prior to its passage, the proposed legislation attempted to incorporate both ends of this spectrum. For example, section 4 of the proposed Act stated:

4 It is recognized and declared that
  a. the protection of society and the administration of justice are well served by the early detection, arrest and conviction of offenders, which can be facilitated by the use of DNA profiles; and
  b. to protect the privacy of individuals with respect to personal information about themselves, safeguards must be placed on
    (i) the use and communication of, and access to, DNA profiles and other information contained in the national DNA data bank, and
    (ii) the use of, and access to, bodily substances that are transmitted to the Commissioner for the purposes of this Act.

Nevertheless, the government failed to bridge the gap between the two sides that were forming around this distinction, and a number of rupture points developed among the stakeholders involved in policy development.

The first rift to become apparent in the policy debate was along a pre-existing fissure within the criminal justice system. Front-line law enforcers, represented by the Canadian Police Association (CPA) and by victims' groups, argued for a strong public protection approach. Their chief antagonist was the Canadian Bar Association (CBA), which argued for a strong focus on due process and individual rights.

The CPA was the most vocal champion of enhanced crime control. It justified its position by aligning itself with victims of crime, arguing that it was police, victims, and victims' families who really experienced the anguish of crime (Canadian Police Association, 1998a: 2–3). Lawyers, judges, and legislators wanted to impose clear limits on DNA testing and banking technology, yet they were too far removed from crime and could not claim to know what was needed in the war on crime. In response, the CBA and the Solicitor General repeatedly asserted that if DNA legislation intruded too far on individual privacy and if the DNA net were cast too broadly in terms of the types of offences to which it would apply, it would be found unconstitutional. This argument satisfied neither the CPA nor victims' groups.

The responses of the CPA and certain victims' groups to the Solicitor General's concerns indicated a second rift among stakeholders, based on differing opinions about the place and the value of the Charter of Rights and Freedoms in Canadian society. In a radical critique of the effects of the Charter, the CPA once again asserted the primacy of public safety over individual rights:

> The *Charter* is there for all of us, not just those who come into conflict with the law, which is why section 1 exists. It says that even if we violate one or more of the rights granted to Canadians, it may be justified because of the greater common good. None of the rights under the *Charter* are guaranteed absolutely. There are limits placed on them to recognize that sometimes the good of the majority is more important than individual rights. And if the *Charter* is standing in the way of ensuring that Canadians receive the maximum protection available to them, then we suggest there is a problem with the *Charter*. (1998a: 6)

Although this condemnation of the Charter was radical, it had a certain resonance among the public. For example, a citizens' lobby group, Victims of Violence, argued: 'The rights of the offenders have outweighed the rights of society for far too long. There is no justification to not allow a technique that can do so much good. DNA is a reality, and it is a part of the criminal justice system. It must be allowed to reach its full potential – to exonerate the innocent and implicate the guilty' (Victims of Violence, n.d.: 8).

In statements such as these, Victims of Violence reflected a common view in Canadian society. Canada is unique among Western nations in the degree to which the public has a positive opinion of the police. At the time the policy debates were occurring, the 1996 International Crime Victimization Survey found that Canada ranked highest among eleven industrialized nations in its approval rating of the police. While the average approval rating was 62 per cent, Canada's was 80 per cent (CCJS, 1999: 109). In the 1999 GSS, only 15 per cent of Canadians rated the criminal courts as doing a good job of helping victims; 33 per cent rated them as doing an average job, and 35 per cent rated them as doing a poor job.

However, this positive perspective on law enforcement is not true of all segments of the public. Interestingly, many women's groups objected to the very idea of a DNA data bank – which was ironic, given the government's legitimating rhetoric invoking the need to protect women from sexual predators. Their critique of the entire DNA scheme formed a third rift among the stakeholders struggling to define the place of this new technology, and it was a critique as radical as the CPA's critique of Charter rights. According to outspoken groups such as the Vancouver Rape Relief and Women's Shelter (Kubanek and Miller, 1997), the issue in most sexual assault cases is not the identity of the attacker, but the consent of the victim. DNA evidence cannot address that question. Also, women's groups objected to the costs involved in establishing a DNA data bank at the same time that women's shelters were being shut down and public funding of women's advocacy groups was being cut back, apparently due to a lack of government funds. These feminist critiques posed the most dangerous challenge to the government's DNA policy because they denied its grounds for existence. However, because the question of whether there should be a DNA data bank and warrants was not asked within the government's consultation documents, the concerns of those who opposed the very idea could be dismissed easily as irrelevant to the discussion. The original framing silenced the most fundamental and damning critique, and the feminist argument was quickly consigned to an occasional footnote in the Solicitor General's speeches on the matter.

A fourth rift among the primary stakeholders involved the ongoing criticisms by the Privacy Commission, which held to the position it had articulated during the DNA warrant policy process: the DNA data bank is a public good in principle, but its use should be strictly limited to serious violent offences, and it should have draconian privacy safeguards.

These various rifts, based on location within the criminal justice system, on different perspectives as to how to enforce the Charter, on different views as to the legitimacy of DNA technology in criminal justice, and on different views as to how strictly to limit use of the technology, became the points of debate that ultimately structured the framework of official meaning defining this new technology.[4]

Interpreting the Policy Discourse: Framing DNA Technology in Criminal Justice

Throughout the policy process, stakeholders were involved in a meaning construction enterprise during which they hegemonically framed the significance and implications of these new DNA technologies for public discourse. In addressing the question of what meanings these policy framers attributed to the technologies, I turn to communications scholars who have analysed similar questions largely in the context of the media. I suggest that their analyses can be extended beyond the media to interpret other forms of public communication, including policy texts.

Framing analysis studies how specific meanings are produced through the production of particular frames that embed, organize, classify, and interpret for the reader the immense amount of information in public circulation. As meanings are produced in this way, publicly circulating texts contribute to the social construction of reality (Gamson, 1989; Edelman, 1993; Tuchman, 1978; Altheide, 1997). Through a process of 'selection and salience,' frames privilege particular understandings of reality (Entman, 1993: 2; see also Gitlin, 1980); they teach the receiver how to make sense of facts and how to contextualize problems, information, and characters. When used repeatedly in the media, frames construct the reality for the community in which they circulate. The range of interpretations available to the public is configured and delimited through this sense-making process. The question then becomes: What frames were employed in publicly circulating policy and media texts to define DNA testing and banking in particular ways, and how did these frames contribute to the normalization of these new technologies?[5]

The Privacy 'Debate'

All of the primary policy and media documents examined in this analysis, as well as all of the secondary social science, natural science, and legal discussions, eventually refer to the privacy debate as central to the development of DNA warrants and data banks. There are a number of reasons why privacy has become the dominant public framing. First, the Solicitor General's consultation document of 18 January 1996 sets the issues in such a way that there is an obvious sensitivity to privacy. Interestingly, all of the questions this document raises are technical in nature and do not open up the possibility of challenging the data bank's existence on moral grounds. The second (related) reason for situating the issue as a privacy debate is that this framing renders the question resolvable. There is a pre-existing mechanism, the *Charter*, for actually settling the debate by ensuring that the legislation falls within the limits prescribed by sections 7 and 8.

As discussed in chapter 2, there are also pre-existing legal mechanisms available for defining the central issue as privacy. In Canadian common law, discussions of DNA testing and storing are grounded by the legal concept of 'bodily integrity.' Prior to the enactment of Bill C-104, sections 254(3) and 256 of the Criminal Code allowed police officers to seize blood samples from suspects in impaired driving offences. Case law around these sections clearly limits their application in terms of the degree of interference with bodily integrity. Bill C-104 and Bill C-3 were designed to resolve contradictions in common law and legislation relating to seizure of bodily substances; they do so by omitting the doctrine of bodily integrity and by authorizing the use of as much force as necessary to execute DNA warrants.

These governmental and legal parameters provided the context in which the DNA data bank was framed as primarily a privacy issue. In the public policy discourse, two agencies emerged as central to the debate – the federal Privacy Commissioner and the Canadian Police Association (CPA) – with the Solicitor General acting as referee between them. Other agencies participated as well, but it was these two that really defined the issue and to which the government responded.

In taking up the privacy issue, the Privacy Commissioner expressed two main concerns. First,

> retaining a databank of genetic samples from convicted offenders will inevitably attract researchers who want to analyze the samples for purposes that have nothing to do with forensic identification. This scientific curiosity, coupled with growing pressure to reduce crime by whatever means, no matter how intrusive, will almost certainly lead to calls to use samples to look for genetic traits common to 'criminals'. This type of

research, while perhaps of scientific interest and possible social value, raises complex legal, ethical and moral problems that we have yet to resolve. (1998: 4)

A number of fears were being expressed here. There was the fear that growing concern about crime rates would lead to diminished concern for individual privacy. There was the fear of the absence of moral constraints on scientific research. Finally, there the fear flowing out of the recognition that genetic research is increasingly informating the human body and the human person – that it is illuminating and codifying the very foundations of our physical and personality attributes. Yet the Privacy Commissioner was not, ultimately, concerned about the increased visibility of the individual offender. Rather, his main concern was DNA technology's potential to identify and code a segment of the population as criminal. Caution over state bio-power rather than individual discipline characterized the Privacy Commissioner's recommendations around Bill C-3. Nowhere did he call for abolition of the bill.

A second issue of privacy raised by the Privacy Commissioner related to the danger of 'casting the net' too broadly:

The range of offences for which samples can be taken from convicted offenders may be unnecessarily broad. Casting too wide a net will result in privacy intrusions on a massive level. For example, Bill C-3 allows a judge to order the taking of a DNA sample from someone convicted of what can be very minor offences involving minimal violence, such as common assault. In 1995, about 85,000 individuals were charged with common assault and about 48,000 charged with break and enter ... The bill includes both offences as 'secondary offences', meaning that a court can order DNA samples from convicted offenders. Thus many relatively minor offenders could have their DNA added to the databank which eventually could encompass a large segment of the Canadian population. (1998: 5).

Other agencies, in particular feminist organizations, also commented on the breadth of the list of designated offences. The government, however, did not shorten the list during the policy consultation process.

In the privacy debate, the primary antagonist of the Privacy Commissioner was the CPA, which took a highly aggressive stance in advocating widespread use of DNA sampling and banking. In emotive and moralistic language, the CPA attacked the arguments of privacy advocates:

> The argument against using the broad base gathering [of DNA samples] currently employed in fingerprinting via the *Identification of Criminals Act*, is based on 'what ifs' and potential abuses imagined by those who oppose the use of this tool. No doubt, had the Office of the Privacy Commissioner existed 100 years ago, similar 'objections' would have been trumpeted to fingerprinting. (1998a: 3)

The CPA was not greatly concerned with genetic privacy; rather, it was asserting the need to combat crime as the top priority. It advocated obtaining DNA samples at the time of arrest rather than conviction; storing both biological samples and digital information for an indefinite time; and broadening the list of designated offences. In these respects, its perspective was the polar opposite of the Privacy Commissioner's.

In arguing their positions, the Privacy Commissioner and the CPA drew from certain metaphors and key terms to characterize the privacy debate in a particular manner and to suggest what stakes were involved in implementing a DNA data bank. The CPA and other groups advocating a broad application of DNA technology in criminal justice employed the metaphor of 'fingerprinting.' The CPA argued that DNA samples had the same investigative relevance as fingerprints. They were a means of linking suspects with specific crimes (or eliminating suspects). Where there was no other evidence, crime scene evidence could be matched to previously collected DNA evidence kept on file (1998a: 2).

The other comparison suggested by the Privacy Commissioner and other privacy advocates related to the rules of search and seizure. From this perspective, the body was a special terrain; within the common law tradition, the state did not have the right to violate bodily integrity except under 'compelling circumstances of pressing necessity' (*R. v. Dyment*, 1988). In other words, the violation of a person's body by agents of the state was a much more serious matter than the search of a place, so the standard for justifying it needed to be very high.

Having delineated the two positions on the privacy issue as fingerprinting versus search and seizure, the parties involved began converting their positions from moral to technical ones. Each of the tropes of fingerprinting and search and seizure invoked certain technical rules for regulating its uses and impacts. The issue thus became which regulatory regime should be employed in DNA sampling and data banking. Fingerprinting has a broader application as well as fewer rules restricting its processes and uses; search and seizure is viewed as a more intrusive process that must be more tightly regulated. Thus the issue shifted from an ethical one – 'should the state have a particular power over its citizens?' to one of how far that power should extend.

At this point the government intervened in the 'debate' to complete the technicalization of the question, by characterizing it as a Charter issue: How could DNA data bank legislation satisfy Charter requirements? Here, a particular event became crucial in settling the issue and defining the government's position. The government asked three former appeal court justices to consider whether it would be constitutional for DNA samples to be taken at the time of being charged with an offence rather than on conviction. In early 1998, each justice responded that it would violate the Charter. A few weeks later the CPA held a press conference denouncing this finding and condemning Bill C-3 as 'foolish' and a 'fraud' (1998b: 1). However, the technical point had been settled, and the course of the legislation was set.

In a speech to the Senate Committee on Legal and Constitutional Affairs, the Solicitor General pointed out that the government was sensitive to the larger issues at stake:

> We have proceeded cautiously with this legislation to ensure a full examination and public debate on privacy and *Charter* issues. We know that DNA has the potential to reveal much more about a person than a breath sample can, or a fingerprint or even a routine blood test. As a result, we've been careful to examine the individual privacy rights of today, while also carefully looking at how this legislation might affect those rights in the future. (1998c: 2)

The Solicitor General proceeded to describe how privacy rights would be protected within the legislation through strict rules for collecting, accessing, and using DNA samples (1998c: 2). This apparently resolved the privacy debate. The privacy issue had become the dominant frame for conceptualizing the entire range of issues surrounding the data bank; it had also been contained and made manageable through the placing of limits on the use and communication of DNA information and samples. These limits became the new ground for debate, and as a result, the privacy debate shifted to a terrain of instrumental rather than ethical considerations. There were no more pro or con positions, only questions of degree.

Within Bill C-3, the language of search and seizure is employed in order to satisfy the Charter. Strict procedures must be followed in gathering DNA evidence for the data bank. In many ways, however, the legislation seems more in keeping with fingerprinting in the sense that samples and information are kept on file indefinitely unless convictions are overturned. A due process approach has seemingly been taken to the DNA data bank; in this way, the ethical question of whether such a thing should exist has been elided altogether. While seeming to take the more liberal approach, the government has enhanced its ability to interfere with the bodily integrity of citizens. As part of this, it has maintained a very broad list of designated offences. The privacy debate had been resolved in such a way as to move the criminal justice system farther in the social control direction of the governmental continuum. By the end of 1999, the privacy debate had been resolved within policy and media texts. Journalists could confidently report:

> Where privacy is concerned, there is less at risk than some would have us believe. The Canadian DNA data bank, like the system used by the FBI in the United States, records information from only 13 loci within the genome. These loci are not known to provide any meaningful genetic information ... except to the extent they mark the bearer's identity. Finally, Canadians should not forget that DNA evidence is just as commonly used to exclude suspects as it is to incriminate them ... From the point of view of the innocent, the idea of DNA testing is not really frightening at all. (Kay, 1999)

The Surveillance Society

The privacy debate served to situate the DNA data bank in terms of social control versus individual rights; it also provided a dominant public framing. In the same vein, the frame of *perpetual surveillance* served as a legitimating discursive device. It answered these questions: Why do we need a DNA data bank? What are the benefits of employing DNA technology in this way? Here, the Solicitor General attempted to position DNA technology in criminal justice within a problem-setting/ problem-solving framework by setting a social problem in a particular way and then presenting the DNA data bank as the obvious solution to that problem.

How was the problem set? In analysing the policy documents cross-textually, I found that a number of key terms were employed in order to legitimate the policy. These terms included 'repeat offenders,' 'high-risk offenders,' and 'dangerous offenders.' For example, the Solicitor General pointed out:

> Stored DNA information will enable police to quickly identify suspects and repeat offenders across police jurisdictions. In addition, by targeting certain high-risk offenders already in custody, the data bank will offer the hope of solving long outstanding crimes. And it will make the most dangerous offenders think twice about committing a violent offence again because their genetic imprint will be in the data bank for future identification. (1998c: 2)

Comments of this sort were common across the policy documents. They were employed even by privacy advocates such as the Privacy Commissioner and the Canadian Bar Association. There was almost unanimous agreement among participating agencies that the DNA policy was justified by the need to control repeat and dangerous offenders. In particular, this policy was aimed at sexual and violent offenders because it was they who committed the most serious crimes and it was they who were most likely to leave DNA evidence behind. The Solicitor General expressed faith that the data bank would act as a deterrent to offenders, who would know their DNA was in the data bank. Also, it would allow for faster and more certain identification of serious offenders and would lead to the 'closing' of unsolved crimes.

Within this frame, there was a constant focus on the risk of dangerous offenders reoffending. An easy assumption was being made that this was a serious problem that could be addressed, in part, through a DNA data bank. The Solicitor General argued that 'the banking of DNA evidence is based on the likelihood that certain kinds of offenders tend to re-offend' (Solicitor General, 1996a: 5). Similar assumptions were made about young offenders, many of whom 'will become adult offenders who may commit serious violent offences' (1996b: 3). The expressed hope of the Solicitor General and victims' groups was that a DNA data bank would somehow deter recidivism. This led to fantastical claims about the nature of the problem. For example, Victims of Violence stated: 'Released murderers are 5 times more likely to be arrested for murder than are other offenders, and released rapists are 10 times more likely to be arrested for sexual offenses than are other criminals. It is estimated that 60 per cent of offenders who commit 3 violent offences will re-offend, and 80 per cent of offenders who commit 4 violent offences will re-offend' (n.d.: 7).

These numbers are frightening, but Victims of Violence did not cite its sources, nor did the numbers match statistics for recidivism and reoffending published by the Solicitor General. The Correctional Service of Canada reported that 46 per cent of male inmates had served a previous term of incarceration, but they did not indicate for which offences (Solicitor General, 1998a: 26). In 1996–7, 15,222 offenders were released from correctional facilities; only 195 of them were charged with serious offences while on conditional release (1998a: 52). This is not to say that recidivism is not an important social problem; the point is that most individuals do not commit serious violent and sexual crimes upon release.

The main antagonists within this discursive frame were feminist groups versus everyone else. Feminists and certain civil liberties groups opposed the very idea of a DNA data bank on two main grounds. First, it would not help women who were victims of violence because most women know their attackers and the issue at trial is consent, not identity (Kubanek and Miller, 1997: 2). Second, the DNA legislation marked a shift to greater social control on the part of law enforcement agencies: 'Conservative "law and order" groups are demanding harsher prison sentences, abolishment of the parole system and/or the Young Offenders Act, reinstatement of the death penalty. Widespread use of DNA evidence to identify suspects is another such demand' (1997: 2).

Concerns like these were all but ignored in subsequent discussions. Instead, the Solicitor General glossed them over and reinforced the government position:

There are those who believe that resources earmarked for a DNA data bank would be better spent on family violence programs or women's shelters. In response, I would agree that spending in those areas is important. Governments and society need to do more to address the important issues of family violence and violence against women. But at the same time, there is no doubt in my mind that a national DNA data bank will add to the safety of all Canadians. (1998b: 4)

All of the other agencies involved in the consultation process embraced this perspective. Once again, the debate was being restricted to a technical question of the *degree* of surveillance.

Why was there such widespread agreement on this issue, even among privacy advocates? Implicit in this legitimating discursive frame was criticism of the corrections system and its prevailing philosophy of rehabilitation. Rising prison costs, the apparent failure of past rehabilitation schemes, the politicization of penal policy, and a general climate of scepticism regarding social welfare have led to a decline in the rehabilitation ideal. The idea that criminals can be transformed into productive citizens has been replaced in policy discussions by notions of 'selective incapacitation' (i.e., removing the law-breaker from society) and 'situational crime prevention' (i.e., reducing opportunities for crime). Implicit in these strategies is the idea that criminal tendencies, whatever their origin, are fundamental and unchangeable.

Newer approaches to crime focus on risk management. The DNA data bank has been legitimated as a tool for enhancing the risk management capacity of the criminal justice system. Within the policy documents and in Bill C-3, no consideration is given to rehabilitation. Violent offenders are assumed to be beyond reform. Even after a long term of imprisonment, they remain social risks who must be kept under perpetual panoptic surveillance. Such offenders can no longer be put to death; thus, they will eventually be unleashed on the public. But through the DNA data bank, they can be kept under a type of permanent, symbolic incarceration. Their essence is being incarcerated and coded, to be read and matched if they reoffend. In this sense, any and all violent offenders can always be put to the question whenever DNA material is left at the scene of a violent crime. The government, anxious to appear in control of crime, is counting on the data bank to serve as a deterrent; this hope has yet to be tested.

Science as Objective Truth

A third narrative frame employed to make sense of the DNA data bank in the public sphere centred on notions of *objectivity*. Here, the frame addressed questions relating to the adequacy of current systems for gathering and employing evidence. Because of its apparent objectivity, genetic information was becoming more than a source of evidence – it was becoming a form of proof: '"The reason why DNA evidence has become so popular in criminal justice is because it approaches mathematical certainty in terms of proof. It is one of the few mechanisms that allow us to transcend subjective decision-making. It gets us away from the fallibility of the human process which we call justice"' (Alan Young, law professor, in Bindman, 1997: A2).

In the policy discourse, DNA evidence was viewed as promising a level of certainty and objectivity impossible within the current methods of the justice system. For example, Victims of Violence expressed the view that 'DNA evidence can provide more definite and objective proof of guilt or innocence than can often be provided by eyewitness identification or other such subjective means' (n.d.: 1). The government concurred with this perspective. The Department of Justice stated: 'DNA typing is a powerful comparative identification tool. Since its forensic introduction in Canada in 1988–89, it has been instrumental in securing convictions in hundreds of violent crimes, from homicide to assault. It has also helped to eliminate suspects, sometimes in the face of damaging allegations' (Department of Justice, 1995: 1).

Common terms present across the texts and instrumental in framing the issue included 'powerful investigative tool,' 'accurate,' and 'objective proof.' In media coverage, descriptors commonly used to make sense of the science included 'fingerprinting,' 'bar code,' and 'powerful investigative tool.' Such terms signified something pragmatic, utilitarian, effective, reliable, and familiar in everyday life. Yet the science of DNA was never explained in any detail. Government agencies and victims' groups offered these metaphors and keywords as proof of the technology's effectiveness and went even further, asserting that DNA evidence had the potential to expand to other types of criminal investigations beyond violent crime: '"The burgeoning science of genetic fingerprinting was once used only in murder and rape cases. But demand is exploding as improved technology makes it helpful in everything from break-ins to arson," said Pam Newall of the Centre for Forensic Sciences' (Canadian Press, 1996). The implicit conclusion was that given the ability of DNA testing to solve crimes of various sorts, both new and old, with such great certainty, what grounds could there possibily be for criticism? These groups were expressing the hope that guilty offenders would not be able to escape justice through the deficiencies of more equivocal forms of evidence. At the same time, DNA evidence promised to exonerate the innocent. Policy documents cited the Morin and Milgaard cases in this connection; both provided a ready-made shorthand for the value of DNA testing and banking (see chapter 4).

At the same time, lawyers, represented by the CBA, were opposing the widespread use of DNA evidence in criminal courts, mainly because the technology wasn't foolproof, and also because the laboratories were not governed by clear regulatory standards for laboratories.

While the protocol for identifying DNA may vary from laboratory to laboratory, the science itself is well known and widely accepted within the scientific community. Improved methods of analysis are being developed, but quality control and the risk of contamination are ongoing concerns. The Canadian Society of Forensic Science and the Standards Council of Canada have not yet created a regulatory regime of accreditation for private laboratories. It is apparent that DNA is a developing science, and there is a continuing need to establish reliability in the field of DNA testing. (CBA, 1996: 3).

The CBA was drawing from a line of argument that had developed alongside the reliability argument for DNA testing: there had been cases where DNA testing had proven less than reliable, as in *New York v. Castro* (1989). Eric Lander, one of the experts consulted in that case, pointed out a number of problems in gaining accurate forensic DNA analysis: degradation of samples due to environmental factors; mixing of samples from different individuals; and the use of samples too small to allow for retesting. Also, the results must be interpreted, and this raises the possibility of human error. For example, determining whether band patterns from two samples match often requires careful judgment. If they do appear to match, scientists must then assess the probability that the match occurred by chance (Lander, 1993: 196).

William Thompson (1997) raises another criticism of DNA science. He contends that the scientific objectivity of forensic DNA laboratories and scientists is compromised by their role as service providers for law enforcement agencies. In that position, they must adopt the goals of the police and prosecutions who are their clients, and these goals sometimes conflict with the professional goals of scientific neutrality and objectivity. In the United States, some scientists have actually been prosecuted for misconduct involving the fabrication of incriminating DNA data.[6]

During the debate over DNA testing and banking, the Canadian government was aware of these problems and took steps to rectify them:

Canada's forensic labs are establishing accreditation standards. These will provide for an independent body to conduct audits and ensure that forensic labs meet internationally recognized quality assurance levels. In addition, the RCMP works closely with several groups and international committees like the FBI-sponsored Technical Working Group on DNA Analysis methods. It facilitates the sharing of information on the latest technology and provides a forum to ensure that Canada's standards are

at par with those around the world. Since the RCMP will be operating the
DNA data bank, all functions must meet the RCMP's own internal standards, which are among the most stringent in the world. (Solicitor General, 1998c: 3)

The main effect of this discursive framing was to signify a shift in
expertise within the criminal justice system. This points to why the CBA
responded as negatively as it did to the use of DNA evidence. Cases
such as Morin and Milgaard suggested to the public that the existing
legal mechanisms were failing where *scientific* processes were succeed-
ing. The government and victims' groups wanted a more definite, scientific mechanism for ensuring that offenders did not escape justice
through insufficient legal standards of evidence. In this regard, the use
of DNA evidence in criminal law had an undeniable appeal. Science
was perceived as having an objectivity and precision that promised to
increase the accuracy of judicial and jury decision making. Science, in
other words, could increase public confidence in the judicial system.

Lawyers' critiques of DNA evidence were represented as the rear-
guard actions of a declining form of expertise, to the detriment of a
fearful society: '"Courts often resist DNA testing in old cases. Every
case where there's a DNA vindication, what's not really reported is the
hard-won fight to get the evidence accepted"' (a wrongful conviction
activist, in Appleby, 1997: A12). Furthermore, the government's concern over civil rights was seen as holding back the efficiency of the science: 'Although the data bank's conception is straightforward, the
mechanics of drafting, passing and putting into action legislation that
would allow the state to become the keeper of the genetic record of citizens who have been accused of certain crimes is proving tricky'
(Grange, 1997: A6). In the end, this frame leaves little doubt as to the
necessity and efficacy of the science. It is precise, and it is free of the
subjective elements that lead to bad decisions in court.

Defence lawyers did not remain idle in the face of these criticisms of
their expertise. Traditional forms of legal argumentation were being
devalued within the policy discourse. In what was effectively a
counter-attack, the law journals began to fill with articles detailing
common law sources for arguing against the legality of seizing biological samples (Bassan, 1996; Federico, 1990; Pomerance, 1995), and for
arguing against the constitutionality of seizing biological samples
(Astroff, 1996), and with discussion of courtroom strategies for challenging and/or discrediting DNA evidence and expert witnesses at

trial (Brodsky, 1993; Lussier, 1992). The development of professional counter-knowledge on the part of defence lawyers implied that the future of DNA evidence in court would not be as unproblematic as the government and victims' groups hoped.

The Need for Administrative Efficiency

The fourth and final frame in the public policy discourse was managerial and technological efficiency. This frame, which served as an administrative frame within the discourse, addressed questions of how to enhance the administrative effectiveness of the criminal justice system by implementing a new technology. It was about the needs of the justice system rather than of society; it was about the need to enhance productivity through savings in time, labour, and money. It was also about the future and how a DNA data bank could result in long-term benefits in crime management.

Within the policy documents, much of the discussion of efficiency centred around the issue of whether and how to retain biological samples. Should Bill C-3 enable the long-term storage of DNA samples, as well as the digitized DNA information acquired from those samples? Once again, the loudest voices in this debate were raised by the Solicitor General, the Department of Justice, and the CPA on the one hand, and the Privacy Commissioner and the CBA on the other hand. The Department of Justice stated the government position quite clearly: 'Samples of bodily substances used for forensic DNA analysis will be retained indefinitely. This will enable the data bank to keep pace with technological advances without having to re-collect samples should the original analysis become obsolete' (1998: 3).

Ethical concerns were addressed simply by displacing them with the needs of technology:

> On the question of retaining a biological sample once it has been typed for banking purposes, the present state of the science and resulting technology would appear to impose special needs. It is true that retaining a sample could lead to misuse. However, as the U.S. National Research Council pointed out: 'there is a practical reason to retain DNA samples for short periods. Because DNA technology is changing so rapidly, we expect the profiles produced with today's methods to be incompatible with tomorrow's methods. Accordingly, today's profiles will need to be discarded and replaced with profiles based on the successor methods. It would be

extremely expensive and inefficient to have to redraw blood samples for retyping.' (1995: 3)

From the other side, the Privacy Commissioner argued for caution:

> Our strong preference is for the retention of the identification analysis only of the DNA samples, not the samples themselves. This may cause some additional expense and require resampling of convicted persons as forensic DNA analysis techniques change. However, retaining actual DNA samples from convicted offenders requires the strongest possible justification. Administrative convenience and reduced expense are not sufficient. (1995: 4)

This debate centred around a broader question: whether the criminal justice system should import into its operations what Nils Christie (1994) refers to as an 'industrial logic.' This was a prominent theme in government policy statements, in which 'keeping pace with technological advances' was a recurring phrase. Other efficiency reasons were also given: investigations would be more focused, trials would be shortened, the number of guilty pleas would increase, some offenders would be deterred from committing serious offences, and Canada would be keeping up with other countries, especially the United States (Solicitor General, 1996a: 2; Department of Justice, 1995: 1).

Here we see a very direct importation of an industrial logic into the framing of the data bank, with the government drawing from a language of savings, managerial efficiency, technological imperatives, keeping pace with other jurisdictions, and, ultimately, an ethos of crime *management*. Interestingly, notably absent from the policy documents was any evidence that a cost/benefit analysis had been conducted in order to demonstrate the actual economic and administrative efficiencies of the policy. Furthermore, there was no discussion in government documents of potential inefficiencies. These could include the costs of inevitable court challenges launched by defence lawyers as well as problems with the science of forensic DNA testing. From this perspective, the DNA policy could be quite costly over the long term.

There is something unsettling about the absence of actual cost/benefit analysis combined with the government's insistence on retaining samples for future analysis. All of this suggests purposes other than data storage. The Solicitor General's comments implied that the data bank would retain biological samples in order to continually 'reinvent' the data bank, enhance it, and draw more and more information from it. This, of course, was exactly what the Privacy Commissioner feared. Data banks are rarely if ever simply about storing data; they are also about generating ongoing *information* to ensure increasingly efficient management of a population.

As Christie points out, the danger here lies in those values which are beginning to guide criminal justice. He observes that in this era of advanced capitalism, the central administrative values are clear goals, production control, cost reduction, rationality, and the division of labour (Christie, 1994: 150). The drive is for efficiency to achieve clearly defined goals. Criminal justice can be 'produced' more quickly by finding ways to sentence more people with less administrative effort. Thus a scientific basis is sought for more uniform decisions. 'Speed, accountability, similarity, clear messages to potential criminals, a system which offers easily operated control by central authorities' – these constitute a perfect adaptation of the criminal justice system to modernity (1994: 151).

DNA data banks appear to fit into such a system quite well. As Benjamin and Weston (2000: 65) point out, the debate around DNA data banks should not focus on whom, how much, and when; rather, it should focus on why, and where do we go from here? It is precisely these ethical questions that were largely suppressed by the Canadian state when the data bank issue was being framed. In each of the frames, ethical questions were quickly transformed into technical ones. At the turn of the new century, all spheres of government administration have been colonized by business rationales. Efficiency and cost minimization are the key imperatives in the present-day criminal justice system. In terms of the DNA data bank legislation, it is likely that these imperatives will result in an even longer list of designated offences and an increased volume of testing to maximize resource use. These developments will cause the data bank to expand and its importance in criminal justice to grow.

Few critical scholars would disagree with the assertion that DNA warrants and data banking are moving the criminal justice system toward greater social control of citizens. It is important to map out the discursive processes by which this is being accomplished and the language by which it is being legitimated. The four narrative frames – privacy, surveillance, science as objective truth, and the need for administrative efficiency – are being employed within public-sphere policy texts to capture this new development in cultural narratives of criminal justice. The

underlying goal of these texts is to render DNA technology understand-
able and to contain it in terms of its social risks. These four frames fit this
new development within pre-existing meaning systems and normalize
it as necessary and inevitable. They define the limits of critical debate
about the technology in the public sphere, and they encourage the public
to accept the state's needs and goals around biotechnology as defined by
certain primary definers.

Of course, it is not quite as simple as this. Within the policy and
media texts, debate is growing heated among institutional authorities
– in particular between police, prosecutors, and scientists on one hand
and government ministers, defence lawyers, and the Privacy Commissioner on the other. Yet few of these groups are actually opposed to
DNA warrants and data banks; they are merely negotiating the boundaries of biogovernance. I suggest, however, that the frames are clearly
promoting a view more in keeping with that of the police and prosecutors – the 'full use' side – rather than with the 'limited use' side of the
debate. This interpretation of the technology is made possible not only
by what is included in the frames, but also by some noteworthy
absences: an absence of questioning of the science, an absence of cost/
benefit inquiry, and in the case of media coverage, an absence of accurate descriptions of the broad range of designated offences included in
the legislation.

How does the public framing of the DNA data bank contribute to a
shift toward greater social control of the citizenry and away from due
process and individual rights? DNA warrants and data banks give the
appearance that governments have new ideas in the 'war on crime'
and can still act to control it. However, the Canadian government's
'action' involves enhancing state power over each individual citizen's
body, as well as acquiring a more intimate knowledge of the aggregate
social body of the criminal population. Combined with a decline in the
rehabilitation ideal in favour of perpetual surveillance, these developments have the potential to foster a less humane approach to criminal
justice. It may well be that crime management is turning away from
moral and clinical intervention at the level of the individual, and turning increasingly to an actuarial language of probability and statistical
distribution of criminal traits. If so, this can only further distance crime
control from questions of public morality.

The public's fear of crime and support for police ensure that the
DNA legislation has popular appeal. Such laws can be framed as democratic even if questions of citizens' rights are never presented to the

public. Only the technical question of how to proceed efficiently has been opened for public discussion. The public has not reacted in any noticeable way to the introduction of the DNA system in criminal justice. Perhaps fear of crime and unthinking adjustment to the late modern 'superpanopticon' have disciplined the public to participate in its own surveillance. In such a context, the DNA data bank is simply one more database in an information society that has normalized and accepted such adminstrative technologies.

As a result of governmental shifts in crime management strategies and definitions of criminality, and the increasingly intimate relationship between information technology and the public, the DNA data bank is being normalized within Canadian society. In the final analysis, the narrative frames of privacy, surveillance, scientific objectivity, and administrative efficiency are instrumental frameworks; they relate to the more general discourse of the fear of crime, and they operate in such a way as to distance crime management from those moral questions which are necessary for public involvement in criminal justice. They promote DNA technology as a major development in risk management due to its near perfect ability to identify, code, and permanently survey offenders.

4 Corrective Justice: Media Events and Public Knowledge of DNA in the Criminal Justice System

In July 1993 an incident took place that seemed incredible, considering that it involved the ordinarily staid, 'peace, order, and good government'–oriented citizens of Canada. Bystanders heckled a judge as he entered his courtroom. This happened at the trial of Karla Homolka, who with her ex-husband, Paul Bernardo, was accused of kidnapping, sexually assaulting, and murdering two teenage girls in St Catharines, Ontario, and dismembering one of them. Over the course of the trial, as Homolka testified against her ex-husband, Mr Justice Francis Kovacs ordered a temporary publication ban on the evidence heard in the courtroom. The stated purpose of the ban was to protect Paul Bernardo's right to a fair trial, which was scheduled after Homolka's, and to ensure that he could not claim a mistrial due to jury bias. Publication bans are not uncommon in Canadian criminal justice, especially for the purpose of concealing the identities of young offenders and victims of sexual assault. Ironically, in the same week that Paul Bernardo was arrested, his father was convicted of sexual offences committed twenty years earlier; again, a publication ban was invoked to protect the privacy of the victims.

Media organizations immediately protested the ban and initiated legal action to have it lifted. The challenge ultimately failed, since the trial judge had the legal right to impose a publication ban and had not erred in law by doing so. Media arguments that the ban would bring justice into disrepute, that the ban would fail because the non-Canadian press was not bound by it, and that the right to an open and fair trial for Homolka would be jeopardized by a publication ban, were not valid legal arguments according to the Ontario Court of Appeal. Consequently, the media turned to the court of public opinion, publishing fiery headlines and articles filled with indignant rhetoric about democracy, public interest, fairness, openness, rights, and justice. The victims in the process were no longer the murdered women and their families and friends, but rather the press and the public that it claimed to represent. A struggle was underway over who properly represents the public in criminal justice proceedings. Was it the police, prosecutors, judges, and juries, or was it the press?

This controversy over the Homolka case was yet another example of a process that in the early 1990s seemed to define the relationship between criminal justice and the Canadian press. A number of high-profile 'media trials' were conducted around that time, each of them framed within narratives of abuse of authority by justice officials. Together, they provided the journalistic context in which DNA testing technology first entered public consciousness in Canada; they also provided a narrative framework for interpreting the meanings of this new technology. Although the press did cover the debates that led up to the passage of the DNA warrant and DNA banking legislation, this coverage was sparse. I suggest that the public came to know about DNA testing and banking through highly publicized criminal trials – trials which provided a particular narrative framework that has done much to shape public opinion about the technology. Specifically, the trials of Guy Paul Morin and David Milgaard – two men accused, convicted, and later exonerated for separate sexual assaults and murders – were the vehicles through which the Canadian press engaged in a problem-setting and problem- solving exercise that defined DNA testing as part of the solution to the problems of the criminal justice system. The policy debates defined the central issue in DNA technology as 'privacy'; in contrast, the media coverage of high-profile cases involving DNA evidence defined the central issue as 'objectivity.' Together, these two frames have shaped the resulting DNA testing and banking system in Canada.

Reporting Justice: The Press and Trial Coverage

Mass media scholars have been interested for some time in the relationship between media coverage and trial processes, especially since the 1980s, when television cameras entered courtrooms in the United States. Live CNN coverage in the early 1980s eventually led to 'Court TV,' a cable television network dedicated to live trial coverage. Over this time, certain trials have come under unprecedented and intimate scrutiny. Three issues are of particular interest to critical scholars. First is how media coverage affects actors within the court system, including lawyers, judges, juries, and witnesses. Second is how media coverage affects verdicts and even state justice policies. Third is how crime reporting affects public perceptions of crime and victimization risk.

Some scholars have contended that the institutional interests of the court and the media tend to converge. David Altheide (1992), for example, maintains that the courts and the media often act in concert to assert social control and moral compliance by creating public spectacles of punishment that stigmatize offenders and valorize crime control agents. This 'Gonzo Justice' is sometimes used to justify abuses of power to apprehend dangerous criminals and impose excessive sentences. It relies on popular support stemming from fear of crime, and it delivers an image of the justice system as proactive rather than reactive. Clinton Sanders and Eleanor Lyon (1995) argue along similar lines, suggesting that the media affect criminal justice agencies by focusing the public's attention on certain types of crime and criminals; this generates pressure for governments to devote resources to these types of crime. At the same time, justice agencies rely on the media to report their successes in fighting that type of crime, to demonstrate the state's concern for the public welfare, and to legitimate their role. Once again, this is a mutually beneficial relationship.

Ray Surette (1996) explores the issue in more detail. He contends that the media affect criminal justice policy either directly (see Sanders and Lyon), or indirectly by acting in concert with an event or chain of events to promote a change in policy. Focusing on the latter, he analyses the passage of the original Three Strikes Law in the State of Washington in 1993. Previous attempts to pass it had failed. However, after a brutal abduction and murder case, the media began championing the law. Surette cautions against this media-based agenda setting since it can result in important public policy decisions being made on the basis of emotion, opinion, and convention rather than rationality, logic, and reason. He characterizes Three Strikes laws as 'the latest in a string of fast-paced, punitive-oriented, heavily media-covered crime panaceas that periodically sweep the nation' (179).

In terms of the effects of media coverage on trial processes and trial decisions, Marjorie Cohn and David Dow (1998), along with many other American scholars, frame the issue as a potential conflict between the First and Sixth Amendments to the United States Constitution, which guarantee freedom of the press and the right to a fair trial, respectively.

Television cameras are now in widespread use in American courtrooms, and concern is growing that they may be having a harmful effect on trials. For example, Cohn and Dow argue that in the retrial of the Menendez brothers, the jury's decision to convict and the judge's behaviour throughout the trial were both strongly influenced by television coverage of the first trial.[1] The defence lawyers in the second trial later claimed that the defence suffered from a lack of television coverage in the second trial; had it received more, judicial misconduct might have been prevented. The concern in all this seems to revolve around balancing the dangers of a tyrannical judge with the dangers of a public lynching.

Other studies suggest that cameras in the courtroom have less impact than this. Ronald Goldfarb (1998) cites a number of studies that have been conducted in the United States beginning in the 1970s that investigated the perceived effects of cameras in the courtroom. A 1970s study in Florida found no effect on jurors and witnesses, nor were there any effects on courtroom decorum arising from the presence of cameras. In 1995, Court TV surveyed judges on the question of cameras in the courtroom. It found that 71 per cent of the judges who participated responded positively to the presence of Court TV, with many reporting that they simply forget that it is present after a time. Also, 65 per cent felt that the presence of the camera was of public educational value. However, other surveys contradict these results. A 1987 Minneapolis survey found that 90 per cent of respondents from the general public believed that a television camera in a sexual assault trial would increase the trauma of the victim. A 1993 study found that 48 per cent of respondents would be less likely to testify at a trial if a television camera was present. In 1990, a study of witnesses in a murder trial found that many reported trying to 'live up' to the perceived expectations placed on them by the media. They reported resorting to a certain performativity in their testimony. Different surveys show contradictory results, so it is difficult to generalize from them, although according to Goldfarb most of the surveys have found some kind of effect on some participants.

A more subtle analysis of media effects on trial processes is provided by Surette (1990), who contends that 'media trials' can have 'echo effects.' Media trials are defined as trials that are media events constructed according to entertainment formats with dramatic, fast-paced narratives. Three recurring categories of media trials recur: abuse of power and trust, the sinful rich, and evil strangers (i.e., either foreigners/marginalized people or psychotic killers who appear outwardly normal). These themes simplify the task of reporting and interpreting a trial by enabling journalists to draw from stereotypes to shape the trial's story. The effects of how media trials are covered 'echo' through the criminal justice system, where they have an impact on how similar cases are covered and even conducted. This is true even if there is no media coverage of the trial. Media images and real trial processes have converged in the public imaginary and are indistinguishable, he argues.

A related question is this: What type of impact does media coverage of trials have on popular perceptions of criminal justice? Altheide (1997), in discussing the role of the news media in producing fear, characterizes the issue in this way: 'Students of the mass media and popular culture agree on two basic social facts: (1) Popular culture includes a relatively large amount of information and images pertaining to fear, including crime and violence, and (2) Audience members perceive social life as very dangerous. It is the relationship between these two "social facts" that remains unclear' (648). So does media coverage of trials contribute to a public sense of fear and risk? The answer probably depends on the outcome of the specific trial. Arguably, the outcomes of the Rodney King and O.J. Simpson trials in the United States contributed to a sense of ontological insecurity among mainstream white Americans, by implying in a highly visible and spectacular way that the criminal court system was unable to deliver justice.

Social scientists also study how crime news is framed and what impact this framing has. Michael Schudson (1989) identifies three key perspectives that shape academic approaches to this question: political economic, social, and cultural. The *political economy* perspective examines links between the political economy of a society and the everyday practices of news journalism. In general terms, he argues that the definition of the situation provided by news reports tends to legitimate the dominant ideology emanating from power elites in society. Perhaps the best-known statement of this position is found in *Manufacturing Consent* (1988), in which Edward S. Herman and Noam Chomsky employ a 'propaganda model' to argue that the mass media serve to mobilize support for the powerful interests that dominate both the state and civil society (xi). The news industry's increasing concentration of ownership, the dependence on advertising for revenue, and reliance on state agents as sources for news ensure that the media remain firmly planted in the ideology of capitalism. However, the political economy approach has difficulty explaining how dissent and criticism become part of news coverage. This approach helps us understand where the connections are among various institutions, but it does not help us understand the disconnections or the ways in which the media can become discredited as the mouthpieces of ideological institutions, as happened in Eastern Europe (Schudson, 1989: 270). Drawing from Habermas, Daniel Hallin (1985) points out that the media are disconnected from other ruling institutions by their need to ensure their own legitimacy just as much as they are bound to those institutions by the project of legitimating capitalism as a whole. If this were not so, they would simply be viewed as tools of the state and/or corporate sectors.

Barry Brummett's (1990) discussion of popular trials draws explicitly from this political economy tradition to characterize televised trials as inevitably ideological in nature. He contends that three processes are involved in the ideological constructions: serialization, personification, and commodification. Serialization is the process by which trials are cast into a narrative form. The 'story' is broken up into smaller segments that bring the audience up to date through the simplest forms of narrative. Personification renders public issues into personal problems by attaching social principles to individuals, who come to represent those principles within a simplified 'good versus bad' narrative. In the process, the backstage elements of the justice system are trivialized; what counts is the character of the individuals, not the operation of the justice system. 'Commodification' valorizes the rich by focusing media attention on their trials and also by seeming to commodify justice itself. That is, it makes justice seem like a commonplace and easily acquired commodity rather than one that is financially ruinous. Through serialization, personification, and commodification, popular trials legitimate a court system that serves the interests of the ruling class; they do so by recasting trials as popular narratives and by making justice seem within reach of all.

The social perspective attempts to address some of the weaknesses of the political economy model by examining the social organization of news work. Study after study comes to the same conclusion: journalism is mainly about the interaction between reporters and officials. A reporter's most important tools are his or her sources within bureaucratic organizations, and a reporter's status within the profession is based largely on the number of such contacts (Tuchman, 1978). Mark Fishman found that the 'journalist's view of the society as bureaucratically structured is the very basis upon which the journalist is able to detect events' (1980: 51). Bureaucracies provide continuous detection of events and a steady source of news. However, this news is highly mediated; it is not a gathering of ontologically independent facts. The news is socially constructed through the perceptions of official sources and through the interaction between these sources and journalists.

In his study of news coverage of criminal trials, Steven Chermak (1998) examines how news coverage of the courts proceeds. At the local level, journalists focus on the most serious crimes in the area. In order to establish stable beats, they cultivate relationships with major actors in the courts, including lawyers, clerks, and judges. These sources are favoured according to ease of access. Prosecutors are the favourite sources because they are fewer in number than defence lawyers; this allows for the cultivation of closer and more established relationships with reporters. However, reporters attempt to have as wide an array of court sources as possible in order to gather the most newsworthy and entertaining commentary. Chermak suggests that when prosecutors are favoured as sources, biased reporting can result; this in turn can damage future trials by tainting jury pools. He also argues that because reporting uses simplified, non-legal language, and because the cases presented are generally high-profile cases involving criminal trials, citizens are not provided with a realistic picture of judicial processes. So one must ask whether the media can truly claim to be surrogates for the public in court proceedings.

The cultural perspective focuses on the relationship between ideas and symbols in news coverage. Cultural approaches go beyond ideological analysis to examine systems of meaning that may transcend particular ideologies in time and space. Cultural symbolic systems may have power effects on society; however, they do not necessarily emanate from extra-discursive power elites. For example, Altheide's (1997) work on fear examines the symbolic means through which a society can become oriented toward a fearful approach to the public sphere in part through generalized mass media narratives that frame social issues as threatening problems. Richard Osborne (1995) draws from Jean Baudrillard's concept of hyper-reality to argue that current images of crime are hyper-real, produced through the implosion of image–reality–representation. The lack of distinction between media representation and reality leads to a state of 'mediachosis' – that is, a state of consciousness characterized by unconscious acceptance of electronically transmitted modes of perceptions and thought. Its effect is to create pathological insecurity through fear of crime. Crime becomes a symbol of our fear of – and cynicism toward – the public sphere.

A major concern that emerges out of all three perspectives is that

increased press coverage of trials – especially on television – can result
in the real being replaced by representations of the real, whether one
defines those representations as ideological, bureaucratic, or culturally
constructed. We end up reacting to the hyper-reality of crime rather
than to its actual incidence. Media representations of criminal justice
arguably have their strongest impact at the point where image and reality implode – at the point where we begin reacting to media formats of
crime and justice and stop distinguishing them from actual processes.
How are media representations of crime and justice actually constructed, specifically in relation to criminal trials? Sanders and Lyon
(1995) note that trial narratives in the news media are generally built
around adversarial experts with conflicting perspectives. The narrative
highlights a conflict between rule breaking and rule abiding, with minimal background and dramatic narratives (31). Surette (1990) goes farther than this, outlining some of the basic strategies involved in
creating these dramatic narratives. These strategies include the following: highlighting extra-legal facts; closely scrutinizing 'characters' such
as the defendant, lawyers, the judge, witnesses, jury members, and so
on, often giving them celebrity status; focusing on personalities, personal relationships, and physical appearances regardless of their relevance to the case; including conjecture and sensationalism; and
providing personalized and simple explanations for the crime such as
lust, greed, immorality, jealousy, revenge, and insanity.

Case studies of specific media trials provide further insight into the
nature of coverage. For example, Susan Drucker and Janice Platt
Hunold (1990) analysed CNN's coverage of the Claus von Bulow retrial.
Certain recurring rhetorical messages characterized the coverage: justice, which is produced through the balance struck by an adversarial
process; violation of the 'golden rules' of personal conduct, which produces judicial action to reinforce these values; and entertainment, which
involves imposing dramatic narratives on the trial process. The authors
employ a genre analysis to show how these themes were organized
through generic conventions typical of certain types of daytime television programming, including talk shows, soap operas, and game
shows.

Larry Williamson (1990) utilizes the narrative analysis methodology
of Vladimir Propp's *Morphology of a Folktale* (1968) to map out the narrative structure of the 1984–5 trial process of Roger Hedgecock, mayor
of San Diego, California, who was accused of fourteen counts of perjury
and one count of conspiracy relating to financial wrongdoing during

his election campaign. Williamson argues that besides drawing from certain archetypes to create a set of characters within a dramatic narrative, media coverage of trials also proceeds through the use of 'media histories' and 'stylized characterizations.' Media histories establish a context for the trial by relying on past accounts of media trials. Legal precedents, which are generally unfamiliar to journalists, are not a part of the media history. Stylized characterizations are stereotypes that serve as role models for characterizing trial participants. They are drawn from entertainment programming, popular culture, and past media trials. Williamson found that journalists often compared Hedgecock's case to the Claus von Bulow and John DeLorean trials, which had recently been held.

Altheide (1997) adds that when entertainment formats are combined with a problem frame for understanding social processes, one result is that criminal justice stories are recast as morality plays. Stories about crime and justice have a narrative structure that provides a storylike coherence; they combine universal moral meanings with an actual person in an actual location; they reduce complex and ambiguous events to simple moral truths that have cultural resonance for the audience; and they constantly present these scenarios in a way that teaches the audience about the nature and causes of social disorder. The cumulative effect is to produce a discourse of fear that becomes a resource for the audience in interpreting subsequent reports.

To show how media narratives of crime and justice in Canada were actually constructed during the trial coverage of the Morin and Milgaard cases, and the role of DNA evidence in those constructions, I have drawn from the ideas of the above media scholars to develop a template. In analysing the newspaper and magazine articles of those two cases, I ask nine questions of each article in order to draw out its narrative structure. (1) What are the central elements of the story, and which elements recur across the articles? (2) What narrative type is used to structure the story – abuse of power and trust, the sinful rich, evil strangers, or some other type? (3) Are references made to past media trials and past defendants in order to characterize this trial? (4) To what extent are extra-legal facts used to frame the trial and the people involved? (5) Who are the main characters identified by the press, and how are they characterized? (6) Does the coverage focus on recurring moral principles that can be drawn from the trial? (7) How does the coverage employ elements of the problem frame by identifying the existence of something undesirable and widespread that can be changed? (8) According to the press, how can the problem be resolved? (9) What role does DNA evidence play in the narrative? In other words, I am interested in determining how the media set the problems of the criminal justice system through trial coverage, and how they came to suggest DNA testing as a solution to those problems.

The Morin and Milgaard Appeals: Canada's DNA 'Media Trials'

Two of the most heavily publicized cases in recent Canadian legal history have been those of Guy Paul Morin and David Milgaard. Both were accused and eventually convicted of sexual assault and murder. Both spent time in prison – Milgaard twenty-three years, Morin eighteen months – all the while proclaiming their innocence. Both were eventually exonerated by DNA evidence. Given their importance in the policy discussions and media coverage of DNA technology in criminal justice, and given their prominence in Canadian public consciousness, these two cases are emblematic of how DNA evidence has been framed in public discourse. They also suggest how a particular perception of the technology is produced in the public sphere.

After Morin was convicted in July 1992, press coverage began to elevate the case to one of national concern. National headlines shouted: 'Scales of justice out of balance,' 'Morin trial judge was biased lawyers say,' and similar. Later, as DNA evidence became a factor, headlines stated: 'DNA results cast doubt on murder count,' 'DNA on trial,' and 'Modern science gave Morin his freedom.' The same year as Morin's conviction, Kirk Makin, a *Globe and Mail* reporter, published a sharply critical account of the investigation and trial, *Redrum the Innocent*. The CBC investigative program *The Fifth Estate* aired a one-hour documentary, 'Odd Man Out,' to coincide with the release of the book. It reported on various questionable elements of the Morin conviction, interviewed many witnesses, and pointed to the presence of other suspects. The *Toronto Star* conducted a telephone poll of its readers in the days following the trial. Of the 834 responses, 91 per cent answered 'no' to this question: 'Did the murder trial of Guy Paul Morin leave you satisfied with the workings of the justice system?' Public awareness of the trial was high across the country. In this atmosphere, Morin's lawyers launched an appeal of the conviction – a process that would be cut short through the intervention of DNA evidence.

David Milgaard's saga began in January 1970, when as a teenager he was convicted of the sexual assault and murder of Gail Miller, a twenty-year-old nurse's assistant, in Saskatoon. Over the next twenty-eight years, Milgaard's case shifted in and out of public consciousness as his mother launched a campaign to have the case reviewed and her son's innocence established. All avenues of appeal were attempted and were unsuccessful. In 1988, as soon as DNA testing technology became available in Canada, a test was attempted on the remaining crime scene evidence, but the technology was in its infancy and the tests were inconclusive. Later that year, Milgaard's lawyers called on the justice minister to review the case, but he refused. Not until 6 September 1991 did Milgaard catch a break. On that day, Joyce Milgaard, David's mother, confronted Prime Minister Brian Mulroney on the street outside his Winnipeg hotel and asked him if he could do something to reopen the case. The prime minister, who was caught off guard and had little knowledge of the case, promised to look into the matter. It is at this point that I begin to analyse the events and the coverage of the events that led to Milgaard's release and exoneration through DNA testing. Media coverage of this process between 1991 and 1997 was extensive and coincided with the coverage of Morin's case. Like Morin, Milgaard became the subject of many print and television news investigations as well as a book, *When Justice Fails: The David Milgaard Story* by Carl Karp and Cecil Rosner (1991b). In 2000, the CTV television network aired a made-for-television movie, *Milgaard*, dramatizing Milgaard's arrest, conviction, and struggle for exoneration. The Morin and Milgaard cases became key references for each other in the media. Together, they generated an ongoing media critique of the problems endemic to the criminal justice system in Canada. Next, I analyse how this critique was constructed and came to incorporate DNA testing.

Guy Paul Morin

It is difficult to summarize the complexities of the Morin case. Kirk Makin provides an exhaustively detailed account, *Redrum the Innocent*, which was republished and updated in 1998. A bare outline would have to include the following. On 3 October 1984, in Queensville, Ontario, a small village an hour's drive northeast of Toronto, nine-year-old Christine Jessop disappeared while on her way home from school. In the early evening her mother contacted the police and a search was organized. It was unsuccessful. Almost three months later, on 31 December, her partially skeletonized body was discovered in a field 56 kilometres east of Queensville. An autopsy showed that she had been sexually assaulted and fatally stabbed and bludgeoned. The investigation continued until 22 April 1985, when police arrested and charged Morin.

At trial, a number of significant pieces of evidence were tendered by the chief prosecutor, John Scott. Clayton Ruby, a high-profile defence lawyer, defended Morin. Forensic evidence was key to the trial. Three hairs found in Morin's car were similar to Christine's hair, but on cross-examination, one of the scientists involved in the investigation, Stephanie Nyznyk, conceded that they were not necessarily Christine's. Also found in Morin's car, and on a recorder bag at the crime scene, were five red-dyed animal hairs that were similar to fibres found on Christine's clothes. Once again, Nyznyk could not state that these fibres were uncommon or that they could not have ended up in Morin's car in some way other than through Christine's presence. Nyznyk also testified that there were microscopic indications of blood in Morin's vehicle; however, during cross-examination she conceded that this was a 'presumptive' test – that is, it did not actually prove that there was blood in the vehicle, that the blood was human, or that it was Christine Jessop's blood. Finally, a black hair had been found on Christine's necklace at the crime scene. Nyznyk reported that the hair was microscopically similar to Morin's hair and could have originated from him. However, the hair type was not uncommon and was also shared by two of Christine's classmates.

Prosecutors also relied on testimony from jailhouse informants. One of these was an undercover police officer, Sergeant Hobbs, who pretended to be a fellow inmate charged with murder. A hidden microphone recorded Hobbs's interactions with Morin; Hobbs also used it to dictate notes about his conversations with Morin. In his testimony, Hobbs argued that many of Morin's often strange and nonsensical comments were actually a code that he and Hobbs had worked out to communicate about their crimes. However, the tape recordings were generally inaudible and what was audible could be interpreted in many ways. Only Hobbs's written notes included self-incriminating comments from Morin. There were two other jailhouse witnesses. One was Robert Dean May, who was in prison for a long list of crimes of dishonesty including fraud, forgery, and cheque kiting. The other was Mr X, who had been convicted of pedophilia but could not be identified by name because he had been convicted as a juvenile offender. Both testified that they had heard Morin confess to the crime while in prison and that in return for testifying they were to receive reduced sentences. Not surprisingly, Ruby attacked their credibility as witnesses.

Next, Morin was put on the stand and questioned about his activities on the night Christine went missing, his lack of involvement in the search for Christine, his comments to Sergeant Hobbs, and his supposed confessions to Robert May and Mr X. Following this, psychiatric experts for both sides were called, at which point Clayton Ruby made an astonishing move: he told the jury that even if they found that Morin had committed the crime, they should find him not guilty by reason of insanity. The defence's psychiatrist testified that Morin was schizophrenic and that this explained some of the strange and equivocal statements he had made to Hobbs. At the end of the one-month long trial, on 6 February 1986, Morin was found not guilty. Insanity was not the basis for the acquittal.

Not long after the acquittal, the Crown appealed the decision to the Ontario Court of Appeal on the basis of conflicting statements from the judge to the jury regarding the nature of reasonable doubt. The appeal court ordered a retrial. Morin was allowed to remain free on $40,000 bail and proceeded to appeal this decision to the Supreme Court. On 17 November 1988, the Supreme Court agreed with the Ontario Court of Appeal and ordered a retrial.

Clayton Ruby, knowing that Morin would need a fresh perspective for the retrial, advised him to retain Jack Pinkofsky. The new lawyer considered different avenues of defence – for example, he conducted a search for more plausible suspects. At this point, Ken Jessop, Christine's older, adopted brother, confessed to the police and prosecution that he and two of his friends had had sex with Christine on a number of occasions beginning when she was four years old. However, he insisted that he loved Christine and that the activity had stopped about one year prior to her murder.

Another revelation at this time was that Sergeant Michael Michalowsky, the chief identification officer responsible for collecting and preserving crime scene evidence at the body site, actually kept two sets of notes about the findings, which differed significantly from each other. After a two-month investigation by the Ontario Provincial Police, Michalowsky was arrested and charged with perjury and obstruction of justice. Finally, on 5 November 1991, seven years after the crime, Morin's second trial began in London, Ontario. It was heard by Provincial Court Judge Donnelly and prosecuted by Leo McGuigan.

During the six-month trial, the longest and most expensive in Canadian history, 109 witnesses were called. Besides reiterating evidence presented at the first trial, the Crown offered witness testimony intended to highlight the strangeness and suspiciousness of Morin as a person. A friend of Christine Jessop testified that in 1984, she saw Morin's knuckles turn white while he was carrying on a conversation with Christine. A police officer testified that on the night of Christine's disappearance, he stopped at the Morin house and spoke briefly with Morin's mother at the door. While there, he saw Morin staring fixedly at the television. Also on the night of the abduction, two volunteer firemen testified that they saw Morin's father outside working with a concrete mixer. One of them recalled wondering if he was burying a body. Christine's mother testified that she had seen a figure scream and run through the snow on the night of Christine's funeral. She suddenly recalled that the figure was Morin. None of these 'incidents' had been recorded in police investigation records. The prosecution also made much of the fact that Morin did not participate in the search for Christine and did not attend her funeral.

Apparently, these anecdotes, along with evidence from the previous trial – especially the testimony of the two inmates who claimed that Morin had confesssed to them – were enough for the jury. On 30 July 1992, despite considerable evidence of police wrongdoing and questionable Crown tactics, Morin was convicted of the murder of Christine Jessop. Many were stunned by this conviction. Morin hired a new team of lawyers, headed by James Lockyer, to begin the appeal process. While Morin was serving his time at Kingston Penitentiary, his lawyers prepared an eight-volume, 1,900-page appeal application detailing wrongdoings at the second trial. This was submitted to the Ontario Court of Appeal in February 1994. Their most pointed arguments were directed toward the judge, Mr Justice James Donnelly, whom they accused of bias in favour of the Crown. Justice Donnelly had refused to allow Pinkofsky to introduce evidence pointing to other suspects. He had treated Sergeant Michalowsky in a very friendly manner even though Michalowsky had been charged with perjury and obstruction of justice before the trial.[2] According to the appeal application, Donnelly had greeted Michalowsky with great warmth and later congratulated him on his testimony. He had even gone so far as to require that the lawyers dress in street clothes while Michalowsky testified in order to make him feel more at ease. Morin's lawyers argued that this must have swayed the jurors, in that it strongly suggested that defence claims about police wrongdoing had to be incorrect. Furthermore, Justice Donnelly's jury instructions, which lasted four days and consumed 550 pages of transcript – emphasized the Crown's case over that of the defence and referred sixty times to Morin's guilty conscience.

Further, While preparing the appeal, Lockyer asked the Ontario Centre of Forensic Sciences for any written materials the lab still held about the case. While going through these documents, the lawyers were shocked to find records stating that much of the fibre evidence in the case had gone missing. Even more shocking, the evidence had probably been contaminated by red fibres from a sweater worn by one of the laboratory technicians. The contamination had not been recorded within the centre until 1991 and had not been reported at Morin's second trial. The exact timing of the contamination was unclear, but it could have happened as early as 1985, thus tainting all subsequent claims about fibre matches. Finally, Robert May, one of the jailhouse informers, had reportedly recanted his testimony that he had heard Morin confess.

The appeal was granted, but days before it was to be heard, Morin's lawyers called for another DNA test. DNA testing had been conducted before the 1992 trial but had proved inconclusive because the technology was still in its infancy. However, by 1995, when the test took place, PCR technology was available. A semen sample from Christine's underwear was sent to a Boston laboratory, accompanied by representatives from the Crown and the defence. This time the test was conclusive. Morin was definitely not the perpetrator of the crime. The Ontario Court of Appeal moved quickly to acquit Morin and cancel the appeal process. As well, it called for an inquiry into the investigation and prosecution of the case. The inquiry got underway in 1997, headed by Fred Kaufman, a retired justice of the Quebec Court of Appeal. It lasted ten months and resulted in a 1,400-page report condemning the conduct of the case and calling for a number of measures to be taken that would help prevent similar situations from arising again. Morin was eventually awarded a $1.2 million compensation package.

Constructing the Media Narrative of the Guy Paul Morin Case

These are the basic facts of the case, but it is important to analyse exactly how the press framed the narrative as well as the role that DNA testing came to play in the process. I limit my discussion to the period following the second trial, when DNA evidence became significant and ultimately determinative. During this later press coverage, a number of characters in the drama became emblematic of problems and solutions in the criminal justice system. At this point a particular kind of critique emerged from the narrative framing that constructed the problem and asserted the solutions that were necessary to address it.

At the centre of the case, of course, was Guy Paul Morin. Initially an ambiguous figure, by the end of the second trial he was clearly being cast as an innocent victim of a powerful and corrupt justice system. Headlines at the time captured this sense of Morin's victimization: 'Innocent for 10 years,' 'How can Morin still be on the suspect list? Police reluctance to exclude Guy Paul Morin raises new questions about justice and fairness,' 'Morin's inner strength,' 'Morin's story both infuriating and inspiring.' This picture of Morin developed gradually during the judicial process. Earlier, he was 'an odd duck of 25, living with his parents and given to gardening, beekeeping and his clarinet' (Coyle, 1995: A13). His family was 'eccentric,' 'their house an eyesore, the lot a junkyard' (1995: A13). Yet by the end of the process, the emphasis was on Morin's inner strength in the face of his victimization:

> At 35, Guy Paul Morin has already endured far more trauma than most people could expect in a busy lifetime. For 10 years, he was falsely accused of murdering nine-year-old Christine Jessop, put through two lengthy trials, spent 18 months in jail and faced the prospect of spending the better part of his life in a federal penitentiary. But there is little in his relaxed, animated manner that betrays his pain. While others might have become guarded and humourless, Morin has retained a boyish, spontaneous side even as he has grown into a worldly adult. (Chisholm and Driedger, 1995: 60)

By this stage in the press coverage, Morin was striking the right balance of seeking justice for what had happened and remaining unvengeful. Gone were the earlier doubts about his mental stability and the notion that his personal characteristics pointed to his guilt. In other words, within the narrative frame, Morin had become a certifiably innocent and harmless victim. As if to emphasize this, his case was repeatedly linked with those of David Milgaard and Donald Marshall, who had also been wrongly convicted and later exonerated – 'Milgaard, Marshall, Morin a reproach to system' (Makin, 1997a: A7).[3] Around this time, a number of articles recited lists of wrongly accused people in contemporary Canadian, American, and British legal history; all of these emphasized the role that scientific evidence played in the cases (for example, Makin, 1997b: A12; Nichols, 1995; Tyler, 1998b: F4).

Another important character who appeared throughout the Morin case was Ken Jessop, Christine's older brother. By the time of Morin's appeal in 1992, his sexual misconduct with Christine had become known. In *Redrum the Innocent*, Kirk Makin describes a number of incidents after the first trial in which the teenage Ken terrorized his neighbours, the Morins. His developing alcoholism, a reckless car accident, and a number of emotional outbursts in the courtroom served to demonstrate his emotional instability and untrustworthiness. Even at the Kaufman inquiry into the Morin case, Ken was overwrought: 'While Janet Jessop [Christine's mother] remained relatively calm at the inquiry, her son seemed overwhelmed. The stocky 28-year-old, who was only 14 when the murder occurred, repeatedly broke down in tears on the witness stand' (Fennell, 1997: 21). Ken was a suspicious character and there was a sense that he had never been properly investigated.

If Morin was the innocent victim, his lawyer during the appeal and inquiry, James Lockyer, was a crusader for justice. His team's 1,900-page appeal document, which documented questionable aspects of the second trial in painstaking detail, received plenty of press (Tyler, 1998c: A5). He advised Morin to seek another DNA test. He came out in the press against double jeopardy – the practice of trying a person twice for the same crime, something that is not permitted in the United States (Schneider, 1997: A24). At the Kaufman inquiry, Lockyer became an avenging prosecutor of the criminal justice system: 'Lawyer at Morin inquiry takes apart "garbage evidence"' (Makin, 1997a: A1). The press also noted that he had taken on similar cases – for example, the case of Gregory Parsons of St John's, Newfoundland, who had been convicted of murdering his mother and had won a retrial on appeal. When DNA samples from the crime scene did not match Parsons, the charges against him were stayed. Lockyer was representing him in his claim for an apology and compensation.

A fourth character in the drama was the second trial judge, Justice James Donnelly. Canadian judges are at a disadvantage in the press, because in order to maintain their dignity and impartiality, they have traditionally refused to speak to the press about cases. Lockyer and others had no such restraints, and they proceeded to tell the press all about Donnelly's indiscretions at the second trial. Thus he was painted as a corrupt, small-town hanging judge who was too friendly with the local police and prosecutors and who was predisposed to convict Morin despite clear indications of tainted evidence and questionable police practices. In the end, Justice Donnelly's side of the story was never heard.

There were other important characters after the second trial, including police investigators, forensic scientists, and jailhouse informants.

Sergeant Michael Michalowsky was represented as a corrupt, small-town, police officer who acted out of self-interest to procure a quick conviction and then covered his own dishonesty by cooking his notes about the evidence. Bernie Fitzpatrick, another officer involved in the investigation, was similarly corrupt; he pressured witnesses to change their stories to fit his version of the facts, and he refused to acknowledge that Morin was innocent even after the DNA evidence had cleared him. Stephanie Nyznyk, the forensic scientist who testified at the two trials, was represented as careless and unethical in her laboratory practices and as conspiring with police and prosecutors to procure convictions instead of adhering to scientific thoroughness to find the truth. Robert Dean May, one of the jailhouse snitches, was represented as thoroughly unreliable; it was reported that after the second trial, he told his parents and three of his friends that he had lied at the trials.

All of these people served as the cast in an unambiguous morality play that exposed the corruption at the heart of the Morin prosecution and also, perhaps, in other prosecutions. Constant references to the Milgaard and Marshall cases reinforced the perception that corrupted trials might well be a widespread problem. Lists of the wrongly accused in Canada and elsewhere heightened concerns that malfeasance in the justice system could well be a pathological social fact, a widespread problem that needed to be thoroughly addressed by society. The ambiguity that surrounded the first trial was completely erased from the press coverage after the second trial, by which time the issue had shifted from a legal to a moral one – specifically, how to correct the functional balance of the criminal justice system. Morin and other media trials highlighted a widespread problem that was producing disorder. That disorder was especially dangerous because it was arising within the justice system. We rely on that system to produce fair outcomes and to uncover the truth. We also rely on it not to abuse its substantial power, for it is within that system that the state exercises force over its citizens in the most blatant manner.

By tracing the interactions of these characters, the press mapped out the web of false evidence, pressured testimony, shoddy forensic work, judicial bias, and official intransigence in admitting errors. The result was a problem-setting narrative in which a number of themes emerged. Many articles listed the various instances of wrongdoing that were brought to light by the Kaufman Inquiry (Canadian Press, 1997: A5; Canadian Press, 1998: A14; Fennell, 1997; Jenish, 1997: 19; Makin, 1997a: A1; Schneider, 1997: A24). These included the weight given to unimportant and circumstantial testimony such as Morin's white knuckles, his failure to attend Christine's funeral, and the fact that his father was mixing cement on the night of Christine's disappearance; the absence of written records of certain evidence; the way the police convinced the Jessops to change the timeline of their activities on the day of Christine's disappearance; the unreliability of the jailhouse informants; and the unprofessional and potentially perjorious activities of forensic scientists.

Throughout the persecution there had been a series of errors and falsehoods. The press linked these to other media trials such as Milgaard and Marshall and thereby constructed a problem-setting narrative of widespread abuse of authority. A great injustice had been done in this case and had been done in other cases. This injustice had been the product of conscious choices made by individuals acting improperly, as well as of a system that allowed such people to get away with it. This was the morality play element of the case. A terrible crime had occurred, yet corrupt officials were obstructing justice by making mistakes and fabricating falsehoods in order to achieve personal goals and to protect their network of power. As a result, an innocent man had endured a terrible ordeal. This resonated with a public that feared being victimized by powerful state agents, and conjured twentieth-century images of leather-clad police hauling people away in the dark and locking them away for the flimsist of excuses. In a risk society, no one can be left with unfettered discretion.

There was a certain recuperation of the justice system following the Morin case: in the end, justice was restored and the system acted fairly. Powerful wrongdoers were brought to account. Yet the media coverage reflected a sense that this outcome had been the product of journalistic activism and eventually science. Had the justice system been left to its own devices, Morin might simply have vanished into prison. A few months after Morin's second trial, one journalist who had followed it summarized her criticisms of the proceedings:

It is, therefore, our responsibility as citizens of this province to start making some noise. If we want to have faith in our justice system, it's up to us to make it clear that we expect concrete action to be taken so the kinds of things which occurred in the Morin case will never happen again. I urge you all to:

1. Let your MPP know that you're appalled at how the Morin case has been handled.

2. Tune in to CBC television's *fifth estate* tomorrow at 8 p.m. for a one-hour special on the subject.
3. Read the newly published book *Redrum the Innocent* by Kirk Makin, who spent the past three years researching the case.
4. Make a financial contribution to the Justice For Guy Paul Morin Committee. (Laframboise, 1992: A25)

As the appeal process continued, another journalist commented: 'Kirk Makin's exhaustive study of the trials was probably instrumental in winning Morin's release on bail' (Coyle, 1995: A13). Comments like these, combined with the ongoing critique of the criminal justice system made the press an important actor in the appeal as well as in the inquiry that followed Morin's exoneration through DNA evidence. Justice had been done, but only after considerable prompting from the outside. Therefore, the problem remained. Simply stated the problem is this: the justice system enjoys the unrestricted power to make subjective decisions, and too much discretion is placed in the hands of police, prosecutors, and judges. According to the press, the Morin case and other cases have laid bare the state's betrayal of its social contract with the citizenry. Criminal justice should not simply be a means to an end; it should also express the moral relations that form the basis for social solidarity. The indignation emanating from the press was an expression of the fear that something had changed in the justice system so that the values guiding criminal investigation and prosecution were no longer *society's* values. In the press and in the Kaufman Report, these changes were attributed to individuals who were pursuing personal advancement and refusing to admit mistakes, and to systemic problems arising from a lack of oversight. The need for oversight was highlighted during the Kaufman hearings when police refused to admit they had made a mistake and left Morin on the suspect list. Jim McCloskey, a pastor who works to investigate wrongful convictions, has been quoted as saying, 'I've seen it happen time and time again, when the boys in blue go the full mile to protect each other' (Levy, 1995: A17).

Once the problem was constructed in this way, two solutions presented themselves as necessary. If the Morin case was ultimately a drama about abuse of authority and about the mistreatment of citizens by state agents, then the actions of criminal justice authorities would have to be audited more carefully, and more objective means would have to be developed for determining truth in criminal trials. The moral critique would have to be converted into a technical critique that generated mechanisms for exercising perpetual scrutiny over the 'authority of authority.' The first step in this process of developing auditing mechanisms for criminal justice would involve identifying common elements in cases where wrongful convictions had occurred. Several of the 119 recommendations of the Kaufman Inquiry focused on the need to rationalize knowledge about wrongful convictions and to develop methods for auditing justice officials. One such recommendation was that police and prosecutors be educated about the warning signs that an investigation might be going off track: the presence of alternative suspects, 'tunnel vision' (i.e., when an initial theory eventually colours the entire investigation); a rush to find a suspect and convict him or her; poor and circumstantial evidence, and possibly even falsified evidence; the refusal of officials to admit mistakes; and reliance on jailhouse informants. The press duly noted these recommendations along with the inquiry's assertion that a national DNA data bank should be established (Canadian Press, 1998: A14).

The Kaufman Report also recommended that the Criminal Code be amended to allow research into how juries reach their decisions; to empower the Court of Appeal to set aside a conviction when there was a 'lurking doubt' about the guilt of the accused; and to establish a quality assurance unit at the Ontario Centre for Forensic Sciences (Canadian Press, 1998: A14). Kaufman was quoted as saying: 'This case is not unique. This case is not an aberration' (1998: A14). However, only a few similar cases have ever been cited in the press, and it is unclear exactly how many such cases there have been and how untrustworthy the justice system really is. Considering the tens of thousands of cases heard each year in Canadian criminal courts, the five or six cases cited by the press over the past few years could also be interpreted as an imperfect system performing reasonably well.

The press coverage also brought DNA testing into the Morin narrative as a heroic ultimate identifier – an objective truth teller that cut through the inefficient and ineffective rituals of testimony, witnessing, and organizational process to reveal the truth:

After dozens of witnesses, crates of documents and numerous lawyers, Guy Paul Morin owes his freedom to a 10-year-old semen sample and a machine about the size of a microwave oven. New technology allowed Boston scientists to do DNA testing on the sample and conclude Morin couldn't have been the one who raped and murdered nine-year-old Christine Jessop in 1984 ... The tests are 100 per cent accurate, said Jennifer Clay, spokeswoman for a B.C. lab that does DNA testing. (Cox, 1995: A3)

Here, DNA tests were being presented as a liberating factor and their accuracy as unquestionable – as the objective remedy to the subjective biases of the system.

Even before the test results were officially announced, journalists were reporting, 'DNA results cast doubt on murder count' (Canadian Press, 1995: A10). On hearing the news, Morin summed up the problem and solution very succinctly: 'The justice system failed me, but science saved me ... My lawyers did the best they could through the avenues of the justice system. But in the end, science gave the final word. Science is wonderful. I love science' (Canadian Press, 1995: A10). In other words, the justice system was not able to determine the truth – that was only possible through science. A number of similar quotes from Morin were reported in the ensuing days and weeks.

The triumph of science was cited alongside repeated warnings about the evils of the justice system: 'What happened to me was wrong and it could happen to any of you,' Morin stated after being officially exonerated (Dunn, 1995: A3). The system itself was coming under scrutiny, and not only by Canadian journalists. A headline in the *Washington Post* stated, 'Conviction of innocent man spurs questions about double jeopardy in Canada' (Schneider, 1997: A24). The article went on to explain that unlike the United States, Canada has no rule against double jeopardy – trying a suspect more than once on the same set of facts:

'There should not be two bites at the apple' [said James Lockyer]. Yet after the first trial ended in acquittal, prosecutors and appellate judges 'thought a person guilty of the offense had gotten off, so they wanted a second crack at him.' It was not so long ago, Lockyer said, that the justices could have gone even further and actually ordered a conviction. When that happened in the mid-1970s to abortion doctor Henry Morgenthaler – acquitted by a Quebec jury only to have the Supreme Court order his conviction – the Canadian Parliament limited judges to ordering a new trial. (1997: A24)

This report added yet another element to the problem frame. In the Morin case, state agents had abused their power to overturn a jury's finding of innocence and force a second trial. Once again, this pointed to the need for a more objective form of identifying truth.

After all the tainted forensic evidence at the two trials, it was forensic testimony that finally exonerated Morin– an irony not lost on journalists: 'While science – in the form of DNA tests – freed Guy Paul

Morin last week, it's important to remember that science was also used to wrongly convict him. A public inquiry into the Morin case should therefore take a hard look at forensic science as it's now being practiced in the province' (Laframboise, 1995: A17). In the media coverage, the apparent contradiction between exuberant claims about the 100 per cent accuracy of DNA testing on the one hand and faulty forensic analysis on the other was resolved in this way: 'Indeed, science in the form of DNA tests ultimately exonerated Morin. But unlike DNA analysis, which could objectively quantify his innocence, other forms of scientific testing are more subjective. When left in the hands of a scientist willing to exaggerate test findings or suppress evidence, it can lead to disastrous results' (Tyler, 1998a: F1). DNA testing was represented as qualitatively different from other types of forensic science – as more objective. Other forms of evidence were represented as more open to unethical practices on the part of scientists. In the press coverage, individual subjective interests were seen as intruding on the search for truth, and DNA testing was represented as immune from this. Ultimately, the problems with the forensic evidence were traced to individual scientists at the Ontario Centre for Forensic Sciences, who did not follow proper procedures, contaminated and lost evidence, and failed to report these errors at the trials. In this context, DNA testing was going to help overcome such problems in the future by relying less on the whims and actions of individual scientists – or so journalists implied at the time.

The problem of subjectivity (i.e., human error or misconduct) in the criminal justice system was going to be overcome by enhancing two forms of surveillance technologies: the organizational technology of auditing procedures to keep a watch over authorities, and the biotechnology of DNA testing and banking to determine the 'truth' of innocence or guilt without having to rely on subjective human judgment. In sum, criminal justice required more surveillance if it was to function properly. In a risk society, the watchers must also be watched.

The Case of David Milgaard

The facts of the David Milgaard case cover twenty-eight years, twenty-three of which he spent in prison. As in the Morin case, the facts are complicated. On the morning of 31 January 1969, the body of Gail Miller, a nurse's aide, was found in an alley in Saskatoon. On her way to work that morning she had been sexually assaulted and stabbed to death. Her coat had been unbuttoned, her dress had been yanked up at the waist, and her underclothes had been forcibly pulled down. There were bloody cuts and wounds on her throat and stomach. There was evidence of a scuffle, and her frozen fists were still tightly clenched. On 4 April, a neighbourhood boy was walking down the street two blocks from the murder site when he saw a wallet sticking out of the snow. He took it to a friend's house, and the friend's mother called the police. Identification cards inside the wallet indicated that it belonged to Gail Miller. The wallet was found in front of Albert 'Shorty' Cadrain's house, which David Milgaard had been visiting on the day of the murder. The following day, police conducted a door-to-door search of the neighbourhood looking for any other items of evidence. Cadrain's neighbour reported finding a blood-soaked blue toque in front of her house at the beginning of February. She had thrown it into her backyard, and the police now retrieved it.

By this time the police had already identified Milgaard, then sixteen years old, as their primary suspect and were building a case against him. One month after the murder, the police had announced that the investigation was at a standstill. They received their first break when Shorty Cadrain came forward to claim a $2,000 reward for information about the case. He stated that he had seen blood on Milgaard's pants on the day of the murder. Milgaard and two teenage travelling companions, Nichol John and Ronald Wilson, were on a road trip from Regina to the west coast. They left Regina at 1 a.m. on 31 January and arrived before dawn in Saskatoon. They visited Cadrain when they arrived, and left for Edmonton a few hours later. Milgaard and his companions were self-described 'hippies,' taking drugs, engaging in 'rough sex,' and committing petty thefts to fund their trip.

The police turned their attention to Milgaard and began to build their case. During the investigation, they interviewed a man who lived nearby, Larry Fisher, who had been questioned earlier about a knife-point attack on an elderly woman in the neighbourhood. When asked about his whereabouts on the day of the murder, Fisher claimed that he was at work, and the police did not follow it up. A year after Milgaard's conviction, Fisher was convicted of a number of knifepoint sexual assaults in Winnipeg, and later, four more in the Saskatoon neighbourhood where Gail Miller had been murdered.

However, the police had by now focused on Milgaard, and in May 1969 he was arrested in Prince George, British Columbia, for the murder of Gail Miller. The trial took place in January 1970 and lasted two

weeks. During the trial, both of Milgaard's travelling companions testified against him. Two other witnesses came forward stating that Milgaard had confessed to the murder during a drug-filled orgy in a
Regina hotel room in 1969. This testimony, along with Shorty Cadrain's statement that Milgaard had blood on his clothing on the day of
the murder, was enough to seal his fate. On 31 January 1970, exactly
one year after the murder, he was convicted of non-capital murder and
sentenced to life in prison.

This conviction was only the beginning of Milgaard's journey
through the justice system. His lawyers launched an appeal, but leave
to appeal was denied by the Saskatchewan Court of Appeal. At this
point David's mother, Joyce Milgaard, began a campaign to free her
son, appealing the Court of Appeal's decision to the Supreme Court of
Canada. That appeal too was dismissed. As far as the justice system
was concerned, the case was closed and so were all avenues of appeal.
Over the next seventeen years, Milgaard's situation went from bad to
worse. In 1973 he escaped from Stony Mountain Penitentiary near Winnipeg but was quickly recaptured. In 1980 he failed to return while out
on a day pass. He remained at large for seventy-seven days in the Toronto area, supporting himself by selling encyclopedias. When police
caught up with him, he attempted to escape and was shot in the back.
During this period of incarceration, Milgaard twice attempted suicide
by cutting his wrists and by jumping out of a second-storey window.

In 1988 the campaign to reopen Milgaard's case began in earnest. The
Milgaard family hired James Ferris, a pathologist at the University of
British Columbia, to re-examine the forensic evidence from the murder
scene. Ferris concluded that for the murder to have occurred as contended by the Crown, the victim would have to have been raped out in
the open in –40° temperatures – an unlikely occurrence. Ferris then conducted DNA tests on Miller's garments, but the technology was too
new to be reliable, so they were was inconclusive. Ferris also concluded
that yellow fluid found in the snow at the crime scene and presented as
semen by the Crown was actually dog urine. The same year, Milgaard's
lawyer, Hersh Wolch, applied to have the case reopened under section
690 of the Criminal Code, which empowers the Minister of Justice to
direct a new trial or a new hearing in front of any court. The application
was denied. Milgaard's lawyers and his mother continued to pursue
the case, casting further doubt on the trial evidence. They hired the
Reverend Jim McCloskey, an American pastor whose organization,
Centurion Ministries, specializes in researching claims of innocence

among convicted offenders. At the time that Milgaard hired him in 1991, McCloskey's work had already led to nine exonerations in the United States, and many people were seeking his services. According to McCloskey, he moved Milgaard's case to the head of his list because of the strong indications that Milgaard was innocent and the growing evidence that Larry Fisher was the perpetrator.

In part through McCloskey's work, the evidence against Milgaard began to unravel. Shorty Cadrain wrote a statement to Centurion Ministries stating that the police had harassed him into claiming that Milgaard had blood on his clothing. A man who was present at the party where Milgaard supposedly confessed to the murder claimed that there had never been a confession. Ron Wilson, Milgaard's travelling companion, recanted his testimony that he had seen blood on Milgaard's clothing. In February 1991, armed with these statements, Milgaard's lawyers once again approached Kim Campbell, the Minister of Justice at the time. Once again, the application for a review was refused due to insufficient evidence of a miscarriage of justice. Joyce Milgaard now showed her characteristic tenacity. On 5 September 1991, she approached Prime Minister Brian Mulroney directly while he was walking down the street outside his Winnipeg hotel and asked him to take action on David's search for a judicial review. He promised to look into the matter, and the following month, Kim Campbell took the unusual step of not only granting the application for a review, but also referring that application to the Supreme Court of Canada. Normally a provincial court of appeal hears such reviews; only twice in the postwar period has the Supreme Court reviewed a murder conviction, and in both instances, the conviction was upheld.[4]

On 21 January 1992 the review began, temporarily turning the Supreme Court chamber into a trial court, complete with a specially constructed witness box. Milgaard and the witnesses who had testified in the 1970 trial were put on the stand and cross-examined by lawyers representing Milgaard and the Saskatchewan government and by a panel of five Supreme Court justices, including then Chief Justice Antonio Lamer. Larry Fisher was also summoned to the court. When Chief Justice Lamer invited him to confess to the crime, he stated, 'I had nothing to do with the murder of Gail Miller, sir. I'm here to prove my innocence in that department' (Vienneau, 1997: A17). Ron Wilson reiterated his retraction of his trial testimony, claiming that the police had pressured him into stating that Milgaard had blood on his clothes. During his testimony in front of the Supreme Court, Wilson contradicted himself on a number of occasions and was ultimately dismissed by Lamer as a pathological liar. Nichol John, the other companion, had testified in 1970 that she had seen Milgaard stab a woman. However, she often had disturbing 'flashbacks' about violence in an alley and could not say for certain that the visions were based on reality or that Milgaard was part of them. Clearly, conclusive evidence could not be found in the testimony of the witnesses or in the forensic evidence. On 14 April 1992 the Supreme Court ruled that Milgaard's 1970 conviction should be overturned and he should be granted a retrial. It also suggested that the Saskatchewan government consider withdrawing the charges. However, Saskatchewan's Attorney General, Bob Mitchell, instead of withdrawing the charges, elected to stay the proceedings. A stay of proceedings is not an acquittal; it leaves the matter open and allows the Crown to bring the matter to trial within a year. Both the Supreme Court's ruling in favour of a retrial and the Saskatchewan government's refusal to withdraw the charges were troubling outcomes. No one had yet stated that Milgaard was innocent of the crime – only that the evidence was inconclusive and that a jury might have come to a different conclusion had evidence about Larry Fisher been presented to it. These decisions had implications for any future compensation package, since only someone pardoned or acquitted qualifies for compensation.

The Saskatchewan government did not pursue the case further. In the meantime, it asked for an independent review of how the 1970 case had been conducted. The RCMP carried out the review, guided by Alberta's Attorney General. Its 1994 report found that there had been no wrongdoing during the case on the part of government officials and prosecutors. Milgaard had by then filed a lawsuit against two prosecutors and three police officers involved in the case with the goal of gaining compensation. The findings of the RCMP review were not helpful to that suit. Consequently, he again began calling for a DNA test, insisting that it would finally exonerate him.

During the 1992 Supreme Court hearing, the Justice Department had conducted another DNA test, but again the results had been inconclusive, given the age of the sample. Finally, in 1997, a third and final test was conducted on the last bit of DNA evidence from the crime scene. By this time, STR technology had been developed, which allowed for a more refined test. The test was conducted in the Forensic Science Service laboratory in Yorkshire, England, by scientific representatives for Milgaard, the RCMP, the Saskatchewan Justice Department, and the British laboratory. They found semen stains on the victim's underclothes as well as on her nurse's uniform. Authorities had brought along blood samples from both Milgaard and Fisher. The Fisher sample had been taken in 1992 during the hearing in front of the Supreme Court. He had not specifically consented to the 1997 test, but the federal Justice Department approved the use of this sample. Milgaard's DNA clearly did not match the crime scene sample. Fisher's did. This was the outcome the Milgaards had been fighting for for twenty-eight years. David Milgaard had been fully exonerated as a result of DNA testing. The Saskatchewan government admitted its mistake and began negotiations for compensation, which eventually reached $10 million.

Constructing the Media Narrative of the David Milgaard Case

Generally speaking, press coverage of the Morin and Milgaard cases avoided sensationalism of the sort found in American media trials, especially celebrity trials such as the O.J. Simpson and Claus von Bulow cases. However, there was slightly more sensationalism in the coverage of David Milgaard than in that of Guy Paul Morin. This is partly because Morin lived a quiet life, so his personal details were of little interest to the press. Milgaard, in contrast, had been a wild and sexually adventurous youth who had taken illicit drugs and committed petty crimes. While in prison, he had twice escaped and twice attempted suicide. These facts were not pertinent to his case at the beginning of his review process in 1991, yet the press often cited them in order to add piquancy to the coverage – a piquancy largely absent from the Morin case. As one result, ever since Milgaard's exoneration, the press has been following his personal life, reporting on a traffic violation, a speech he gave at a high school, the fact that he has a girlfriend, and the impact of his ordeal on his brother, sisters, and parents.

Another element in the characterizations of Milgaard and others involved in the case is reference to similar cases. This is not surprising, when we consider how the press covered the Morin case and that some of the same people were involved. Morin himself made an appearance, having befriended Joyce Milgaard through a support group for the wrongly convicted. It was reported that it was he who informed Joyce Milgaard about the results of her son's 1997 DNA test. Also, Morin's lawyer, James Lockyer, was Milgaard's lawyer in his efforts to extract compensation from the Saskatchewan government and to arrange the DNA test that would finally exonerate him. Throughout the coverage there were constant references to other famous Canadian cases of wrongful conviction, not just Morin and Marshall but also Truscott, Sophonow, Nepoose, Nelles, and Norris. A number of American cases were mentioned as well. The most famous one was that of Rubin 'Huricane' Carter, but there were others as well. All of these together gave the strong impression that the justice system was broken and needed to be fixed.

A number of characters were important in the construction of the Milgaard narrative. David Milgaard himself is a difficult person to characterize. The press has clearly labelled him as an innocent victim of an abusive system. Yet he is nobody's saint. His past suggests that he is not an innocent *person* even if he is innocent of Gail Miller's murder. Also, there are reports that he confessed to her murder while in jail, although for this we would have to take the word of an alcoholic prison guard who eventually quit his job (Karp and Rosner, 1991a: A4). Furthermore, Milgaard has been vengeful since his release and has had a few brushes with the law. The press has generally dismissed these, however, as the adjustments of a man who was incarcerated as a youth and never properly socialized.

Joyce Milgaard is also a mixed character in the narrative. Her personal background has received almost as much attention as David's, including how she had to quit school when she was young and work at a number of jobs. After David's conviction, she again took on a number of jobs to pay for her campaign to free him. In the meantime her marriage and her family disintegrated and she lost all her money. Her crusade verged on the fanatical, propelled as it was by her embrace of Christian Science and her strong religious faith.

Two other crusaders figure prominently in the case. Hersh Wolch, Milgaard's chief lawyer, took on the case *pro bono* and pursued it with the greatest tenacity. Along with Joyce Milgaard, he explored every possible avenue to bring about a review of the case, and after the review he fought ferociously to exonerate Milgaard. The other was the Reverend Jim McCloskey, a romantic figure, a prison chaplain who took it on himself to begin a crusade to free the innocent.

On the other side were the Saskatchewan government and the federal Minister of Justice. Both seemed motivated by the need to look infallible, which explains why they worked so hard to defend their agents (i.e., the prosecutors and Saskatoon police) who conducted the investigation and trial. The Minister of Justice seemed arrogant in her refusal to even consider reviewing Milgaard's conviction. Her actions suggested that the twenty-three-year incarceration of an innocent man was beneath her notice. The Saskatchewan government looked petty and mean in its refusal to admit a mistake and voluntarily make it right. Chief Justice Lamer, who came to represent the face of the Supreme Court in the review, went some way toward recuperating the system by showing that he cared about justice. He asked penetrating and forthright questions that challenged the participants to tell the truth. However, the Supreme Court lost some credibility when it refused to exonerate Milgaard: the system was still protecting its own.

Finally, always lurking in the background was Larry Fisher, who from the perspective of the journalists was obviously the real murderer. Reporters provided details of his past, interviewed his ex-wife and his mother, and listed his criminal activities to imply that he was the actual culprit. Through all of this, Fisher maintains his silence. He refuses to acknowledge his guilt, which only contributes to the impression that he is a cold-blooded psychopath with no remorse for his victims, who include David Milgaard.

These are the characters whose interactions drove the narrative as it unfolded between 1991 and 1997. In the media narratives, each was a recognizable type; the result was a fairly straightforward story of moralistic crusaders versus impassive authorities, David versus Goliath, truth versus power. In the end, justice was restored, but only because of media pressure, extra-legal crusading, and the final 'truth' as delivered by DNA testing. The fundamental problem of discretion in criminal justice and abuse of that discretion remains. The next victim of this flawed and subjective system may not be as lucky as Milgaard (or Morin).

Once again, the media narrative functioned as a morality play. By 1991, Milgaard was clearly innocent in the eyes of the press, and this clear, unambiguous stance made it difficult to fathom the justice system's denial of Milgaard's appeals. Joyce Milgaard, the Reverend McCloskey, and the defence lawyers had uncovered compelling new evidence and had found solid grounds for challenging the existing evidence, yet the state refused to hear it. At no time was the perspective of the government, police, and prosecutors presented in the coverage, and their silence suggested profound arrogance. The only reported comment from a government official was made by William Corbett, a senior counsel to the federal justice department, who compared those who believe in Milgaard's innocence to those who believe Elvis is still alive (Tyler, 1997: A17). Considering the apparently overwhelming evidence, this comment seemed nonsensical and made the authorities look both ludicrous and cold-hearted. Likewise, the Supreme Court's decision to order a retrial and the Saskatchewan government's decision to stay the proceedings were incomprehensible in the context of the media narrative, which was based on the fundamental assumption that Milgaard could not possibly be guilty. Article after article reiterated the flimsy evidence against Milgaard and the strong evidence against Fisher, whose 1994 release from prison was reported with out-and-out dismay:

> A violent serial rapist accused of a murder that David Milgaard served 22 years for was to be released today from a Fraser Valley prison. Larry Earl Fisher, 44, was considered so dangerous by officials that he wasn't released a day early. He served his entire 23-year sentence for raping seven women – most at knifepoint – in Saskatchewan and Manitoba. Now there is nothing more officials can do to keep Fisher behind bars. (Hall, 1994: A3)

The article went on to detail Fisher's crimes, implicate him in the death of Gail Miller, describe Milgaard's review, point out that Fisher denied murdering Miller, and report Joyce Milgaard's shocked reaction to the news of Fisher's release. Officials were covering up their mistakes in relation to Milgaard; not only that but they were not pursuing the dangerous offender who *had* committed the murder, and they were hamstrung by their own system for keeping the public safe from him.

The morality play went on to detail how the Saskatchewan government was playing politics in order to avoid having to compensate Milgaard and admit a mistake. It called on other state agents – the RCMP and the Attorney General of Alberta – to conduct an investigation into any wrongdoing or cover-ups in the original investigation and trial. Not surprisingly, the investigation found no evidence of wrongdoing. Joyce Milgaard was quoted as saying, 'It somehow seems wrong. The whole thing has been a whitewash and a coverup ... It's real dirty pool that they're announcing the findings of this right now when we're having a civil action before the courts ... What would you expect from Saskatchewan? They've never done right by him to begin with' (Jang, 1994: A8). The Saskatchewan Attorney General was quoted as glibly stating: 'You just have to turn the page on this and consider that the book has been completed and is now closed ... Life goes on.' (1994: A8). The Saskatchewan government seemed satisfied with how it had handled the matter. However, it had resorted to questionable tactics to avoid admitting its mistakes, paying compensation, and dispensing justice.

The state's power interests and its need to appear in control of criminal justice were preventing it from admitting the truth and restoring justice. By this point in the narrative, only one force could reverse this outcome – the intervention of objective science in the form of DNA testing. The government having been cleared of wrongdoing by the RCMP, the press renewed its calls for DNA tests. However, not until three years later were those tests conducted. Prior to this, DNA testing had been referred to at least four times: in 1988, when Joyce Milgaard and David's lawyers initiated the reopening of the case; in 1992, during the Supreme Court hearing; in 1995, after the findings of the investigation into the Saskatchewan government's conduct in the case; and in 1997, when after pressure from Milgaard's lawyers, the federal Justice Department agreed to pay for tests. On each occasion, DNA testing was presented as holding out hope that the truth would finally be determined. In the end, those tests restored justice and found the truth. In 1999 David Milgaard was finally exonerated, and compensated for his ordeal. In 2000, Larry Fisher was tried and convicted for Gail Miller's murder. DNA testing had been necessary – the only remaining avenue for resolving the narrative. Milgaard's innocence could not be left unresolved. In the Morin case there had been some hesitation over forensic science in general because of the personal failings of individual forensic scientists; in the Milgaard case no doubts were raised about the utility of DNA testing. It was presented as the final arbiter; by 1997 any lingering doubts about its accuracy, usefulness, and necessity were gone. The laboratory errors that arose in the Guy Paul Morin and O.J. Simpson cases had been forgotten. DNA testing was now an objective oracle of truth in criminal justice, superior to the politicized power games of self-interested state agents.

Morin, Milgaard, and the Media Critique of Criminal Justice

Throughout the narratives of the Morin and Milgaard cases, the press constructed a problem frame. Something existed that was undesirable – the criminal justice system was making serious errors in finding the truth and dispensing justice. As a result, innocent people were being incarcerated while the real criminals were walking free. To emphasize this problem, the press referred constantly to a number of known cases of innocent people who had been exonerated over the past few years in Canada, the United States, and Britain. The facts of the Morin and Milgaard cases were represented in the coverage as unambiguous – at no time were counter-interpretations suggested. Reporters simply pointed to wrongful convictions, to abuses of authority resulting from too high levels of discretion allowed by the system, and to the self-interest of individuals involved in the cases. The problem could be fixed, however, mainly through closer auditing and reduced levels of discretion to ensure due process and through the use of biotechnology to ensure that truthful outcomes were found. These cases challenged the government to reconstitute the criminal justice system so as to ensure that innocent people were no longer imprisoned. We had the technology in our grasp to reduce the likelihood of wrongful conviction in cases of violent crime.

Contrary to what many media analysts contend regarding the usual relationship between the press and the courts, the Morin and Milgaard cases (and the Homolka case, and the Simpson case, and others) did not reflect a convergence of interests between the two institutions; they were, in fact, rupture points in that relationship. Although justice was restored within the Morin and Milgaard narratives, the problem of abuse of power and trust remained. In their coverage, journalists put the criminal justice system on trial and found it guilty. They charged the justice system with a lack of objectivity in the pursuit of truth and justice: authorities had too much discretion and abused it to torment and condemn innocent people. This perspective placed media consumers in an unusual position. Usually, media narratives place consumers in the position of the crime victim, but in the Morin and Milgaard cases, they were being invited to identify with victims of the justice system. The claims of prosecutors and judges to be representing the public in the system were shown to be false. Although justice was eventually dispensed to Morin and Milgaard, this was only because science and the media had intervened.

The two cases had similar narratives. A horrific crime occurs – a young girl/woman is raped and murdered. The police turn up few clues until someone provides questionable circumstantial evidence that points to the accused. Further investigation turns up more equivocal evidence. In a rush to close the case, the police arrest the accused, who is shocked. During the trial, he is betrayed by friends and neighbours, whom police have pressured to testify against him. On the basis of shaky evidence and as a result of aggressive state prosecution, the accused is convicted and sent to prison. Crusading friends, lawyers, and family members mobilize to free the accused and exonerate him. The media take up the cause. To protect its reputation and the reputations of its agents, the state resists. However, a DNA test provides incontrovertible evidence that exonerates the accused. Thanks largely to DNA evidence – which is not subject to contestation – the state must now provide justice in the form of an acquittal, an apology, compensation, and perhaps an inquiry.

In constructing such simple narratives of good and bad, right and wrong, guilty and not guilty, the media rely on certain techniques. In both cases, the media depended heavily for their information on defence lawyers, family members, and Morin and Milgaard themselves. Justice officials were rarely cited, and only from written comments. News stories repeatedly mentioned other cases of mistaken convictions, and these established the context for understanding Morin and Milgaard and for framing the problem. Morin and Milgaard were represented as simply two more victims in a widespread problem; in this way, their cases become emblematic of a pathological condition in the criminal justice system. Only a handful of similar cases were cited, however, and throughout the Morin and Milgaard coverage they were always the same ones. Such evidence was always anecdotal; no estimates were ever made of the actual numbers of people wrongly convicted and imprisoned. In this way, a type of hyper-reality developed in the coverage, with the press responding to these two cases as though they represented a broader social problem.

In one sense, the critique offered in the above narrative is a critique not of the bureaucratic system of justice, but rather of the system's failure to act bureaucratically. The technical legal rationality of bureaucracy is precisely what was absent from the officials' behaviour: they were acting in an individual and personalized manner. Thus bureaucratic rationality and the system of oversight it entails needed to be restored. In this way, what started out as a moral issue of abuse of state authority became a technical question of finding the science that would restore the system's instrumentality. This is the responsibilization strategy, adopted on a grand scale. In a risk society, individuals cannot be trusted with discretion; therefore, society must protect itself by establishing systems to ensure that people do not pursue their own good through public means.

In the coverage, two technologies for accomplishing this were recommended. The first was further layers of bureaucracy for auditing the decisions and actions of other layers. The Kaufman Report made a number of recommendations along these lines: appeal courts should be granted the power to set aside questionable convictions and to inquire into juries' decision-making processes; a quality assurance unit should be established to review the practices of forensic scientists; and police and lawyers should be trained to spot indications that their efforts may be leading to wrongful conviction. Cases such as Morin and Milgaard have done much to produce reflexivity toward criminal justice expertise that puts expert self-regulation into question.

The second technology – and a much more effective one – is DNA testing. The Kaufman Report called for the institutionalization of DNA testing and certainly the press agreed. In the coverage, DNA was reified as something that transcended human agency and as a force for justice in its own right. Few doubts were expressed about its efficacy. The standard narrative seems to pin all hopes on this technology to rebalance the justice system in its dealings with serious, violent crime. The argument is compelling. Proponents of DNA testing can point to its many proven strengths not only in freeing the innocent but also in convicting the guilty (such as Larry Fisher). Some people would hesitate to implement it because doing so would invade privacy, heighten social surveillance, and possibly lead to genetic discrimination, but there are few cases of abuse of the technology that would support their position. DNA was the determinative factor in the Morin and Milgaard cases. The charisma of genetic science resulted in an immediate acceptance of the DNA verdict in both cases and in government apologies and compensation. DNA simply put, restored justice. Clearly, DNA testing technology has become an antidote to politics rather than an object of politics. Science and scientists are often targets of calls for public scrutiny and democratic accountability in late modern risk society, yet technology seems immune from politicization. In Canadian criminal justice, politicization occurs around the risks implied by rising crime rates and abuse of expert discretion. DNA technology is a means for bringing both criminals and crime experts – including forensic scientists – under control. This is its power within the genetic imaginary and it adds a utopian element to the media narrative. All the more reason, then, for us to discuss what is involved in allowing genetic technology such a prominent place in criminal justice. That is the subject of the next chapter.

5 Opening and Closing the Black Box: DNA Typing as a Regime of Practice

After twenty three years in prison, a reopening of the case in front of the Supreme Court of Canada, a cautious stay of proceedings on the part of the Saskatchewan government, a final exoneration through DNA evidence, and the conviction of the real murderer of Gail Miller, David Milgaard ultimately had his case come to a satisfying conclusion. The same cannot be said for the Guy Paul Morin case. Morin's conviction was overthrown as a result of DNA evidence, but the real killer has never been found, and Christine Jessop's family must live with not knowing. From the perspective of those who wish to see a scientifically objective justice system, there are other disturbing elements to the case. At the Kaufman Inquiry, police stated that Morin became a suspect when a forensic analyst, Stephanie Nyznyk, concluded that a hair sample from Morin and a hair found in Christine Jessop's necklace were likely from the same source. She also spent several months combing through fibres found in Morin's car, and found a number of matches with fibres from Christine's clothing. However, it is likely that she knew even then that fibres from the clothing of laboratory personnel had contaminated the samples.

The Morin case has not been the only one involving questionable evidence from forensic laboratories. The most famous is that of O.J. Simpson, whose defence team had the monetary resources to comb through every step of the forensic DNA collection, analysis, and interpretation process and found a number of deviations from prescribed forensic practices. Crime scene investigators had not consistently worn gloves, had not recorded entries, had spilled substances, had not refrigerated samples, and had not taken photographs. Cross-examination showed racism to be a factor in police decision making, which raised the possibility that evidence had been planted by the police. The prosecutors had based their case on science. When the forensic evidence was shown to be subject to human error and malfeasance, that prosecution failed.

Another example of distortion arising from the human factor is the case of Fred Zain, a serologist at the West Virginia State Police Crime Laboratory, who was found to have fabricated data to produce convictions in more than 130 cases. Investigation into his work began when a man convicted on serological evidence produced by Zain was later proved innocent through DNA tests. In convicting Zain, the West Virginia Supreme Court of Appeals concluded that his behaviour included 'overstating the strength of results; ... reporting inconclusive results as conclusive; [and] repeatedly altering laboratory records' (in Thompson, 1997: 1116). The cases of Zain and Nyznyk illustrate a serious concern regarding the DNA typing system – the context in which forensic scientists' work promotes a pro-prosecution perspective. These scientists are solicited by police and prosecutors to assist in making a case against the defendant – a task that may be contrary to the principles of scientific objectivity.

The Kaufman Inquiry and Simpson and Zain trials point to gaps in the socio-technical network that is supposed to 'seal' the authority of DNA science and its practitioners. A technology is defined not only by its physical artifacts but also by its social organization, political structures, forms of knowledge, and social groupings, all of which come together to produce a working system. From this perspective, technology is a social process comprising social, rhetorical, and material elements, and a socially acceptable technology is one in which the potential conflicts built into this heterogeneous mix have been overcome and the social relations behind the technology have been made invisible and unquestionable. The socio-technical system that supports DNA testing and banking in Canada includes diverse institutions such as the National DNA Data Bank (NDDB), five regional RCMP forensic laboratories across the country, provincial forensic laboratories in Ontario and Quebec, the RCMP, municipal and provincial police departments, the Solicitor General and the Canadian Department of Justice, the FBI and the U.S. Department of Justice, the criminal courts of Canada, victims' groups, the media, and suppliers of laboratory and crime scene sampling equipment, as well as an accepting political culture. In the previous two chapters I examined certain political and social elements in this socio-technical network. In this chapter I focus on the NDDB and how its operations contribute to the seamlessness of this network.

In the chapers on policymaking and media coverage, I addressed questions of ontological security as they relate to genetic privacy and objective justice. The NDDB was designed very deliberately to embody these privacy and objectivity concerns; the point of this was to ensure that the public would perceive its DNA findings as both objective and fair. Through DNA typing and banking, the criminal justice system is trying to produce the appearance of an objectified justice process. Its laboratory procedures and activities are designed to perform the *boundary work* of the expert community of forensic analysts – that is, to legitimate the truths produced in the laboratory and to establish forensic scientists and technicians as the expert community uniquely qualified to generate these truths. Here, I address the following question: How is objectivity achieved in DNA typing? In other words, how is the trace defined, processed, and circulated within the DNA typing socio-technical network to produce objective and reasonably private evidentiary truth?

To produce evidentiary truth, DNA analysis must become a *regime of practice* – a stable set of routinized, ritualized, and institutionalized activities. A regime of practice gives rise to, and depends upon, particular forms of scientific and popular knowledge. It is associated with specific techniques, instrumentalities, and mechanisms through which it achieves its goals. It has a range of effects that flow out of the truths it produces and that lead to institutional actions and social policies. So in order to analyse DNA testing and banking as a regime of practice designed to produce objectification in criminal justice, we must ask three questions. First, what are the processes of representation that define the DNA trace as a particular kind of scientific field open to technological intervention? Second, what are the techniques of manipulation involved in translating the trace into information about the identity of criminals? Third, what are the modes of governmental meaning production that constitute institutionally legitimated interpretations of the trace? Cases such as Nyznyk, Simpson, Zain, and others provide glimpses into how regimes actually operate. Non-experts do not often have the opportunity to scrutinize this. These glimpses serve as rupture points that allow us to analyse the kinds of slippages that are present behind the relatively seamless exterior of DNA testing.

Representing the Gene

Before genes can be manipulated, broken apart, analysed, and converted into information about identity, they must first be imagined. They must somehow be represented as something that is open to human observation and intervention. An image of the gene must be created. This is certainly necessary in order to publicly legitimate genetic research and is an essential component of the genetic imaginary that is beginning to form in Western culture. This process of imagining is the theme of a growing number of works, including those of Nelkin and Lindee (1995), Turney (1998), and Van Dijck (1998). I would go even further and argue that scientists themselves require images and narratives of the gene in order to imagine directions of research and develop rationales for that research. Images of the gene do not develop strictly in laboratories or in science fiction stories; they also develop in scientific and popular cultures. Furthermore, these two sites of cultural production interact with each other.

In her analysis of popular genetic visions over time, José Van Dijck identifies four dominant images of genetics that have arisen from the interactions among science, science fiction, environmentalism, feminism, and business since the early 1950s, when the DNA double-helix was first discovered. Early in DNA research, the image of DNA as an alphabet, language, or code developed. The four bases of DNA – A (adenine), G (guanine), T (thymidine), and C (cytosine) – form the letters of the alphabet or code, and their endless combinations constitute the 'book of life.' Through the code/language metaphor, DNA has become a concrete entity and the object of molecular biological research. DNA allows the body to be understood as a rule-governed system of communication that can be read by those who have the expertise to do so. The gene has become reified as the site of vital activity (37).

In the 1970s, environmental consciousness affected the image of the gene, promoting it from neutral and relatively benign matter to an agent capable of independent acts. Geneticists were reconceptualized through representations of the irresponsible scientist and of the sloppy lab worker who has an incomplete understanding of genetic processes and also allows strings of modified genes to escape the lab and contaminate nature in a harmful way. Van Dijck relates this negative image of the scientist to the doubts raised about scientists' ethics in the wake of the development of the atomic bomb (65). Would genetic R&D proceed with a similar disregard for the consequences? In this cultural context, the gene was increasingly defined as a type of germ that could infect the natural gene pool of the planet in unforeseen ways. Scientists were losing their power to define the situation, and at a number of scientific congresses they began to pay some degree of attention to the need for public accountability. Mainly, this involved using the media to promote more positive images of genetic science. At this point, geneticists began to explore social marketing techniques to counter negative, politicized images emerging from popular·culture and the counterculture.

The third image of genetics developed during the 1980s and can be characterized as the gene as factory manager. As the political importance of environmentalism declined in the 1980s, the agency of the gene took on a different meaning, aided by the development of sociobiology. The idea that gene sequences determine the kinds of proteins that organisms will make led to an image of the gene as a master molecule that directs an organism's development. The autonomy of the gene was reinterpreted as positive: humans are machines created by genes within a competitive context. Our function is to preserve and disseminate our genes. At the centre of this industrial metaphor is the gene as manager, running our bodies in a manner similar to how businesses are run in order to survive and flourish in a competitive environment.

The fourth and final image is that of the map. This image developed in the 1990s as a byproduct of the Human Genome Project and its quest to detail the entire human genome. The Human Genome Project consisted of two related projects: the mapping of the relative positions of genes on the chromosomes, and a more detailed DNA sequencing of the exact order of base pairs along the chromosomes. The resulting representation allows for the actual locating of specific genetic aberrations – a guide to defects that scientists hope to correct in the future, a tool for navigating the terrain of the human genome.

Metaphors of mapping may provide the dominant language of genetic research in the early twenty-first century, but the images of language, germ, and factory manager are still present. They form stratigraphic layers of imagery that are periodically mined for meaning at different times and at different biotechnological sites. Unlike these earlier conceptualizations, defining the gene as a map of a person's structural make-up suggests a fixity of genetic characteristics. This has drawn criticism from noted analysts such as Daniel Kevles (1997) and Richard Lewontin (1995). Kevles contends that mapping the genome and identifying aberrations based on this map can lead to a return to eugenics:

Biology still knows little about the role of genetics in behavior, but it might someday learn – or claim to have learned – more. In that event, the definition of 'defect' might become once again a hereditarian cloak for social prejudice. One can hardly be confident that principles of political and social equality will, as a practical matter, remain unscathed by scientific contentions of racial differences in such traits as intelligence. The ancient impulses setting group against group survive. (1997: 299)

Lewontin echoes these sentiments, suggesting that a map is a deterministic image that reinforces sociobiological notions by fixing a norm that becomes the new basis for past ideological claims justifying male dominance, meritocratic class systems, aggression, fear of strangers, and other hierarchizing processes (1995, 22). The 'map' can become a basis for moral claims and judgments. In a risk society, these claims could lead to calls for public control over the right to bear 'aberrant' children, for example (Kevles, 1997: 300).

The image of the map as a fixed representation of the gene does not capture the complexities of what is currently happening in the genetic imaginary. There is a qualitative difference between the map metaphor and earlier images of the gene. In the 1990s, genetic research merged with informatics. The gene became the 'genome,' genetics became 'genomics,' and the geneticist became a combination of molecular biologist and computer scientist. As a consequence, the map has become an information map that is not entirely static. It is interactional rather than unidirectional – part of a complex organic network of data. Yet there are still some deterministic qualities to this vision of the genome. The human body is still a predetermined route that scientists can travel to trace diseases and defects. But, the fact that this image of the map is inscribed in the form of a digital code adds another level of complexity. As Van Dijck points out:

Sequencing genes – the activity that constitutes the core of the HGP [Human Genome Project] – now fully consists of processing digital information. The idea that the human body can be coded in a decipherable sequence of four letters, and hence in a finite collection of information, is based on the epistemological view that computer language – like molecular language – is an unambiguous representation of physical reality. (1998: 123–4)

Converting DNA sequences into digital codes is not simply a *repre-*

sentation of molecular language; it is a *translation* into an informational realm. It converts the genetic make-up of the body into a series of bits and bytes with a number of consequences – it *informates* the genetic sequence. Informating the gene has a number of implications. First, the body recedes from view in biological discourse and becomes part of an informational network as an exchangeable commodity, along with the political body, the corporation, and the population. The patenting of genetic information and of the processes involved in decoding and manipulating that information result from this reconceptualization. Second, the simultaneously material and digital nature of current conceptions of the genome allows for an easy slide between representational and ontological languages. Editing, copying, and deleting are common terms in genomics as well as in computer science; this leads to an understanding of the genome as open to manipulation. Third, the digital genome data emerging from the Human Genome Project inscribe the model body. Digitized data about the genome can be recorded and rearranged to form an 'ideal' genetic sequence. However, the map of the human genome is a standardized composite from thousands of donors, expressed as a formula in a mathematical language. It has no referent in reality – it is not a real person's genetic sequence but rather a hyper-real sequence. To the extent that this digital map of the human genome represents a norm, it is not based on an actual human being.

What are the implications of the digital mapping concept for DNA typing in criminal justice? Increasingly, criminal investigation and identification are about identifying the suspect not as a person or as even a body, but rather as an abstract coded sequence. Mapping is central to conceptions of DNA typing in the form of the 'DNA fingerprint' or 'bar code.' Fingerprints and bar codes are types of maps taken from traces and compared to the map of the suspect body. Use of the fingerprinting analogy was not accidental. Alec Jeffreys himself commented on use of the term: 'One of the reasons we called this "DNA fingerprinting" was absolutely deliberate. If we had called this "idiosyncratic Southern blot profiling," nobody would have taken a blind bit of notice. Call it "DNA fingerprinting," and the penny dropped' (in Cole, 1998: 706).

Since each person's genetic map is theoretically unique (with the exception of identical twins), the trace becomes a powerful identifier of the offender's genetic terrain. This map bears the dual legitimacy of digitization and genetics; it combines the power of two charismatic techno-sciences to produce levels of certainty expressed as astronomical odds against false matches. Bar codes and fingerprints, however, are not really unmediated images of genes; they are representations that leave room for interpretation. DNA identification is the highly mediated end product of a set of techniques that process the gene, reorganize it into a readable format, and interpret the resulting image. Yet processes of representation and human judgment tend to be erased from narratives of how the testing is done. Embedded in the techniques of this technology are practices that close the 'black box' of the technology and produce claims that are legitimated as truths. The map becomes the reality, a simulacra; the processes of representation are thereby rendered invisible.

Techniques of Manipulation

Given the concerns expressed in media coverage of trials and in policy debates about DNA testing and banking, the NDDB's practices for translating the trace into information on identity are constrained by two principles. First is the need for privacy – a code word within the policy debates for observing certain levels of bodily integrity rights and for restricting exchanges of genetic information. Second is the need to demonstrate objectivity when handling and processing the trace in order to legitimate this technology as a remedy to the problem of subjective justice. The DNA Identification Act and the internal protocols of the NDDB were written in such a way as to enforce these two principles in a strict and highly visible fashion. They establish a series of *technologies of distance* that erase the world of representation by separating institutionalized routines from individual human fallibility.

DNA Typing in Canada

The NDDB came into operation in July 2000. It is located at RCMP headquarters in Ottawa. It is the centre of the DNA typing network in Canada, and $11 million was spent to establish it. Once it is fully operational and running at full capacity, its operating costs will be around $5 million a year. At present, twenty-five people work there; eventually this will increase to thirty-three (NDDB, 2002b: 15). This is a very small staff compared to other countries. For example, more than four hundred people work in the United Kingdom's DNA data bank facilities.

The hiring process is rigorous. More than four hundred applications were received for positions on the DNA analysis team that processes the samples. Initially, four analysts were hired; two more were added later. Successful applicants, who must have a degree in biology, genetics, or a related field, are put through four or five months of training, during which they must learn the laboratory's protocols, demonstrate an ability to work with small samples, and practise with the robotics machinery that carries out the data bank's basic functions. Practical lab tests and a written examination test their skills. They must then pass a final qualifying examination before being allowed to process convicted offender samples. Once they are fully authorized to carry out the work of the laboratory, they must pass proficiency tests every six months.

In conjunction with six regional RCMP laboratories in Ottawa, Edmonton, Vancouver, Regina, Winnipeg, and Halifax, as well as two provincial forensic laboratories in Toronto and Montreal, the NDDB matches crime scene DNA profiles to convicted offender profiles. Two indexes are kept at the NDDB: the Crime Scene Index and the Convicted Offender Index. Regional and provincial laboratories are responsible for processing crime scene samples gathered by trained police officers. They then submit the digitized DNA information from the crime scene to the NDDB, where it is entered into the Crime Scene Index and compared with other crime scene DNA in the database as well as to the Convicted Offender Index to see if there are any matches. If there is a match, police investigators are notified. Samples taken from suspects through DNA warrants are not submitted to the NDDB. Only convicted offender samples may be stored there. As of 14 May 2003, 40,097 DNA profiles had been entered into the Convicted Offender Index and 9,090 into the Crime Scene Index. There have been 762 matches of crime scene samples to offenders and 50 matches from crime scene to crime scene (NDDB, 2003: 1). Although the law allows for sampling of blood, hair roots, and saliva, 97.9 percent of the samples received are blood samples. Another 1.9 percent are buccal swabs, and 0.2 percent are hair roots. Blood samples are simply easier to collect and process.

Privacy

Throughout the processing and storage of samples, one of the main concerns is privacy. In the DNA Identification Act, sections 6, 7, 8, and 10 address matters of privacy in terms of who has access to samples and information in the data bank, the circumstances in which it may be communicated, and to whom. Section 11 establishes penalties for violating these rules; doing so is an indictable offence that can lead to imprisonment and/or a fine. Only NDDB personnel have access to the DNA samples for the purposes of analysis and training. As well, the RCMP Commissioner has the authority to grant access to anyone whose presence is necessary for the preservation of DNA samples. Profiles can be used only to investigate and prosecute a criminal offence. Information as to whether a person's DNA profile is present in the Convicted Offender Index can be communicated to authorized users of the RCMP's automated criminal convictions records retrieval system. Primarily, this means Canadian police officers and foreign law enforcement agencies. Requests from the latter must be approved by the RCMP Commissioner. All other uses, including medical, are punishable under section 11.

Besides all this, the NDDB's processing procedures have privacy built within them. This begins at the sample collection stage. When an officer collects a sample from a convicted offender, he or she randomly selects a sample collection kit, each of which has a unique serial number printed on it at the manufacturing stage. These kits were field tested by the RCMP during the Swissair Flight 111 disaster in 1998 and were found to work very well for processing large numbers of samples at a time.[1] A sample kit for blood samples, which are the majority of all samples, includes the following: a fingerprint identification form, an ink strip for fingerprinting, a sample collection card on which the blood sample is placed, an alcohol prep pad, a lancet, a mylar envelope for storing the blood sample, three desiccant pouches placed inside the mylar pouch along with the blood sample, disposable gloves, a disposable mask, and an eight-by-ten-inch Ziplok bag to contain the completed kit for submission to the NDDB. Once collected, the kit is couriered to Ottawa.

Once the NDDB receives the kit, data bank personnel compare the fingerprints on the fingerprint identification form with those placed on the back of the sample collection card to confirm that they are from the same person. At this point, the two forms of information are separated. The fingerprint form, with the name and other identifying data from the offender, is sent to the RCMP's Canadian Criminal Records Information Service (CCRIS). The blood (or hair or buccal) sample is retained by the NDDB, but is identifiable only by the bar code on the sample collection kit. In this way, someone can establish a link between the sample and an actual person only by accessing two separate and secure databases located in two different places. The personnel who process the samples at the data bank do not know the identity of the offender who submitted the sample; however, they can trace the sample's journey while it is being converted into information using an optical scanner on the bar code. This records the sample's passage from station to station. This procedural information trail is vitally important, given the volume of samples processed each year.

Once the sample has been processed, it is digitally coded and entered into the Convicted Offender Index. At this point it is compared to coded information in the Crime Scene Index. If a match occurs, the CCRIS is contacted. Personnel at the CCRIS match this information to the name of the offender and contact the regional laboratory that submitted the crime scene sample and data to the NDDB. The NDDB will also inform the submitting laboratories if there is a match between two or more crime scene samples.

Yet another privacy safeguard involves administrative oversight in the form of the NDDB Advisory Committee, which was appointed by the Solicitor General in early 2000. The committee has eight members: the RCMP Commissioner's representative, a representative from the legal profession, an officer from the Privacy Commission, a population biologist, a medical geneticist, a biomedical ethicist, a human rights advocate, and the director of the NDDB. This committee reports annually to the RCMP Commissioner and is responsible for reviewing the NDDB's operations – in particular, the relationship between the Crime Scene Index and the Convicted Offender Index. As well, the Privacy Commissioner has the right to audit the NDDB's operations at any time. There will be a full Parliamentary review of the data bank and the DNA Identification Act in 2005, after five years of operation.

Genetic privacy is thus produced and protected in a number of ways. Scientific: DNA testing examines only thirteen points from the entire human DNA structure, and these points do not allow for the identification of physical or behavioural attributes other than gender. Methodological: Personal data and genetic data are separated into two highly secure databases. Physical: Unauthorized personnel cannot enter NDDB premises to view or retrieve data. Legal: Unauthorized use of the DNA information or samples leads to criminal penalties. Administrative: Both the NDDB Advisory Committee and the Privacy Commission scrutinize the the data bank's procedures and decisions to ensure proper protocols and respect for human rights.[2] In all of its public communications, including its website and its annual report, the NDDB strongly emphasizes all of these processes.

Objectivity

Privacy safeguards contribute to the appearance that the system is objective, but objectivity involves more than this. Abstract notions of expert boundary maintenance serve to establish DNA forensic analysts as the sole authorities on DNA identification. Forensic expertise is 'blocked off' from the public through a number of technologies of distance which together suggest that the work of DNA technicians is uncontaminated by subjective judgments and interpretations. However, as Thomas Kuhn (1964) pointed out, at some point there is always a gap between the ideal type and the actual result of the measurement – in this case the ideal of the clear DNA map and the actuality of the messy, degraded, fuzzy, and ambiguous crime scene sample bar code often seem hard to reconcile. Somewhere in the process, a human must make an estimation or a judgment call, and means must be available to weigh the risks of varying levels of competence and care.

The primary technology of distance is the formation of a generally accepted trajectory of events, which together tell the 'story' of what happens during the DNA typing process. This becomes a narrative that can then be told in a number of formats, including news reports, private forensic laboratory brochures, and the NDDB website. The latter contains the following narrative, complete with photographs of the technology involved at each stage:

- Sample Collection
- Kit Reception Room: Kits received and validated – sample receipt initiated
- Punching Room: Samples punched from dried biological stains on FTA collection cards
- Pre–PCR Room: Automated DNA extraction and PCR setup
- DNA Amplification Room: Samples amplified and fluorescently tagged using thermal cyclers and the PCR process
- Post–PCR Room: Sample preparation for gel electrophoresis – automated comb loading
- Sequencer Room: DNA fragments detected and digitized to computers
- Computer Analysis: Gel electrophoresis results processed and formatted for CODIS
- CODIS Room: DNA profiler results up-loaded to Convicted Offender Index – this room also houses the Crime Scene Index termi-

nal. (National DNA Data Bank: http://NDDB-BNDG.org/techno/
Lab1_e.htm)

This is typical of the sanitized version of DNA typing most often
presented to the public and to courts. The technology is presented as
well-understood and relatively simple, as comprising a series of well-
defined steps. Diagrams such as this provide no sense of the scientific
and legal controversies surrounding particular steps or the procedure
as a whole. There is certainly no sense that errors are possible; readers
are provided with only enough information to conclude that it is a logical, straightforward, and trustworthy process. There is also no sense
that the techniques listed are part of a socio-technical network that
extends beyond the laboratory to include validating social and political institutional processes. It objectifies the technology and closes it to a
critical non-scientific gaze. However, if we look at the techniques
involved in manipulating the DNA trace, it is possible to add complexity to the diagram and open the black box a little further to include
potential problem points and controversies. There are three basic
stages in the DNA typing network: sample collection, laboratory processing, and interpretation. At each stage there are potential problems.

DNA samples are collected by specially trained police officers.
When the NDDB was opened in 2000, there were already 1,200 trained
officers across the country, and that number is increasing as those
officers train others (Kerr, 2000: 26). Collection from a convicted
offender or a suspect seems fairly straightforward. Each collection kit
contains a checklist of instructions, including which authorization
forms need to be filled out by the judge and the police officer, and
which report forms must be sent to the judge after the test. There are
also step-by-step instructions for each type of sampling – blood, buccal, and hair. The NDDB also provides a Sample Collection Handbook,
which provides extensive details on how to get the necessary authorization for sampling, the forms necessary for processing the offender,
the protocols for taking samples, and the steps for processing the sample for submission to the NDDB.

Included in the kit are the following statements to be read aloud to
the offender:

I am detaining you for the purpose of obtaining a DNA sample for the
purpose of the National DNA Data Bank pursuant to an order/authoriza-
tion issued under the Criminal Code of Canada. It is my duty to inform

you that you have the right to retain and instruct counsel without delay. You have the right to telephone any lawyer you wish. You also have the right to free advice from a legal aid lawyer.

Do you understand? Do you wish to call a lawyer now?

Pursuant to Section 487.07(1) of the Criminal Code:

1. It is my duty to inform you that I have an order/authorization issued by a Judge to take bodily substances for forensic DNA analysis. (Show or read order/authorization to offender)
2. A blood sample will be taken from you by piercing your fingertip with a sterile lancet and depositing blood droplets onto a collection card which will be forwarded to the National DNA Data Bank for analysis.
3. The National DNA Data Bank will analyse your blood sample and generate a DNA profile which will be maintained by the National DNA Data Bank and compared against evidence received from crime scenes.
4. I must advise you that during this procedure, if required, as much force as necessary will be used to obtain this blood sample.

This sort of collection is relatively straightforward and is usually done in controlled surroundings in the courthouse or in prison. These are relatively 'pure' samples that will yield clear DNA profiles. However, there are potential problems with this type of sampling, involving legal technologies of rights as well as material technologies of lancets, swabs, and envelopes. In an attempt to anticipate ruptures in the collection process and to prevent them from occurring, the Sample Collection Handbook warns officers to watch for certain risk factors, including the following:

1 Judge is not asked or does not issue order to obtain DNA sample.
2 Order is not pursued or is lost during transportation of offender.
3 A sample is rejected.
4 Protocol is not observed or recorded.
5 Confirmation form 5.07 is not completed or sample is lost during transportation.
6 Failure of NDDB to notify police officer that a sample has been rejected; failure of the crown to request order for re-take.

Despite the great care that has been taken to ensure proper collection techniques through training, checklists, and the Sample Collection Handbook, several sorts of problems can arise. What is collected, how it is collected, who collects it, how it is labelled, who handles it, how it is stored and transported, whether proper authorization was obtained are all potential points for courtroom challenge. For example, as of January 2003, of the 34,654 convicted offender samples received, 357 were rejected. Reasons for rejection included the following: non-designated offences (195); inadequate biological sample (71); use of wrong kit (67); lack of court order (4); 'other' reasons, largely administrative and clerical (20) (NDDB, 2003). This rejection rate of only 1 percent suggests that the collection process is effective as it pertains to convicted offenders. Even so, in its electronic newsletter which is sent out to a list of regular contacts, and in its regular videoconferences with police around the country, the NDDB has repeatedly expressed concern about the problem. The most common error involves failing to place the offender's fingerprints on the back of the sample collection card. This form of identification is at the heart of the privacy claims of the entire DNA identification system; in its newsletter, the NDDB has labelled this an 'urgent' issue (NDDB, 2001).[3]

Similar statistics are not available regarding the rejection of crime scene samples by regional laboratories. Samples taken at crime scenes are less pristine. They may be very small (merely a few cells), and they may be contaminated as a result of being mixed with other people's DNA. The following areas are often searched for DNA evidence at crime scenes: the handle of a baseball bat or similar weapon; the inside of a hat, bandanna, or mask; nose pieces, ear pieces, and lenses of glasses; facial tissues, cotton swabs, and dirty laundry; the tips of toothpicks; cigarette butts; licked areas of stamps and envelopes; the inner and outer surfaces of tape; the sides and mouth areas of bottles, cans, and glasses; used condoms; surfaces of blankets, pillows, and sheets; bite marks on skin and clothing; and scrapings from under victims' fingernails (National Commission on the Future of DNA Evidence, 1999). DNA-bearing evidence is collected with cotton swabs, tweezers, gloved hands, scissors, and so on. Each individual sample is placed in a labelled bag by a forensic technician or a police officer for later analysis.

Collection of samples from suspects during an investigation is less regulated and controlled than collection from convicted offenders. There is no central body such as the NDDB to manage the process – regional laboratories carry out the DNA typing process – and kits for this type of collection must be purchased directly from private suppliers. In its 14 March 2001 newsletter, the NDDB posted the following warning:

> It has come to our attention that NDDB collection kits have been used for a variety of investigative samples, including Bill C-104 DNA Warrants. *It is important that this practice cease immediately.* NDDB Collection Kits should *only* be used for collecting convicted offender samples that will be submitted to the Data Bank under the DNA Identification Act (Bill C-3). A sample collection kit specifically designed for C-104 Warrant samples is under development and should be available by early fall. In the meantime, the supplies required for DNA Warrant and other investigative sample collections can be purchased from a number of different suppliers. (NDDB, 2001, emphasis in original)

A successful challenge of the collection process can render the evidence entirely unusable as happened in the O.J. Simpson case. Interestingly, however, collection methods are rarely challenged. Courtroom challenges and scientific debates have focused on the technical and scientific procedures followed to process the traces, and on how sequence frequencies are calculated within populations. Forensic experts have come to determine the terms of debate, and as a result, most controversies now focus on their expertise. Collection, which falls outside of laboratory expertise, has become a less visible feature of the entire process. This is, perhaps, less true in Canada than in the United States. In Canada, because the NDDB is centralized and under RCMP management, there is a closer connection between collection and laboratory processing and the NDDB is more actively involved in prescribing and controlling collection techniques. In the United States, much of the processing is performed by private laboratories, so there is less connection to police investigators. The Canadian arrangement is more seamless in the sense that laboratory administrators play a more active role in collection. One obvious way is by providing collection kits to police. Also, through communication strategies such as the regular newsletter and videoconferencing, NDDB personnel receive feedback and communicate about problems in collection. They can thus work to bring collection processes more closely into the idealized narrative of DNA typing.

The second stage of the DNA typing process is laboratory work. This is where the technical work of the socio-technical network takes place – work that comes to represent the entire network and that provides the focus for debates and discussions about the entire process of DNA typing. Lab work is the 'black box' that is largely insulated from legal, scientific, and journalistic scrutiny. In Canada, this stage begins when the sample, separated from its source and identified only by a bar code, is passed on to the *punching room* (assuming that all administrative details have been properly carried out during the collection phase). In the punching room, dried samples on the collection cards are punched out of the card by machine and then prepared for DNA extraction. In the case of blood samples, each card contains two or three drops of blood placed on each of four separate circles. The card has been coated with preserving chemicals similar to those used to preserve cosmetics. These chemicals cause the cell membranes to rupture in such a way that the DNA is trapped in the fibres of the paper. Next, the sample passes to the *pre-PCR room*, where the punched-out disks of paper with blood samples are placed on a process plate that contains ninety-six wells. Some of the samples in the wells are control samples; if they produce the expected results, this indicates that the system is working properly. A robot extracts the DNA from the samples using a liquid reagent; the DNA is then sent to the *DNA amplification room*, where it is 'amplified' through the PCR process, which replicates the DNA, thus eliminating the need for large samples (see chapter 2). During the amplification process, the DNA is fluorescently tagged for easy detection by laser scanner equipment.

In the next stage, samples go to the *post-PCR room*, where a second robot loads each DNA sample onto one of the teeth of a membrane sample 'comb.' From there, the samples pass to the *sequencer room*, where an electric field pulls the DNA from the sample comb into a gel-like substance. Within the gel, the DNA fragments move toward a laser detector, which records the fragments as they exit the sequencer in ascending order of length. This creates a profile of twenty-eight bands resembling a bar code, displayed by the sequencer as twenty-eight coloured, horizontal bands called an autoradiograph or autorad. For each sample two analysts verify the results. On top of this, two separate sample discs are processed for each sample card and the results are compared to ensure that the procedure has worked properly. The entire process takes three to five days. For the sake of efficiency a large number of samples can be processed at the same time.

Two software applications are at the heart of this process. The first is STaCS^{TM} (sample tracking and control system), which has been developed in conjunction with Anjura Technology of Ottawa. It automatically tracks and records every step in the analysis process for each sample; in this way an accountability record for sample manipulation is provided along with a record of the results of each step of the process for easy comparison of the parallel tests run on each sample. STaCS is the first major intellectual property to have been developed by the NDDB, which, as part of its mission, is developing licensable technologies that will help the data bank pay its own way. The second important computer application is CODIS (combined DNA index system), which has been developed by the FBI and the U.S. Department of Justice and which is provided at no charge to law enforcement agencies that follow similar codes of quality assurance. CODIS is a database that allows for the storage and comparison of digitally coded DNA sequences. CODIS is used by all six of the RCMP forensic labs across the country, by the provincial labs in Montreal and Toronto, and by laboratories in the United States; it is the North American standard, and it allows for easy communication of crime scene and offender DNA information. The final step in the DNA analysis process involves formatting the results of the gel electrophoresis process for CODIS, entering the results into the Convicted Offender Index in the CODIS room, and running comparisons between the offender's DNA information and information contained in the Crime Scene Index.

In its public communications and also in its organizational communications, the NDDB emphasizes how highly automated its laboratories are. This is a way of emphasizing how objective the process is and how carefully privacy safeguards have been built in. Automation reduces the likelihood of human error and/or malfeasance. It also legitimates the results as more accurate in the sense that they involve less human judgment. All of this, and the stability of the biological science that underpins DNA typing, means that the results of DNA tests are less likely to be challenged in court.

Yet, the DNA matching process is neither seamless nor automatic, and there are a number of sites of potential subjective variation. Analysts must measure precisely the length of DNA fragments and decide whether two fragments match each other. Bands are often very faint, which means that analysts must decide whether they are present on the basis of barely visible marks on an imperfect film. Broad bands or smeared bands from overloading the gel, as well as DNA degradation or the overexposure of an autorad, throw analysis back on the expert's visual matching. Band shifting can occur when one or more lanes are vertically displaced from their matching bands into other lanes. This is probably a result of loading the gel with too much DNA, or contamination of the DNA, and it may lead analysts to relax their standards of error measurement in order to avoid falsely exonerating a guilty suspect (Derksen, 2000: 813). Some of these problems have been reduced through technology – most notably the problem of too little DNA, which is counteracted by PCR technology. In Canada, there have been fewer cases than in the United States involving challenges to the processing technology; arguments in Canadian courts focus more on rights and due process. Canadian courts have been largely content to allow American courts to work out the scientific controversies.

Most of the concerns that have arisen over laboratory processes in Canada are about the third stage of the DNA typing process – interpretation – rather than the scientific techniques themselves. The technologies are rarely challenged, and when they are, those challenges tend to be restricted to localized instances of misconduct or carelessness. The strategy is to question individual practitioners rather than to raise doubts about the technology or the system as a whole.

The third stage of the DNA typing process involves interpreting the results of the laboratory analysis and presenting those results in court. In the past, this has been the most controversial stage of the process because it is the most difficult one to free from subjectivity. Interpretation of the results is less easy to contain within a particular expert community. This is partly because interpretation involves human visual comparison of two autorads, which can be done by anyone. Also, judicial and scientific standards for providing truth come into conflict at this stage (see chapter 6). Basically, a match, exclusion, or inconclusive result must be drawn from the autorad comparison. This is done by estimating the size of the DNA fragments of any particular band and then comparing them to size estimates from other relevant samples.

It is here that another technology of distance comes into play – the translation of potential error into a numerically expressed measurement error. As Linda Derksen (2000) points out, numbers can compensate for the gap between theory and observation; we simply employ them to establish a stable limit for a wide array of personal, subjective, and technical sources of variability in measurement (806). All of these factors become invisible when experts agree on a 'reasonable' level of measurement error for purposes of courtroom evidence. There are two forms of error measurement in DNA typing. The first expresses the agreed-upon potential for error when two autorads are compared and estimating the acceptable variation in length between two fragments that will still allow the expert to declare that they match. Both visual and computerized estimations are used to arrive at a conclusion on a match. Analysts will declare a match if the bands fall within a certain range of variation in their length, usually 1.5 to 2.5 per cent. Once a match is declared, population geneticists must draw the implications for guilt or innocence. The second form of error measurement involves calculating the statistical likelihood of a false match within a given population. These calculations are performed using databases of enzyme frequencies within racial groups. Experts present this number to the court to give weight to the inference of a match gained from the comparison of autorads.

As noted earlier, much of the controversy in the early years of DNA typing centred on interpretation, especially as it related to population genetics calculations. However, much of that controversy has subsided since the establishment, within the expert community, of a set of agreed-upon standards. The NDDB follows standards set by accreditation bodies, most notably the Standards Council of Canada's Program for the Accreditation of Laboratories Canada (PALCAN). Although the NDDB is not yet accredited, it will be shortly, and there is little doubt that its processing, information management, and record-keeping procedures will receive accreditation. Accreditation helps close the leaky black box of interpretation, since it indicates that independent outside assessors have given their seal of approval to the accredited organization and thereby declared its outcomes trustworthy. Once the NDDB is accredited, the implication will be that its standards of error measurement are appropriate and should not be questioned in the courts. Also, that the visual authority of the forensic experts should be accepted along with their population genetics calculations.

Another basis for the authority of forensic DNA expertise relates to the absence of defence experts. RCMP forensic DNA experts generally provide uncontested evidence on behalf of the prosecution and are not available to the defence. In this way, DNA evidence is unlike other forms of expertise – for example, psychology, which is often solicited by both sides in a criminal trial. This creates the impression that DNA is an exact and unambiguous science in which human interpretation plays no part. In this way, DNA tilts in favour of prosecutors. Add to this the fact that the NDDB and the regional RCMP laboratories are under RCMP management and so their forensic experts are not subject to accusations that they are motivated by profit (unlike their counterparts in the United States, many of whom operate in the private sector).

Overall, the techniques for manipulating the trace are designed to produce legitimate outcomes in terms of privacy and objectivity. Broader ethical questions relating to whether we are creating a social environment that increasingly involves greater surveillance and less freedom from state observation has been converted into technical questions regarding whether identity information and DNA samples should be stored in separate data banks and how many points in the DNA sequence should be included in the testing process. Distrust of the social technologies of criminal justice and their attendant forms of expertise is addressed by checklists, standardized kits, STaCS, CODIS, robots, autoradiographs, and population genetics calculations. These characteristics of genetic justice convert certain evidence-gathering processes into automated laboratory techniques, which in the name of privacy are relatively closed to public scrutiny. Given the demonstrated impact on juries of calculations of chance matches, this technicalization of criminal investigation and testimony has effectively removed judicial decision making from the reason of juries and judges and placed it in the hands of technicians and their machines. Over time, the narrative representing the socio-technical network surrounding these processes has become increasingly closed; it is now forensic analysts who define acceptable standards, and lawyers and judges are deferring to those analysts. In this sense, DNA typing is now producing more than autorads or maps of DNA profiles. It is producing social outcomes in the form of verdicts, new institutional configurations, public opinions, expert communities, and government policies and legislation. All of these are reinforcing the centrality of the technology itself.

Modes of Truth Production

How do the processes of representation and the techniques of DNA manipulation render the issues of crime management and genetic justice governable and productive of certain forms of truth for purposes of social governance? In other words, how are DNA's representations and techniques employed to produce and legitimate criminal justice policies and legislation? This was the subject matter of chapters 3 and 4; however, some reiteration is valuable at this point because it is at this level of truth production that DNA typing, as a regime of practice, mobilizes elements of the broader socio-technical network to limit the grounds for questioning the technology and its associated representations of the trace. Authorization of the technology and the associated definition of the situation occur through acceptance by stakeholders in the socio-technical network of DNA typing's claims to privacy and objectivity. Privacy and objectivity are the two risks emerging from the public sphere and from government policy processes. Both issues must be addressed in order to counter the public's ontological insecurity – insecurity that arises from the surveillance potentials of the technology and the generalized fear of crime.

David Kaye, a law professor at Arizona State University, argued in 1993 that in the United States, DNA typing as courtroom evidence had already passed through three stages: first, enthusiastic acceptance; second, a reduction of enthusiasm and a more cautious approach after *New York v. Castro*; and third, a period of mixed decisions that reflected a cautious approach to certain aspects of DNA evidence (Kaye, 1993). During the first stage, judges, juries, and lawyers did not have the knowledge or the tools to open the black box of DNA typing. During the second stage, defence lawyers began to probe into the possible sources of human error in the technological system. By the third stage, after the National Research Council reports and debates about the science of population genetics, the evidence produced by DNA typing was more open to courtroom challenge. Kaye wrote his article before the second NRC report (1996) that replaced the controversial calculation standards (1992) with a more accepted and authoritative standard for calculating odds of false matches.

I argue that in Canada, DNA typing in the courts developed in a different manner, passing through five stages between 1988, when it was first used as evidence in a Canadian court, and 2000, when the NDDB began operations. As it passed through these stages, different institutional processes and forms of expertise became responsible for authorizing the technology and for promoting its acceptability to the public. During the first three stages, the court was the dominant institution involved in assessing and defining DNA evidence. The first stage, as in the United States, involved an enthusiastic acceptance by the courts. This was apparent in one of the first cases, *R. v. Parent* (1988), in which DNA evidence exonerated the accused. The first major case involving a conviction based on DNA evidence was *R. v. Legere* (1994). Allan Legere, a New Brunswick man, was accused of four counts of murder, three of which involved sexual assault. Public scrutiny was intense, and DNA evidence became the central feature of the prosecution's case and of the press coverage of the trial. DNA from semen samples at the crime scenes was compared to DNA extracted from blood on a discarded tissue that the police had picked out of the trash. During the trial, forensic experts for the prosecution testified that Legere's DNA matched that of the semen samples with the odds of a false match ranging from one in tens to hundreds of millions. Legere's lawyer challenged the experts on two grounds. He asked one of them how much he was being paid to testify, implying potential bias in favour of the Crown. He also attacked the science as new and untried, suggesting that Legere's DNA pattern could not reliably be compared with that of the general Canadian population because he was ethnically Miramichi, a First Nations group. These arguments were rejected by the jury and by a subsequent appeal court. The DNA evidence was decisive.

The second stage followed closely on this first stage of enthusiastic acceptance. As in the United States, it involved sharper questioning of DNA evidence and a confusing mix of legal decisions. However, in Canada the key issue was not scientific accuracy; Canadian courts were content to leave that debate to their American counterparts. Rather, the courts focused on the social technologies of collection and how they related to the Charter. This was a question of citizen rights rather than scientific measurement, and as such it dealt with the place of DNA evidence along the continuum between individual rights and public safety. Some courts decided that police techniques for gathering DNA evidence were acceptable within the bounds of the Charter; others found certain collection processes in violation of Charter rights to security of the person and unreasonable search and seizure. Generally, evidence was considered acceptable if it already resided outside the person, but this was not adequate for police purposes.

The third stage was a short period initiated by the Supreme Court decision in *R. v. Borden*. In that case, the Supreme Court upheld the Nova Scotia Court of Appeal decision to throw out evidence linking Borden to an earlier sexual assault because he had not been informed that his volunteered DNA sample would be used to investigate that crime as well as the crime for which he was currently charged. Consequently, the police received no relief in their quest for more easily obtainable DNA samples. On the contrary – the court was saying that under common law, their resources for obtaining such materials were quite limited. The courts had imposed substantial limits on DNA evidence gathering.

At this point, responsibility for managing DNA typing as a sociotechnical network passed largely out of the hands of the courts and into the hands of the legislature. This constituted the fourth stage in the development of the technology. In response to public pressure based on fear of crime, the federal government began developing a DNA warrant scheme and a national DNA data bank with the goal of utilizing the new technology to promote ontological security in Canadian society. During this phase, negotiations among institutional stakeholders produced the meanings that would come to define the purposes and justifications of the technology. The objectification of justice and the privacy of DNA codes became the central issues when the risks of crime and of the technology came to be addressed.

The fifth and current stage involves the institutionalization and normalization of the DNA typing network through the NDDB. At this stage, the dominant institutional processes involved in maintaining the network and authorizing DNA typing flow from science and the police. Throughout the first four stages, the expertise of forensic analysts was never seriously questioned the way it was in the United States. However, since the NDDB was established, the possibility of challenging that expertice has become increasingly remote, The authority of these experts is tightening now that systems – and, more importantly, narratives of systems – are being established that can be taken for granted and left largely unexamined by outsiders. The NDDB's success closing the black box speaks for itself – in this regard, witness its statistics on matches between the Crime Scene Index and the Convicted Offender Index. As the data bank expands, we can anticipate further positive outcomes in the future.

Throughout these phases, a particular truth about DNA typing has emerged – one that now forms a closed narrative regarding the effectiveness of the science and its astonishing results in capturing violent criminals. The gene as a digital map was easily accepted in criminal justice, when it assumed the status of a super-enhanced form of fingerprinting. As a laboratory technology, DNA typing was never scrutinized in Canada to any great degree. The social context in which the new technology developed was open to its claims to objectivity; DNA typing incorporated technologies of distance in the form of software, automation, and statistical expressions of measurement error. However, it posed certain risks to privacy by opening the door to an expansion of genetic surveillance of the entire population. To counter this risk, legislators and the NDDB's management developed social technologies sich as legislative safeguards, coded identities, and an oversight committee. By 2000, when the NDDB began operations, the boundary work of the socio-technical network was complete. All phases of DNA typing had been brought within a closed narrative of technical processes, one that would produce accurate and objective outcomes – true outcomes. It seemed that Canadian criminal justice had found a reason for overcoming subjective discretion – one that at the same time utilized technical, legal, and administrative safeguards to protect the privacy of those whose DNA codes were entered into the data bank.

As a mode of governmental meaning making, the DNA typing system in Canada is an example of biogovernance in action at the intersection between risk management and biotechnology. The system is designed to produce a particular kind of truth that addresses Canadians' needs. In a perfect world for police, the DNA data bank would contain samples from every resident of Canada and the police would be able to seize samples at will. However, the primary purpose is not to manage crime, but, rather to manage the frameworks of meaning that emerge from public perceptions, governmental debates, and the policy consultations surrounding DNA typing, crime, and risk. The characteristics of the NDDB and the DNA warrant provisions of the Criminal Code very delierately address these concerns in ways that are not present in other countries. For example, in most American jurisdictions there are few privacy safeguards and forensic analysts often know the identities and backgrounds of the persons being typed. Thirty-one states authorize the use of DNA samples for purposes other than law enforcement and identification, including five states whose legislation seems to open the door for outside agencies to conduct research on DNA samples from offender data banks.[4] Fewer technologies of distance are deployed, and the system's objectivity is more open to challenge.

Over the course of the 1990s, DNA typing became increasingly beyond question. The scientific community resolved the debate over population genetics calculations. Technological developments in PCR and STR analysis made it possible to analyse smaller and smaller samples more accurately. Other stakeholders in the socio-technical network worked to develop policies, legislation, and social marketing strategies that would authorize DNA typing and its attendant expertise as safe and productive in terms of combating crime and managing the subjective decision making of justice officials. Also, the absence of a counterexpertise in forensic science – of DNA analysts readily available to the defence – further reinforces the sense that the science and technology are beyond challenge. The perception now is that a forensic analyst can give a definitive answer to guilt or innocence. The NDDB is organized to promote this view with its conscious attention to establishing technologies of distance and privacy. This being so, the question becomes: What is the impact of this technology on the conduct of crime control?

6 From Crime Control to Crime Management: DNA and Shifting Notions of Justice

On 21 September 2001, the Alberta Court of Appeal handed down its decision on *R. v. S.A.B.* The appellant had been convicted of sexually assaulting a fourteen-year-old girl, who became pregnant as a result of the assault. She had an abortion, and police seized fetal tissue for DNA testing. Subsequently, the police obtained a DNA warrant to take a blood sample from the accused. Based on the resulting DNA analysis, forensic technicians identified the accused as the father. He was arrested, charged, convicted of sexual assault, and sentenced to six years' imprisonment.

The defence lawyer, Larry Anderson, appealed the conviction on three grounds. First, he argued that the Criminal Code requirement that there be reasonable grounds to believe that the suspect was involved in the crime before a DNA warrant is issued is not sufficient grounds to allow the seizure of a part of the human body. In other words, this type of search and seizure should require a higher standard in order to meet the requirements of section 8 of the Charter. Second, he argued – as others had in previous cases – that the seizure and testing of DNA material infringe the accused's right against self-incrimination, which has been read into section 7 of the Charter. Third, Anderson argued that the trial judge had erred in relying on a Crown expert witness who testified about DNA testing in paternity cases. The expert stated that the internationally accepted standard in paternity testing is that there must be two non-matching samples out of seven in order to question paternity. One out of seven can be disregarded as a mutation. In this case, five samples matched, one was damaged, and one did not match. Anderson argued that the assumptions behind this test violate the presumption of innocence in criminal trials: mismatches should be given weight in raising a reasonable doubt.

In a split verdict, the appeal court rejected the appellant's arguments. With respect to section 8, Justice Russell, writing for the majority, disagreed that a higher standard of proof is necessary before a DNA warrant is issued: 'It is reasonable to assume that any issuing judge will be alert to the serious concerns and consequences relating to the granting of a warrant which will authorize any interference with bodily integrity and privacy, and that those concerns are implicitly factored into the determination of the best interests of the administration of justice.' The majority also dismissed the appeal in terms of section 7, stating that 'the search for the truth, and the influence of DNA evidence on that search is of sufficient importance to warrant overriding the deeply rooted principle that the accused need not participate in the case against him or her.' Justice Russell went on to state that there is an adequate balance between the principle against self-incrimination and the principle that all relevant evidence should be available in the search for the truth. The balance is maintained by the value of DNA analysis in investigating serious crimes and exonerating the innocent, and also by the restrictions placed on it in the legislation. Finally, on the issue of the admissibility of the expert testimony, the majority found that the evidence was valid and that the trial judge had not erred.

Justice Berger wrote a dissenting opinion: he would have allowed the appeal, set aside the conviction, and ordered a new trial. On the issue of the constitutional challenge, Justice Berger argued that the majority verdict means that 'a credibly-based probability applicable to "ordinary" warrants to search will suffice for searches and seizures that violate bodily integrity and force self-conscription.' He went on to state that reasonable probability is not sufficient grounds for issuing a DNA warrant and that an issuing judge 'must be convinced on a balance of probabilities by clear, cogent and compelling evidence that the information in support of the DNA warrant justifies its issuance.' According to his analysis, 'the invasive nature of body searches demands a higher standard of justification in order to satisfy s. 7 of the *Charter*. Failure to apply such a higher standard results, in my opinion, in a violation of the principle against self-incrimination and a real or imminent deprivation of liberty and security of the person.'

Justice Berger also differed from the majority on the expert testimony issue, arguing that it should not have been given any weight because the guidelines contradicted the presumption of innocence. A single mismatch is assumed to be a mutation even though the likelihood that a mismatch results from a mutation is very low. As well, he argued that the trial judge had erred in adopting and relying on unspecified international guidelines without any evidence regarding who had authored, published, and sponsored them, how widely accepted they were in the field, and how reliable they were.

R. v. S.A.B. is important for criminal justice and DNA technology for two reasons. First, it has been appealed to the Supreme Court of Canada and will be the case in which Canada's highest court makes a final pronouncement on the constitutionality of the DNA warrant provisions of the Criminal Code. Second, it illustrates a number of important effects that DNA typing and banking are having on Canada's criminal justice system. The disagreements between the majority and minority in that case, and in many others, are ultimately about defining the contours of biogovernance within criminal justice – about the roles of objectification, responsibilization, normalization, politicization, and privatization in law enforcement. Will those roles be broad or narrow, open or restrictive, permissive or strictly monitored? Well into the second decade of genetic technology use in criminal justice, we are begining to see the emerging shape of those contours and are beginning to critically evaluate the effects of DNA typing and banking on the Canadian justice system. We are beginning to ask why the relationship between DNA technology and criminal justice is developing the way it is.

In previous chapters, I examined the framework of meaning that emerged out of the policy making process and how it helped shift the emphasis in criminal justice away from individual rights and toward public safety. In this chapter I examine recent approaches to collecting samples from suspects, the admissibility of samples collected in questionable ways, the bases for ordering NDDB sampling after conviction, and the ways that courts have treated questions of privacy and security of the person. I argue that enough time has passed that we can begin to measure the impact that biotechnology is having on the criminal justice system as well as on our society's long-held values of justice.

Constructing and Managing Riskiness in Late Modernity

It is difficult to make sense of the plethora of social control mechanisms that late-modern Western societies have begun to develop. These range from execution, massive expansion of prison populations, longer sentences, dangerous offender classifications, and three strikes laws, to electronic bracelets and stricter public and private surveillance, to community policing, Neighbourhood Watch, community service, parole, and alternative dispute resolution mechanisms, to responsibilization strategies designed to reduce one's likelihood of victimization. Present-day crime control strategies range from zero tolerance to individual responsibility. The question is this: Where does the typing and banking of DNA fit into these apparently diverse processes of control?

Critical analysts often discuss DNA testing and banking in terms of panoptic forms of control. However, a number of governmentality and risk theorists are suggesting that social control at the beginning of the twenty-first century is post-panoptic. This is the result of shifts in the socio-economic order brought about by social adaptations to the global economic environment. Zygmunt Bauman, for example, argues that the panopticon, as a diagram of power, developed to accommodate the needs of early industrial capitalism by isolating those on the margins of the emerging system of production and placing them within 'factories of disciplined labour' (2000: 210). There, they were set to work in the kinds of labour least desired by free labourers. The stated aim was moral reform and rehabilitation – socialization into a work ethic that would carry on after the prisoners were released. Despite this aim, prison has never rehabilitated inmates; it has never produced the desired social competence. Instead, it 'prisonizes' inmates, causing them to adopt the habits and behaviours of prison culture. This is the opposite of rehabilitation.

Such concerns are moot in the present era, in which capital is no longer eager to absorb expanding quantities of labour. In fact, markets now reward companies that reduce their workforces, and in this environment the rationales underlying treatment of prisoners have changed as well. Rehabilitation is no longer an important goal of the corrections system. Instead, as Bauman argues, incarceration 'is rather, under the present circumstances, an *alternative to employment*; a way to dispose of, to incapacitate or remove out of sight a considerable chunk of the population who are not needed as producers and for whom there is no work "to be taken back to"' (2000: 211). What prisoners do inside their cells no longer matters; what matters is that they stay there:

> If the concentration camps served as laboratories of a totalitarian society, where the limits of human submission and serfdom were explored, and if the Panopticon-style workhouses served as the laboratories of industrial society, where the limits of routinization of human action were experimented with – the Pelican Bay prison [a new type of high-technology prison in California] is a laboratory of the 'globalized'... society, where the

techniques of space-confinement of the rejects and waste of globalization
are tested and their limits explored (2000: 212)

Other theorists have referred to the resulting situation as 'crimefare'
– an institutionalized means of dealing with excess populations that do
not have the required capacities – whether by choice or otherwise – to
function within the new socio-economic system. Peter Andreas (1998)
asserts that the crimefare state began in the United States, where it
took the form of the 'War on Drugs.' Over the course of the 1980s and
1990s, the U.S. Justice Department's budget tripled and its personnel
doubled as a result of this policy. Between 1990 and 2001, the incarceration rate in the United States rose from 458 to 690 per 100,000, with
approximately 2 million men, women, and youths in federal, state, and
private prisons as of midyear 2001 (Department of Justice, 2002: 2).
Andreas contends that these hyperinflated incarceration rates mark
the emergence of a law enforcement industrial complex at a time when
the military industrial complex is looking for new markets after the
end of the Cold War (1998: 54). It can be argued that since the 11 September 2001 attacks on the World Trade Center in New York and the
Pentagon in Washington D.C., the crimefare state has been extending
its reach internationally – a process that was already underway in the
War on Drugs but now includes the War on Terrorism. Furthermore,
the United States is pressuring other states to become involved both
domestically and internationally.

Bauman relates the end of panopticism to the interests of global capital; governmentality theorists relate it to the corresponding turn to
neoliberalism as a mode of governance – to a trend away from viewing
the state as a director and provider toward viewing it as a regulator
and facilitator. Social solidarity has been replaced by a fragmented
social field of multiple communities, diverse identities, and cultural
pluralities. In the vacuum left by the retreating state, the market is
evolving into the primary medium of social interaction; in this new
world, individuals are required to be responsible for themselves in
terms of acting prudently to ensure their own security. In this milieu,
moral norms governing individual conduct are becoming the basis for
social order.

This is the theme of Gilles Deleuze's (1992) notion of 'societies of
control,' within which control is linked to individual identity. Control
is no longer a matter of disciplining individuals into bodily and behavioural competence and restraint. Rather, it is an ongoing 'modulation'

built into the architecture of all institutional processes through practices such as continuous training, life-long education, constant health monitoring, and continual inducement to purchase. How individuals perform within these processes becomes the basis for coding them in terms of their level of riskiness, their security ratings, their profiles of preferences, and their creditworthiness. These codes in turn qualify us for varying levels of access to privileges. Do you have sufficient funds, are you entitled to enter a particular area, are you a good insurance or credit risk, are you a potential suspect of crime? Nikolas Rose (2000: 327) contends that this coding produces a mode of citizenship that is linked not to the state or to the public sphere, but rather to an array of private and corporate practices, especially working and shopping. In order to gain access to circuits of civility, including those of capital, one must constantly prove one's credentials as a responsible citizen.

One of the means by which citizens demonstrate their individual responsibility is by taking the necessary steps to ensure their own security, instead of relying on the state. David Garland (1996) notes that one characteristic of neoliberal governance is a shift in state policy away from promising to be the sole provider of social control toward pushing responsibility for social order onto responsibilized citizens. Pat O'Malley (1996) traces how securing oneself against crime has become another form of insurance along with private health insurance and private pensions. All forms of insurance become a part of the politics of choice. These sorts of insurance are obtained through the market and are sustained by anxieties about achieving one's desired future.

Similar considerations apply at the community level. Within fragmented late-modern society, each community takes on some of the responsibility for risk management within its own space, be it a neighbourhood, a workplace, or a shopping mall. Consequently, gated communities are emerging, and the architecture of urban zones is being configured to prevent loitering and unauthorized access.[1] Ericson and Haggerty (1997) analyse how, as a result of these developments, the role of public policing is changing. The police collect information through surveillance; they then use it to trace out problem territories and to identify the types of crime and suspects in particular zones. Having done this, they inform communities within those zones by distributing leaflets, visiting schools, and so on. They also work to mobilize communities by coordinating Neighbourhood Watch programs and community policing strategies; in this way, they are employing the community as a means of policing and not simply a territory for it. Meanwhile, the mundane work of guarding and patrolling increasingly falls to private security firms.

What happens to those who are unable to function within this 'society of control,' which operates through individual responsibility based on personal risk management, participation in consumer and corporate cultures, and location within a secured territory? Rose contends that the diverse social control practices currently operating in Western societies reflect two generalized governmental strategies – a network of inclusion and a network of exclusion (2000: 324). Those who have the capital, capacity, and inclination to live within the society of control have access to the former; those who do not are circulated to the latter. These two categories correspond to Bauman's description of seduced and suppressed classes in late modernity (see chapter 1). In other words, people who do not fit in are no longer simply left to wander the margins; rather, they are subject to strategies of control. These strategies come in two varieties. The first are strategies to reaffiliate the excluded with the circuits of inclusion through programs such as workfare, retraining for the unemployed, and the regeneration of disadvantaged communities. The second are strategies for those who are deemed incapable of civility; these individuals are managed through measures intended to neutralize the dangers they pose, such as three strikes laws, prison expansion, and permanent detention for 'dangerous offenders,' pedophiles, and other sexual offenders (Rose, 2000: 330).

Rose contends that the people within this excluded category are the members of the welfare underclass, who are perceived either as rational actors who have calculated that they can live better by not working, or as victims of a culture of dependency nurtured by the welfare state, or as entrepreneurs within a culture of anticivility, living off of the proceeds of crime and drugs (2000: 331). These people are not attached to a moral community, defined as those who ensure their own well-being through formal market entrepreneurship and self-responsibility. For those whose riskiness cannot be managed by reattachment to the network of inclusion, crimefare becomes an important mode of control, one that involves long-term incapacitation through imprisonment. Within this category of incorrigibles, those of a lower risk are managed through measures such as probation and other forms of monitoring.

Individuals involved in exclusion-based forms of control are subjected to various risk management experts such as social workers, psychologists, and health experts, who assess the risks posed by these individuals and add data to ongoing dossiers. Assessments of dangerousness and risk are based on actuarial factors such as housing conditions, employment history, family history, current family circumstances, and substance abuse. This information is organized into databases and schedules and communicated to law enforcement officials, who are removed from the initial collection of data (Castel, 1991). Those who are considered most risky are confined until their riskiness can be fully assessed and controlled. Within this group, certain individuals – serial violent offenders, rapists, and pedophiles – are defined as intractably risky. These flawed human predators will forever be outside the bounds of civility. Various legal strategies are now being developed to contain this group through ongoing surveillance and indefinite incarceration (i.e., classification as dangerous offenders). All of this in the name of community safety. Many are now calling for the return of the death penalty.

Strategies like these are about containment, not about reforming the individual. However, some strategies of reformation are still being aimed at members of the excluded class who are categorized as less risky. Workfare and welfare programs encourage individuals to transform their lives as a condition of receiving benefits. The goal is to reconstruct self-reliance among members of the welfare class, whose problems have been redefined as moral rather than socio-economic. Experts in the field of self-transformation use a language of empowerment; they see self-esteem, self-worth, and self-control as necessary qualities for participation in the world of choice (Rose, 2000: 334). They see the excluded as suffering from a subjective condition – namely, the absence of these qualities. The problems of the excluded can be resolved through moral transformation. In other words, you can be a full citizen if you adopt the proper conduct. Thus, a politics of class gives way to a politics of conduct.

How do DNA typing and banking fit into these broad processes of social control? Critics of DNA banking raise two general complaints in this regard. First, they argue that DNA is a panoptic technology designed to keep the criminal population under constant surveillance, whether that surveillance is justified or not. Second, they argue that it is the first step toward a truly genetic justice system premised on the search for genetic causes of criminal behaviour and for a criminal classification system based on genetic characteristics. Both critiques raise what could be important points; however, I suggest that neither penetrates to a more central and more immediate critical point. Although DNA data banks have panoptic potential, ultimately they are a postpanoptic technology. This is their power. They are not highly intrusive in an Orwellian fashion, and the familiar comment that if you have done nothing wrong you have nothing to fear has considerable validity. Only those who have done something wrong have any need to fear DNA typing and banking. DNA, when cast this way, is simply an efficient and accurate form of identification, like fingerprints but better. Fear of full genetic profiling and identification of criminal genes seems a remote possibility. DNA typing in Canada involves examining only thirteen points on the gene, and these points are not known to be associated with physical or behavioural characteristics. As well, the NDDB's security measures ensure that genetic researchers do not have access to the DNA samples stored there.

I am suggesting something else, however; I am suggesting that DNA banking serves as a method for coding an individual as part of either a network of inclusion or a network of exclusion. It is one means among several for classifying people according to the level of risk they pose to circuits of civility. It serves as a gate-keeping mechanism to separate the responsible from the risky, the seduced from the suppressed. Ironically, it is judges and prosecutors who are responsible for determining whether a convicted person's DNA will be sampled and banked – the very roles that have come under attack as containing too much discretion. An examination of judicial decisions surrounding DNA sampling indicates that the factors judges consider are actuarial in nature. In this sense, the NDDB enables us to measure the extent to which risk thinking is becoming the basis for crime management. Has there been a shift in law enforcement practices and attitudes, and if so, how does this shift fit within current trends of social control?

To answer this question I analysed 164 judicial decisions in Canadian courts between July 1999, one year before the NDDB officially began operations, and April 2002, the month of the most recent decisions available at the time of writing. These 164 decisions were not all the ones available, but they constituted a large proportion of them and a substantial representative sample. I organized the cases into categories of legal issues, which included the following: whether DNA sampling should be ordered after the accused is convicted; whether evidence seized under a DNA warrant should be admissible; constitutional challenges to the legislation; how much judicial discretion should be allowed in making sampling determinations; whether DNA samples should be taken from people convicted before the DNA legislation was passed; whether DNA samples should be taken from young offenders; and the veracity of forensic DNA science. I also noted the types of considerations the courts took into account in deciding whether to order DNA sampling.

Besides judicial decisions, I examined professional publications within the Canadian legal community, including *Lawyers Weekly, Canadian Lawyer, LawNow, Law Times, Ontario Lawyers Gazette,* and *Juridique.* The purpose of this was to trace the ways in which DNA technology was being debated within the legal community and to gain insights into community members' positions, concerns, and strategies. I also examined news stories about police actions pertaining to DNA technologies and the uses to which police were putting the technology. A web newsletter edited by two lawyers, *Federico and Rondinelli's DNA NetLetter,* available through Quicklaw, was especially useful here, as it provided capsules of news stories as well as court decisions about DNA-related cases. Finally, I examined recent developments in the Canadian legislation pertaining to DNA technology and criminal identification. Together, these sources provided a range of critical insights into the ways in which DNA technology is being used and how it is affecting the central actors and institutions of the judicial system – police, lawyers, and judges. A careful analysis of these sources revealed three significant impacts on the administration of justice: a changing role for science discourse in the courtroom, pressures to expand the DNA net, and an instrumentalization of justice in cases involving DNA evidence.

Science in the Courtroom

Judges and juries today sometimes find themselves in the position of having to determine the validity of complex scientific evidence.[2] As a consequence, judges and lawyers have had to diversify their reading materials in order to deal with specialized scientific concepts. For example, in *R. v. Murrin* the British Columbia Supreme Court found itself having to rule on the validity of mitochondrial DNA analysis – a first for the Canadian courts. In ruling the evidence admissible, the court had to consider complex scientific and technical issues: 'In my view, neither the discovery of heteroplasmy within the control region nor the alleged danger of 'false inclusions' provide a reason for rejecting evidence of this novel scientific theory or technique. Like the ever present danger of contamination, the existence of heteroplasmy is a complicating factor which requires substantial exercise of judgement by mtDNA analysts' (¶121).

Prosecutors are promoting the shift toward scientization. As one result, technical developments in surveillance and identification technologies are generally favouring the Crown rather than the defence. In the United States, biotechnology's incursion into the courts has been highly politicized. Prosecutors and defence lawyers are falling into separate and highly antagonistic camps and are carrying on their disputes outside the courts. Prominent personalities include Rockne Harmon, the chief District Attorney in the O.J. Simpson case, and Peter Neufeld, who along with Barry Scheck established the 'Innocence Project,' which investigates false convictions by funding DNA tests for convicts who claim innocence and for whom there is evidence of wrongful conviction. Harmon has been an outspoken champion of DNA evidence since the early 1990s. In a 1993 article, published before the Simpson trial, he sets out his case, claiming that DNA evidence is rarely used to convict in cases where a conviction would otherwise have been impossible. It generally provides corroborative evidence only. He takes issue with Neufeld's claim that 'hundreds of innocent people may be behind bars because courts never doubted DNA evidence' (Neufeld, 1990: 3), as well as Barry Scheck's claim that 'there are probably far more people rotting in jail who didn't commit crimes than any of us believed' (in Sherman, 1993: 1). Scheck was calling for increased use of DNA evidence to free innocent convicts.

Harmon characterizes these claims as 'simply rhetoric designed to convince trial courts to continue to allow each defendant to challenge the DNA evidence, whether or not the law affords the right to such challenges' (1993: 176). He goes on to argue that the rules of admissibility for DNA evidence are actually *too* rigorous. This is a result of *New York v. Castro*, in which the trial court ruled that the prosecution must not only show the general acceptance of DNA typing, but also demonstrate the quality of the work actually performed. In other words, the defence must always have the right to challenge the admissibility of the evidence, no matter how well established the science. Some jurisdictions in the United States have accepted the *Castro* standard; others have rejected it as perpetuating the admissibility debate unnecessarily (1993: 178).

Neufeld has countered that there are no enforced standards to ensure the quality of DNA evidence. Contrary to Harmon's implications, only about 2 per cent of criminal cases involving DNA evidence are preceded by admissibility hearings. The normal route for the defence is to seek a plea bargain (1993: 190). More significantly, Neufeld presents instances of prosecutorial and FBI misconduct in promoting DNA evidence. For example, he cites the case of Dr Laurence Mueller, a respected University of California geneticist who had testified for the defence in a number of pretrial hearings and who, in 1990, submitted an article to *Science* that was critical of aspects of forensic DNA typing. Two months later, Harmon wrote to the editors of *Science*, criticizing Dr Mueller's technical arguments and suggesting to the editors that the article was unethical because it could result in violent criminals continuing to prey on society. The editors took Harmon seriously and notified him – and later Dr Mueller – that the article had been rejected for publication.

Neufeld also claims that the FBI interfered with the National Research Council's 1990 to 1992 study of the appropriate statistical methods for interpreting DNA evidence (see chapter 2). The FBI was one of the sponsors of the committee, even though according to the rules of the National Academy of Sciences, government agencies and other sponsors are not permitted to influence the findings of reports. Preliminary drafts of the report are supposed to be confidential until they are released to the public. Neufeld states that John Hicks, the FBI's assistant director at the time, accepted a leaked draft of the report from two disgruntled committee members and wrote a stinging critique of a chapter that focused on statistical methods of population genetics – a subject in which he had no expertise. Despite this improper interference, the NRC report recommended a statistical method not favoured by the FBI. Neufeld suggests that the FBI worked informally to bring about another NRC committee to review the issue. In 1996 a second report overturned the conclusions of the first report, establishing a measure that was more in keeping with FBI standards (1993: 196).

If Neufeld's claims are correct, prosecutors and police agencies in the United States are vigorously promoting the aggressive use of DNA evidence in the courts. As a result, judges and lawyers have had to become conversant in the language of genetic science. In Canada, there is no evidence of improper influence on the part of police and prosecutors; however, the Canadian Police Association (CPA) has been lobbying strongly for expanded use of the technology.

Obviously DNA evidence is here to stay and consequently, defence lawyers and judges have had to begin mastering the science behind it. Professional newsletters and magazines commonly include stories, interviews, and editorials about DNA evidence. Explicitly or implicitly, these exhort defence lawyers to become conversant with DNA science and its techniques in order to defend their clients properly. In an interview, Leo Adler, the defence lawyer in the high-profile case *R. v. Terceira* (1998), set out what is required of defence lawyers in the scientized courtroom: 'The first question you want to ask yourself is have [the scientists] done all the work up to the production of [autorad] properly ... Take a look at the various samples and follow the chain of continuity right into the lab and through the various lab procedures' (*Lawyers Weekly*, 1993: website). Adler went on to detail a number of steps including examining the lab notes of the technicians for signs of carelessness and looking at the computer matching to see if the operator has overruled the computer's assessment or disagrees with the computer's determination of band measurements. He states: 'If they would just allow the computer to do it that would be one thing, but they don't so you end up with subjective points of view.' The next step is to determine the reliability of the match by applying the population databases. This requires the assistance of a population geneticist who can determine whether the proper databases have been used and whether the Crown expert's calculations are valid. Adler also recommends running independent tests of samples found at the crime scene instead of simply accepting the Crown tests. The point of all this is to add up all of the margins of error that may be involved in calculating a DNA match.

The problems inherent in this kind of defence are immediately apparent. Janne Holmgren and John Winterdyk (2001) interviewed twenty-two Canadian defence lawyers, each of whom has defended at least two cases involving DNA evidence, to see what kind of impact DNA evidence has had on their ability to defend their clients. One of the concerns the respondents reported was the gap between the assessment of the evidence and the need to understand the assessment. Defence lawyers often feel vulnerable to DNA evidence; many feel that 'DNA evidence is so overwhelming that it is not possible to contest the evidence in court' (2001: 11). In Canada, relative to the United States, there has been little consideration of the admissibility of novel scientific evidence. This suggests to defence lawyers that 'the legal system has difficulty keeping up with this continuing state of development with regards to the changes that are so rapidly occurring within the expanding areas of forensic sciences' (2001: 11).

All defence counsel agreed that they needed to learn about DNA evidence in order to adequately defend their clients; they also pointed out a number of problems in acquiring that knowledge. One is that lawyers simply don't have the time to read large amounts of technical literature. Another involves funding. Many defence cases are funded by Legal Aid, which has limited resources to help lawyers acquire the knowledge they need. Also, the funds are often not available to pay independent expert witnesses to conduct their own tests of crime scene evidence. The Crown can use RCMP and provincial laboratories for the DNA testing or utilize a private laboratory; the defence cannot use the same laboratory and often must resort to expertise in another country, as happened in the Morin and Milgaard cases. However, independent laboratories charge between $800 to $3,000 per analysis, and expert witnesses charge around $1,200 per day for their testimony. For most criminal defendants, these costs are prohibitive. Legal Aid will not necessarily cover these costs, and according to respondents, lawyers require a certain level of DNA expertise before they can convince Legal Aid of the need for expert witnesses (2001: 13). Holmgren and Winterdyk conclude from these findings that 'the end result may be that justice is being compromised by the seductive uses of science in some cases' (2001: 13). They echo the Kaufman Report's findings on the Morin case, which call for a joint education program between forensic scientists and the legal community to enhance understandings of forensic science.

Among practitioners, the process of scientization underway in the courts raises two types of concerns. First, there is concern over whether 'the scientist's lab coat [will] one day replace the lawyer's judicial robes in the courtrooms' (Daisley, 1993). Is forensic expertise replacing legal expertise as the arbiter of justice? A story in *Canadian Lawyer* illustrates defence lawyers' fears:

> Michael Neville begrudges the extracurricular reading he's had to tackle over the past six years. Not that he's particularly averse to science, which has been the general topic of his evening studies, or that he's had more self-fulfilling things he'd rather do with his time, like watching sports on television. As a criminal lawyer, Neville's annoyance stems from his obligation to acquire scientific expertise well beyond what's necessary to provide his client with a solid defence. On top of proving that toxicology tests on the alleged victim in the case were botched by the Centre of Forensic Sciences (CFS), its scientists were unrelenting and perpetuated the contest round after round perhaps hoping Neville would just tire and quit. (Carlson, 2001: 37)

Lawyers are facing increasing pressure to ignore legal principles and argue with forensic scientists on their own terms.

The second concern relates to good science versus bad science. Neufeld points out that 'scientists agree on the need for a government regulatory scheme. There is a consensus in the scientific community that, although the laboratory procedures for comparing genetic evidence are fundamentally sound, the validity of any particular case will depend on the inclusion of proper quality controls and the performance of laboratory personnel' (1993: 191). In Canada, the Kaufman Report on the Morin case echoed these sentiments. It pointed out how serious shortcomings in the procedures of the Ontario Centre of Forensic Sciences, and in the attitude of its personnel, contributed to Morin's wrongful conviction. Thirty-three of the Kaufman Report's 119 recommendations targeted 'bad science' at the CFS and called on scientists to adopt the scientific method of trying to disprove a hypothesis (i.e., instead of setting out to prove one); to establish protocols for preventing contamination of evidence; to develop policies that would compel technicians to record their work; to establish a quality assurance unit; and to produce protocols that would allow defence lawyers to obtain forensic work in confidence.

Yet this focus on scientists in the courtroom and on managing bad science may only be addressing the surface symptoms of a problem that goes much deeper. It may well be that forensic experts for the defence could counter forensic experts for the prosecution if enough money were available to pay private laboratories. Bad science can be overcome through accreditation processes which ensure that laboratories are following prescribed procedures. Once a laboratory has been accredited, it can be virtually impossible to question the results of its tests. McMaster University molecular geneticist John Waye often works as a defence consultant on DNA evidence. He points out that attacking test procedures is a waste of time: 'The RCMP, Ontario and Quebec labs use test methods that are universally accepted and reliable.' He also suggests that it is no longer even useful to highlight mistakes in the laboratory procedures; they are no longer seen as having a significant impact on the end result: 'Errors just show the technicians are human. But they generally do a competent job, and the test works out eventually' (Papoff, 1996: website).

In the wake of the O.J. Simpson trial in the United States and the Kaufman Report in Canada, laboratories have become aware that they are being scrutinized more closely and are acting quickly to gain accreditation. The Ontario Centre for Forensic Science gained accreditation from the American Society of Crime Laboratory Directors shortly after the Kaufman Report was released. Despite accreditation, defence lawyers are still discussing strategies to cast doubt on the evidence. Since 1998, York University's Osgoode Hall Law School has been hosting the Annual Canadian Symposium on Forensic DNA Evidence; this conference brings together forensic experts, lawyers, judges, and other experts to discuss developments in law and science. A common topic is strategies for attacking the outcomes of DNA testing. However, these strategies almost always involve attacking 'bad science.'

Good versus bad science, and equal access to forensic experts for defence and prosecution, are symptoms of a more pervasive shift in twenty-first century courtrooms. As the tools of forensic science – and DNA typing in particular – continue to be refined, politicization continues to take hold within the 'field' and 'habitus' of the courtroom (Bourdieu and Wacquant, 1992). Pierre Bourdieu uses these concepts to characterize social spaces of conflict and competition in which people struggle for authority and control. A *field* is like a game in which people employ appropriate forms of 'capital' – economic, cultural, informational, social, symbolic – in order to win control (Bourdieu, 1987). *Habitus* describes a set of dispositions that agents develop through their socialization and education; these dispositions give them a certain level of facility within the given field. Put simply, habitus is a 'feel for the game.' A change in the field thus requires a new habitus for managing the game. Technological change in the form of DNA typing affects courtrooms by changing the field so that those involved in the judicial process require new forms of expertise. DNA analysis and other developments in forensic science are not simply another element added to the existing legal process; they are changing the very nature of the legal process by redefining the nature of the game and transforming the necessary habitus. From now on, criminal lawyers – along with family lawyers, immigration lawyers, and others – will require a facility with genetic science and DNA typing techniques. In many cases, scientific capital is becoming as important as legal capital.

Within the scientized field of the courtroom, the defence lawyer is at a disadvantage. His or her main enemy is the alliance between forensic laboratories and prosecutors – an alliance that allows prosecutors to push for higher levels of scientific discourse within the courtroom and to draw from the charisma of genetic science. This cannot help but have a powerful impact on standards of evidence and proof in criminal cases. Without similar allies, defence lawyers must don white lab coats themselves and enter the courts as amateur scientists/technicians.

They may not wish to do so, but they recognize that a technological imperative is at work, and many of them accept that they must acquire scientific capital and exhort others to do the same. Statements such as the Kaufman Report, which examined a case involving an overreliance on scientific evidence and unquestioning acceptance of the pronouncements of forensic experts, do not reassert legal principles of evidence over scientific standards of proof. Rather, they blame individual technicians and recommend more careful oversight of the production of scientific evidence. Thus, it is no longer an issue of scientists replacing lawyers and judges as arbiters of justice; rather, it is a matter of everyone getting involved in adopting a scientific discourse and scientific standards of evidence and proof.

Expanding the DNA Net

Even before the DNA Identification Act was passed, there were calls for expanding its scope, especially from the CPA and victims' rights groups. These calls have grown louder since this bill's passage now that the efficacy of the DNA system has become apparent. For example, in May 2002, Toronto's police chief, Julian Fantino, publicly called for a loosening of DNA collection laws – specifically, for an expansion of the list of designated offences for DNA warrants to include drug-related offences, child pornography, domestic assaults, prowling, and indecent acts (Yourk, 2002: A22). New Brunswick's Attorney General has also been pushing hard for an expansion of designated offences to include lesser property offences such as vandalism (Schmitz, 1998: website). In 2001, Ontario's Attorney General, David Young, published an open letter to the federal Minister of Justice, Anne McLellan, urging her to close a number of 'loopholes' in the legislation by expanding the list of crimes for which DNA samples may be obtained. He argued for the following crimes to be added to the list for retrospective sampling: one count of murder and another of manslaughter, two counts of manslaughter, first-degree murder and a criminal record of sexual assault, and gross indecency or indecent assault involving children (Canada Newswire, 2001).

While there have been calls from governmental corners to expand the scope of testing and banking, certain processes of legislative expansion are already underway. Bill C-3 called for an expansion of the list of designated offences in Bill C-104, and the Senate review of Bill C-3 resulted in a further expansion in the form of Bill S-10, which added military offences to the list of designated offences. Currently, there are thirty-eight primary designated offences and twenty-one secondary designated offences. On 24 December 2001, in the wake of the terrorist attacks of 11 September, six secondary offences were redesignated as primary. All six are related to terrorism: piratical acts, hijacking, endangering the safety of an aircraft or airport, seizing control of a ship or fixed platform, using explosives, and hostage taking. These offences now require mandatory sampling on conviction.

On 30 July 2002 the Minister of Justice and Attorney General of Canada announced that the Department of Justice would soon begin another public consultation relating to the NDDB legislation. This process would collect opinions on the legislation and proposals for changes to it in advance of 2005 Parliamentary review of the legislation that was provided for in the initial DNA Identification Act. The consultation document includes five issues for discussion: (1) whether there is a need to amend the current lists of designated offences in s. 487.04 of the Criminal Code; (2) whether there is a need to amend the Criminal Code to allow DNA samples to be taken from individuals found not criminally responsible by reason of mental disorder for inclusion in the DNA data bank; (3) whether there is a need to amend the Criminal Code to expand the 'retroactive' aspect of the DNA data bank legislation; (4) whether there is a need to amend the Criminal Code to address certain procedural issues (to resolve any problems inherent in making sampling orders after sentencing); and (5) whether there is a need to provide for resampling in some cases where access to the offender's DNA has, by operation of law, been permanently removed from the NDDB (Department of Justice, 2002).

The last two issues are technical issues that were not foreseen when the initial legislation was drafted and concern the authority of judges to order samples in certain cases. It is likely that the legislation will be changed to ensure that judges have this authority. The first three issues, however, operate at a different level and are about potentially expanding the scope of who can be included in the NDDB. The first concerns expanding the list of designated offences and possibly reclassifying some secondary offences as primary. The second issue concerns including people not convicted of an offence by reason of mental disorder. Should judges be empowered to order DNA samples for them? The third issue concerns expanding the retroactive sampling scheme. Currently, only dangerous offenders, serial murderers, and serial sex offenders can be retroactively sampled. Should this list be expanded? How the legislation is revised in 2005 will serve as an interesting measurement of the impact that DNA technology is having on criminal justice in Canada.

Another measurement of expansive tendencies in DNA sampling and banking is the actual number of samples entering data banks. In Canada, during the consultation process for the DNA Identification Act, the Solicitor General's office estimated that roughly 10,000 samples would be entered into the Convicted Offender Index each year. As of 14 May 2003, the number of convicted offender samples received totalled 40,097 with 9,090 crime scene samples also entered (NDDB, 2003: website). In other words, two years and six months after going into full operation, the NDDB is slightly ahead of the 10,000 samples anticipated each year. According to the NDDB, the goal of the data bank is to process 30,000 samples per year (NDDB, 2001: 17).[3]

Other countries have pursued DNA banking even more vigorously. The U.S. Justice Department estimates that there is a national backlog of 750,000 samples, with another 50,000 coming in each month (CNN.com, 30 August 2001). Currently, there are 600,000 convicted offender DNA profiles just in the United States' national DNA data bank. This figure does not include the numbers held in state and local data banks (Crimtac, 2001: website). In Britain, around 300,000 samples are processed at the national DNA data bank each year; in September 2000 the British government announced an extra £109 million for police to take samples from approximately 3 million people suspected of lesser offences. The government was concerned that because of limited funds, police were able to use DNA for investigating only more serious offences (Kite and Ford. 2000). Currently, Britain's national DNA database holds close to 2 million profiles from suspects and convicted criminals (2001: website).

In the short time since Bill C-3 was passed, there has been constant pressure to expand the data bank's scope. The list of designated offences is not sacrosanct and seems open to calls for change. The direction of change has so far been toward adding more offences to the list and toward reclassifying secondary offences as primary and thereby requiring automatic DNA sampling. Expansion is partly a result of pressures from the law enforcement community, including police and politicians. It is also a result of pressures from outside sources such as the American-led War on Drugs and War on Terrorism. Furthermore, Western nations such as the United States and the United Kingdom are providing models of expanded DNA testing and banking systems that could prove attractive to Canadian authorities, as evidenced by the current consultation process on the DNA system. There is little evidence that these internal and external pressures will subside, so it is likely that Canada's genetic justice system will continue to expand.

Instrumentalization of Justice

The scientization of legal knowledge and law enforcement's lobbying to expand the DNA net are clear indications that genetic technology is affecting criminal justice. That said, the most important indicator of this is what is happening in judicial decisions. How are the DNA provisions being applied, and what are the cumulative effects of those provisions on the system? Having analysed 164 cases, I contend that DNA evidence and the sampling of convicted offenders are having an instrumentalizing effect on crime management; there is a trend toward applying instrumental rationality over value rationality, and as a result, forensic DNA techniques are trumping legal protections for the accused. This instrumental rationality manifests itself not only in judicial decisions but also in police tactics for acquiring DNA evidence, in government policies, and in the increasing privatization of the DNA testing industry.

Judicial Trends

Of the 164 cases sampled for this analysis, 102 dealt directly with the question of whether or not to order a DNA sample on conviction of the accused. In 72 of these cases, sampling was ordered; in 30 it was not. Obviously, each case is unique in terms of its fact situation and a strict numerical accounting cannot convey the complexities of the decisions. However, for this many cases the fact situations can be factored out to some extent. Thus we find that in roughly 70 per cent of the cases, sampling was ordered. Around two-thirds of the cases involved primary offences and one-third secondary offences. Secondary offences allow for more judicial discretion, and in these, 19 sampling orders were granted. However, in 14 cases sampling applications were denied, which suggests that where judges have discretion, they are willing to exercise it. That said, when a sampling order was denied, the case usually involved a young offender or an offence internal to a family.

Overall, the courts tend to open the door to the DNA warrant and banking system without necessarily placing stronger restrictions on it due to its invasive nature. This statement is supported by an examination of cases involving DNA sampling on conviction and cases where the admissibility of DNA evidence was an issue at trial. As well, an examination of how Charter challenges and the issue of judicial discretion have been dealt with highlight trends in the application of the DNA provisions.

The present law in Canada regarding sampling upon conviction comes out of *R. v. Briggs* (2001). Briggs was convicted of armed robbery, a secondary designated offence, and the court ordered a DNA sample. His lawyer appealed the sampling order, arguing that the court should use the same standard in ordering sampling for secondary designated offences that it uses when issuing DNA warrants – there should be reasonable and probable grounds that the samples will have future evidentiary value. The court disagreed, ruling that there are two exceptions in common law to the reasonable and probable grounds standard: when the state's interest is not simply law enforcement, and when there is no threat to bodily integrity. In terms of the DNA data bank, the purpose is not simply law enforcement, but also to ensure that innocent people are not convicted. In terms of bodily integrity, the procedure is unobtrusive. Brigg's lawyer appealed the decision to the Supreme Court of Canada, arguing that this standard makes it too easy for the Crown to get a sampling order, that it does not include the constitutional safeguards that should be part of the process, and that there should be reasonable and probable grounds, even after conviction. However, the Supreme Court refused leave to appeal the case, and *Briggs* is now the standard for ordering data bank sampling. This has opened up the possibility of making sampling orders with few restrictions.

The same openness is characteristic of the standards for granting DNA warrants. Generally, the courts have not placed many restrictions on the admissibility of DNA evidence; in fact, they have sometimes gone a considerable distance to allow questionable evidence. For example, in *R. v. Eakin* (2000) and *R. v. Rennie* (2002), DNA evidence at trial was found to be of little value because of high odds of a mismatch. Yet, in both cases, the trial judges' decisions to consider the evidence were upheld on appeal. In *R. v. Xie* (2000), the Alberta Court of Queen's Bench ruled that calculations of a mismatch probability based on a Caucasian database were acceptable despite the accused's East Asian ancestry. In *R. v. D.M.F.* (2001), police staged an interview with the accused and took cigarette butts he left behind. They also searched his bedroom and took a pair of boxer shorts, without a warrant, from which they retrieved a DNA sample. Based on this evidence, they obtained a DNA warrant and seized a blood sample, which was used to convict him of sexual assault. The question on appeal of his conviction was whether the evidence had been improperly obtained, which would have made the application for the DNA warrant invalid. The evidence was found to be valid. Trickery was also used in *R. v. Nguyen* (2002) in which the accused refused to consent to a DNA test but accepted chewing gum from officers, who later retrieved it and used it to obtain a DNA match. The court allowed the evidence, arguing that it did not violate bodily integrity. In more and more cases, DNA evidence is being admitted despite the questionable means by which it was obtained and/or its questionable reliability. It seems that the courts are beginning to make a standard practice out of admitting DNA evidence because of its power to identify individual perpetrators in a highly efficient and relatively foolproof manner.

Some decisions have attempted to limit the extent to which questionable DNA evidence may be admitted. For example, in *R. v. Van Osselaer* (1999) the British Columbia Supreme Court ruled that a DNA warrant which failed to inform the accused that the results of a DNA analysis might be used in evidence against him, produced evidence that was unconstitutional and that must be excluded from trial. In *R. v. Turner* (2001), the first Canadian case in which a jury acquitted the accused despite DNA evidence linking him to the victim, the Newfoundland Supreme Court placed limits on the evidence. Traces of the murder victim's DNA were found on a ring worn by the accused, but it was mixed with the DNA of three other people, including a lab technician involved in the DNA analysis; this suggested that contamination had occurred in the laboratory. A DNA expert hired by the defence testified that the evidence could only be reliable in excluding someone. As a result, the court ordered that the Crown could only describe to the jury the exclusionary probabilities of the evidence. *Van Osselaer* and *Turner* are exceptional, however, and the trend is toward easier admissibility.

A third indication of the increasingly instrumental view being taken of DNA evidence relates to the handling of Charter challenges by the courts. Many challenges have been made; not one has been successful. There have been three main grounds for challenging the DNA system on the basis of Charter rights. The first is the *ex parte* provision of section 487.05(1), which allows the police to apply for a DNA warrant without notifying the suspect and allowing him or her to appear at the hearing. The first major case to consider this claim was *R. v. S.F.* (2000), in which the Ontario Court of Appeal dismissed the section 7 challenge to the *ex parte* hearing provision. Justice Finlayson stated:

> It is important to remember that applications for search warrants and other judicial warrants traditionally have been heard ex parte to avoid not only the flight of the suspect but also the destruction of what is sought under the warrant. Even accepting that the destruction or alteration of DNA evidence is not a possibility and there may be cases where notice might be ordered by the issuing judge, these are not reasons for the court on a constitutional review to start rewriting customary procedures. One must keep in mind that these DNA warrants are an investigative tool. If their use is to be overly restricted by procedural impediments and interlocutory proceedings, the investigation may be frustrated. (¶40)

Subsequent courts have adopted the same position. This has closed down an avenue for suspects to contest the DNA provisions and provide police with relatively simple and uncontested access to DNA warrants.

A second and more fundamental issue is the argument that DNA evidence violates the accused's right against self-incrimination – a right that courts have read into section 7. The first case on this issue was *R. v. Brighteyes* (1997). In its decision, the Alberta Court of Queen's Bench determined that although the DNA warrant provisions do not violate section 8, they interfere with 'the subject's bodily integrity, which in turn is a breach of privacy and an affront to his or her dignity.' More importantly, the warrant provisions clearly violate section 7. Justice Alec Murray noted that the Supreme Court decision in *R. v. Stillman* (1997) clearly stated that the taking of bodily substances is a violation of the right to liberty and security of the person, but could be justified under section 1 because here, the rights of the individual are outweighed by the rights of society.

Since the *Brighteyes* decision, courts have been less liberal in their interpretations of the warrant provisions. The consensus of the courts is that DNA sampling on conviction does not violate self-incrimination rights any more than the fingerprinting requirement (*R. v. Dwyer*, 2000), that the legislation strikes a proper balance between the principle against self-incrimination and the principle that all relevant evidence should be available in the search for the truth (*R. v. S.A.B.*, 2001), and that the physical intrusion and inconvenience are trivial in the context of someone convicted of a designated offence (*R. v. Murrins*, 2002). In other words, the courts are upholding the notion that seizure of DNA material for evidence or for sampling is not an issue of fundamental justice and does not violate section 7.

The third Charter issue is whether or not DNA warrants and post-conviction sampling violate the section 8 right against unreasonable search and seizure. This issue was considered in a number of the cases mentioned above, and dismissed. In *R. v. Anderson*, defence counsel argued in front of the Ontario Court of Justice that the postconviction sampling provision of the Criminal Code places an onus on the offender to show that if a DNA order were made, it would be grossly disproportionate to the public interest in the protection of society and the proper administration of justice. In criminal cases, the onus of proof always should be on the prosecution. Also, obtaining a sample for use in future investigations would amount to a 'fishing expedition' without a reasonable basis for linking the offender to the crime. The court responded that even if the provision places an evidentiary burden on the accused, a reverse onus is not necessarily unconstitutional. It is not unreasonable to expect a convicted offender to establish why the privacy and security of his or her person outweighs the public interest in identifying offenders. In terms of fishing expeditions, the NDDB is nothing more than a neutral record of a person's identity. It is in the nature of fingerprints and criminal records and has the positive goal of establishing the identity of offenders. There have been many other cases on section 8 that are fact specific, but in all of these, the courts have decided that the DNA provisions do not violate the right against unreasonable search and seizure (see for example, *R. v. Larsen*, 2001; *R. v. Brosseau*, 2001).

It is apparent that the courts are deeply hesitant to strike down any provisions of the DNA system as unconstitutional. They have been more apt to defer to legislative intent and to limit their own discretion. Section 487.051 of the Criminal Code states that in the case of primary designated offences, the court 'shall' make an order for sampling DNA. The court is not required to make such an order if it is satisfied that the 'impact on the person's or young person's privacy and security of the person would be grossly disproportionate to the public interest in the protection of society and the proper administration of justice, to be achieved through the early detection, arrest and conviction of offenders.' For secondary designated offences, the court 'may' make an order for sampling but must consider 'the criminal record of the person or young person, the nature of the offence and circumstances surrounding its commission and the impact such an order would have on the person's privacy and security of the person and shall give reasons for its decision.'

In other words, discretion has been built into the legislation for both primary and secondary designated offences. A number of cases have considered the nature of that discretion, and there has been a clear trend for courts to restrict their own discretion in ordering sampling. In earlier cases such as *R. v. Brochu* (2000), decided less than two months after the DNA data bank provisions came into force, the Ontario Superior Court of Justice interpreted the provisions cautiously. Justice Platana stated:

> My understanding of the operation of the DNA data bank is that it is really premised on the ability to identify high risk offenders who are likely to be recidivists with respect to certain designated offences and who are likely to leave a bodily substance capable of forensic DNA analysis at the crime scene of such an offence. Recognizing that this is a secondary offence and that there is no mandatory operation of this type of testing, I will state for the purposes of the record, that I do not consider the circumstances of this offence to be such as ought to require the accused to be subjected to what can only be categorized, while perfectly legal, as a very intrusive type of testing for purposes of potential use against him in the future. (¶52)

A number of other provincial and superior court decisions during the first year of operation of the data bank provisions concurred with this sort of reasoning and applied a cautious approach to sampling on conviction. In *R. v. Gillis* (2000), which involved the secondary designated offence of robbery, Justice Wilkie stated: 'So that when we look at the impact that such an order would have on a person's privacy and security of the person we must go beyond simply the notion that we are interrupting his day with a five minute procedure; there are consequences. It is a very symbolic matter, in my view, when the state is authorized to take such a sample' (¶14).

After a year, however, the tone of the court decisions began to change; they were becoming more and more favourable to a 'large and liberal interpretation' of the provisions (*R. v. Penney*, 2001). By late 2001, a number of appeals of DNA sampling orders, or refusals to order, had reached the appeal court level. Appeal courts are now going even farther in limiting judicial discretion. A representative case is *R. v. Jordan* (2002), in which the Nova Scotia Court of Appeal determined that on conviction of a primary designated offence, an order is mandatory unless the offender establishes that he or she falls within the exceptions:

> There was no evidence of any exceptional risk to the offender's privacy other than that inherent in the scheme itself. There was no evidence that the taking of the sample would involve more than minimal and brief discomfort. There was not evidence that it would put Mr. Jordan's health at risk in any way. There was no suggestion, let alone any evidence, that the taking of the sample in the circumstances of this case would result in a violation of the offender's Charter rights. There was, in short, no basis in the record or in matters of which judicial notice could be taken upon which the order could be refused. (¶79)

Although the courts of appeal were dealing with primary designated offences in these cases, it is interesting to note the different attitude shown toward the very concept of DNA sampling compared with earlier cases such as *Brochu* and *Gillis*. The earlier decisions were cautious about this new technology and noted its *socially* invasive nature; the later decisions have defined intrusiveness *physically* and have limited their discretion to cases where the sampling would be physically harmful – a rare circumstance. As well, for primary designated offence convictions, the legislation places the onus on the offender to demonstrate a negative impact on his or her security and privacy; the Crown is no longer required to demonstrate a need for the order. The courts have interpreted this as a clear presumption that on conviction, the offender has a reduced expectation of privacy and assumes the burden of proof.

For secondary designated offences, there seems to be a balance of probabilities test. From a review of 102 cases dealing with the question of whether or not to grant a sampling order, the following list of considerations emerge: dangerousness of the offender, cooperation of the offender, violence of the offence, the remorse of the offender, risk of reoffending, prior criminal record, youthfulness of the offender, intrusiveness of the sampling, nature of the offence in terms of leaving bodily substances at a crime scene, deterrence potential of sampling, and necessity for public safety. Many of these factors are actuarial in nature and address the need to code certain offenders in terms of their riskiness, with the goal of determining whether they might be able to enter into networks of inclusion at some later time.

I contend that the cumulative effect of these developments in judicial decision-making has been to instrumentalize the judicial system. Partly owing to the presence of DNA-based technologies in crime management, there has been a relatively easy bypassing of the spirit of evidentiary rules, if not the rules themselves. An open stance toward sampling applications is being adopted; all Charter challenges are being refused; and judicial discretion is being interpreted very narrowly. If these trends continue, the future of DNA evidence and sampling in Canadian courts will likely involve a certain erosion of evidentiary rules designed to protect individual rights in favour of an easier crime management through technological means.

Police Tactics and DNA Sampling

It is clear that DNA sampling technologies are affecting police practice and are enabling an instrumentalization of law enforcement administration, primarily through new strategies of criminal identification. DNA technology is evolving to the point that police will soon be able to apply it at street level. At the forefront of this evolution is the United Kingdom, where government scientists have developed handheld DNA testing kits that will be electronically linked to Britain's national DNA database. The idea is to allow police to use these on suspects for an immediate match between their DNA and DNA found at crime scenes (Carcknel, 2000: A9). Similar research is being done in the United States, where the National Institute of Justice is funding a number of research projects to develop credit card–sized devices for analysing blood, semen, and skin samples at crime scenes (Sinha, 1999: 48).

This sort of technology needs further refining, yet it seems to be on its way. In the meantime, an emerging tactic of police is also the oldest tactic, one that was employed in the very first DNA typing case involving Colin Pitchfork – the DNA dragnet. DNA dragnets are police investigations in which people are asked to submit to mass DNA testing so as to to exclude themselves from the suspect list. To date, there have been three major DNA dragnets in Canada. The first was in Vermilion, Alberta, a town of 3,800 people 200 kilometres east of Edmonton. There, beginning in November 1994, men were asked to submit to testing in an effort to identify a rapist who had been active in the community for at least three years. Initially, ninety men were asked to surrender blood samples because they were known to be out on the town during the evening of the last attack or because tipsters had mentioned their names. The dragnet was conducted quietly, with nobody in the town talking about it. According to one resident, 'nobody's saying whether they have or haven't given blood because who wants to be stigmatized with that? In a small town, as soon as they think you have one foot in the police station door, they think something's happened' (in Plischke, 1995a: A1).

During the initial investigation, no one refused to give blood. This was because of the obvious stigma attached to a refusal. RCMP Corporal Craig Smith, an investigator at the time, commented: 'I'm sure if someone were not to give blood and that were found out, he would be really, really unpopular' (in Plischke, 1995b: A3). A number of men in the town reinforced this view, telling reporters that they would not look favourably on someone who refused to give a sample (1995b: A1). However, by June 1996, after eighteen months and 240 tests, there still was no match. The police, fearing a loss of enthusiasm on the part of the community, called a town meeting to motivate people and to reveal a psychological profile of the rapist in the hope of gaining new leads. The mayor spoke out in support of the ongoing DNA dragnet, saying that she favoured banking DNA samples at birth: 'Anyone who wants to protect the system and wants to live in a safe society, why would we have anything to hide' (in Plischke, 1996a: A1)? About two hundred people attended the town meeting, where they listened to a psychological profile of the rapist, which described him as a loner who selected his victims by peeking through windows. He was nocturnal and likely had few friends. He perhaps selected his victims by breaking into their homes or by making obscene phone calls. People who knew him would likely describe him as polite and respectful. At the meeting, two men spoke out against the mass testing as a violation of privacy; they were shouted down by the other residents, who supported the investigation. Following this, the police praised the community members for their cooperation and warned that anyone who did not give a blood sample on request would face an intrusive background check (Plischke, 1996b: A6). Despite these tactics, the case has never been solved.

The second DNA dragnet in Canada was conducted in Port Alberni, British Columbia, a town of 18,000 on Vancouver Island. On the evening of 31 July 1996, eleven-year-old Jessica States disappeared after watching a baseball game at a local park. The next day, her body was found nearby; she had been sexually assaulted and beaten to death.

After approximately 5,000 interviews, 1,100 tips, an emotional public plea from the parents of the victim, and a $110,000 reward, no useful evidence emerged. At this point, Staff Sergeant Dale Djos, who headed the investigation – and who had recently read Joseph Wambaugh's account of the Colin Pitchfork case, *The Blooding* (1989) – began a DNA dragnet. The RCMP were helped by the fact that the DNA warrant legislation had come into force (this had not been so in Vermelion). This meant they did not need to rely on voluntary sampling, although all of the 411 samples were volunteered, as they were in Vermilion. Police also worked with the FBI to try to find DNA matches from crime scene and offender indexes in the United States. Finally, in August 1999, three years after the investigation began, the police arrested Roderick Patten, a twenty-year-old inmate serving time for break and enter and theft. He had been identified through a DNA sample he had given.

The third major DNA sweep was conducted in Sudbury, Ontario, in 1998. Renee Sweeney, an adult video store clerk, had been stabbed twenty-eight times. Police found a blood-soaked High Sierra jacket at the crime scene and decided to conduct a DNA sweep. Over the next two years, 485 suspects were tested with no result. Police reported that four men had had to be coerced through DNA warrants. To date, no suspect has been found.

Canada is certainly not unique in conducting DNA sweeps. The largest to date was carried out in Germany in 1999, when 16,400 men were tested to identify the person who raped and killed an eleven-year-old girl. The assailant was eventually identified (Leonard, 2001: A1). A number of sweeps have been conducted in Britain as well. American commentators tend to point out that DNA sweeps are less likely in the United States than elsewhere. When interviewed by a reporter covering the Vermilion case, Joseph Wambaugh suggested that many American men would refuse to submit to testing; in contrast, Canadians (like the British) were more 'civic minded' and would be less likely to refuse testing on the grounds of civil rights (in Plischke, 1995a: A1). Kenneth Kidd, a Yale professor of genetic psychology and biology stated: 'I don't think anything like this has occurred in the United States. I think there would be a great hue and cry raised if it were tried here. I don't have this sense that Canadians have this paranoia that the Americans have about the police' (1995a: A1).

However, the United States has been far from immune from DNA sweeps. Since the early 1990s, sweeps have been carried out in the Bronx, in Los Angeles, Costa Mesa, Huntington Beach, San Diego, and

Palo Alto in California, and in Ann Arbor and Lawrence in Michigan. The widest sweep was conducted in Miami, where 2,300 people were tested. Only the Lawrence sweep turned up a suspect, after employees in a nursing home were tested to determine who had sexually assaulted a comatose patient (Leonard, 2001: A1). Another interesting development in the United States involves corporations hiring private forensic laboratories to conduct sweeps of their employees. Cellmark, a major private testing company in the United States, says that it conducted six corporate sweeps in 1999 and 2000. In one case, a midwestern company tested 350 employees in order to identify the individual who had sent a letter threatening to tamper with the firm's product. DNA was taken from the saliva used to seal the envelope (2001: A1). There are no regulations regarding what happens to such samples.

In fact, there are no regulations or laws about mass DNA testing at all, in Canada or the United States. No one has challenged the practice in court, and informal public pressures to submit to such sweeps will likely mean that no one will challenge them for some time. The practice has in its favour the possibility of identifying a suspect who is hiding among the general population; at the very least, it may act as a deterrent to would-be criminals. At the same time, DNA sweeps have shown themselves to be highly inefficient in a cost/benefit sense; they rarely lead to identification of perpetrators despite the effort and resources that go into them. More important are the ethical questions that sweeps raise regarding the use of state authority to compel individuals to cooperate with criminal investigations. In effect, DNA sweeps are a form of police interrogation. The public often supports DNA sweeps because they assuage fears of criminal victimization; even so, this practice erodes certain principles of justice, such as presumption of innocence and bodily integrity, which exist to protect citizens against state power.

Privatization

A final component of the instrumentalization of crime management through DNA testing is privatization. DNA testing in Canada is not as heavily privatized as in the United States, but there are signs that this is changing. Currently there are seven private forensic companies in Canada compared to about five hundred in the United States, where private firms are heavily involved in DNA testing for criminal investigations as well as civil cases. This industry has been slow to develop in Canada partly because of the nature of the market. There are no individual proprietary rights to the technology, and the Canadian market is not very big. That said, private labs are becoming more viable for two main reasons. First, the costs of private tests are falling, making them an increasingly viable option in civil cases as well as for criminal defence lawyers and even prosecutors who need a fast turnaround time. The cost varies with the number of loci on a DNA strand that are required for matching. Costs can be as low as $300 per test in a private laboratory (Cohen, 2001: 48). Second, since April 2001, police and prosecutors have been required to pay 55 per cent of the costs of testing in the RCMP laboratories; some of them have begun taking their business to private laboratories to save money.

The first private laboratory to be accredited by the Standards Council of Canada was Maxxam Analytics Inc., which is modelled after the Ontario Centre for Forensic Sciences and is staffed by a number of ex-employees of that facility. Maxxam is based in Montreal and has seven laboratories in Ontario and three in Alberta. According to the head of Maxxam's human DNA department, Wayne Murray, the firm is already negotiating with the RCMP to help ease the DNA testing backlog in government laboratories. Interestingly, Maxxam Analytics has formed a partnership with the private investigation firm King-Reed & Associates Ltd., based in Toronto, to carry out DNA-based investigations. Private investigators from King-Reed – many of whom are former police officers – are receiving training in police-style DNA collection practices at crime scenes. They are also being trained to identify and collect 'voluntary discards' such as saliva on envelopes, discarded cigarette butts, chewing gum, and coffee cups. After the samples are properly collected and stored, they are shipped to a Maxxam laboratory, where they are analysed for a match. Joint enterprises such as Maxxam/King-Reed hope to fill in the gaps for understaffed police forces and to investigate more minor crimes, which police do not always have the resources to pursue.

Such partnerships between public and private agencies fit well with current government policies for reducing the costs of government departments. This orientation is built into the NDDB's mission statement, which states:

In today's dynamic business environment, many government departments and agencies are taking steps to identify intellectual property (IP) assets, recognize their value, and manage them as strategic levers to future innovation. This is certainly the case within the National DNA Data Bank. From the outset, National DNA Data Bank managers have fostered a corporate culture that encourages employees to innovate and to pursue creative partnerships with both public and private sector organizations. A project as complex and science-oriented as the National DNA Data Bank created a number of very progressive and potentially lucrative intellectual assets. Intellectual properties are being protected to preserve their value and to provide valuable tools and knowledge to the national and international police communities. Taking advantage of IP assets is also contributing to Canadian industrial competitiveness and providing other socio-economic benefits. (NDDB, 2001b: 10)

The NDDB has already developed one technology for marketing – the Sample Tracking and Control System (STaCS), a software system that monitors, controls, and reports on samples as they pass through the analysis process. The NDDB intends to license this technology to other laboratories (NDDB, 2001b: 7). Given the government's orientation toward partnership with the private sector, and given the private sector's preparations for such partnerships, it is likely that even more cooperation will develop as more private firms enter the market.

To some extent, privatization is built into the NDDB's mission, both in terms of its goal of developing marketable technologies and in terms of importing private-sector management rationales into its operations. If corporations such as Maxxam Analytics become increasingly involved in DNA investigations, as in the United States, we are likely to see a growing willingness on the government's part to partner with the private sector in the name of more efficient crime management. At present, such partnerings are problematic in terms of the lack of regulation of forensic corporations. The strict privacy safeguards of the DNA Identification Act do not apply to them. The capitalist logic at work in these different modes of privatization has a rationalizing effect. Efficiency, profitability, productivity, and entrepreneurialism may well become goals of criminal justice, displacing more traditional, value-based objectives. If that happens, crime will become a problem to be managed rather than merely controlled, as the skills, values, and measures of management practice increasingly refer to a corporate rather than a state-based model.

From Crime Control to Crime Management

To date, the few criticisms levelled against DNA typing and banking have focused on the issues of genetic privacy and bodily integrity. These are important, but the technology has more immediate, systemic impacts on criminal justice. Viewing the issue through the lens of biogovernance allows for a more complex critique in that it allows us to focus on the technology's rationalizing and normalizing effects. I suggest that an important impact of biotechnology on criminal justice relates to the ongoing instrumental rationalization of the system. This apparent shift in the way justice is distributed is making some people think hard about the technology of DNA testing and banking. Several effects of this rationalization process are beginning to make themselves felt. First, privatization is entering the justice system through this technology. I use the term privatization here to denote the importation of what Nils Christie (1994) refers to as an 'industrial' logic and what David Schichor (1997), drawing from George Ritzer's work on the rationalization of consumption, calls a 'McDonaldization' process in which the principles of efficiency, calculability, predictability, and control become the overriding means and ends of the system. As market logic becomes the dominant management paradigm across Canada's public institutions, the language of enhanced productivity – in terms of increasing the quantity of people flowing through the system and assisting in cost effectiveness – becomes the basis for assessing the system's quality. This was evident in the policy justifications provided during the drafting of the relevant legislation, and it is evident now in the annual reports of the NDDB with their proud statements of the number of samples processed and in the decisions of judges to allow the storage of offender samples.

Combined with changes in the language of management is the entry of private laboratories and private investigation firms into the justice process for the sake of cost efficiency. Crown and defence lawyers are beginning to resort to private laboratories, and this trend will likely continue as the industry linked to this technology grows. As well, the NDDB will likely continue developing technologies that can be marketed within this industry as the line between the public and private sectors continues to blur. Concerns over efficiency and cost-effectiveness are certainly not new in criminal justice; however, the danger is increasing that they may replace justice and fairness as the ends of the system.

Related to this concern is the increasing scientization of trial discourse. Like the language of industrial management, the language of science is technical and non-normative. It reduces questions of guilt or non-guilt to technical, objectified questions that do not depend on circumstances, rights, or values. Industrial logic and scientific language are rationalities external to the justice system, yet both are increasingly affecting how justice is managed. DNA typing and banking are bearers of these rationales – they are entering the justice system attached to the technology. This is happening in part because the system is adapting to the needs of the technology rather than the other way around. The DNA warrant and data-banking laws were all passed quickly and with little debate. The overriding concern – especially for the data bank legislation – was privacy. The impact that the technology would have on the justice system was not seriously considered.

Arguably, the same is true for how the courts are actually implementing the DNA system. Canadian courts have barely considered how to deal with DNA evidence as novel scientific evidence. Such evidence has entered trials with little debate even though judges and juries have only a limited ability to understand the significance of the evidence and how it was produced. All attempts to question the constitutionality of DNA evidence have failed on a number of fronts. Questions of evidence collection have also been passed over; an excellent indication of this is that DNA dragnets have never been challenged in court.

Despite all of this, DNA typing and banking are largely depoliticized forms of biotechnology. Fear of crime and the acceptability of surveillance technologies in the name of community safety have legitimated the technology as well as calls for expanded use of it emanating from government officials, police associations, and others. The current round of public consultations on the DNA warrant and banking legislation may very well result in more property offences being added to the list of designated offences. To the extent that the technology has been politicized, it is only within the legal community, where defence lawyers are accusing prosecutors and forensic laboratories of forming an alliance to maximize convictions at the expense of scientific neutrality. However, even this criticism is pulling the trial process farther into the scientific arena.

Changing the Values of Justice

These effects are the material traces of a more fundamental change happening in criminal justice – a shift in legal regimes away from an ideal type based on political values about the relationship between the individual and the state toward one based on values imported from the technological, scientific, and corporate domains. Both ideal types value objectivity. However, in the former, objectivity is the outcome of a social game in which the actors are constrained by rules designed to equalize, to some extent, their power differentials. In the genetic justice system, objectivity is an outcome of odds calculations and produces non-normative truth claims that are not influenced by social circumstances. Power differentials are irrelevant because what is being produced is truth, not fairness.

What is wrong with a more efficient, accurate and objective justice system, an objectification of courtroom processes and criminal investigations, and an expansion of the DNA net to include more convicted offenders? When framed in these terms, it is difficult to say. However, when we ask what these developments mean for the long-term administration of justice, a more critical response is possible. I identify three criticisms that can be levelled at this new ideal of justice. First, there are dangers inherent in normalizing the surveillance mentality. In reference to the DNA dragnet in Vermilion, the Privacy Commissioner stated: 'There's a psychological aspect to this and that is getting the public conditioned for mass testing, and I don't like it. We've been poked and prodded enough' (in Plischke, 1996a: A1). Given the prevalence and normality of surveillance in Canadian society, there may be a tendency to simply accept this new form without considering how it empowers state agents. Mass DNA testing is already being conducted and people have been very accepting of it. It has never been challenged in court and it fits well with provincial government policies calling for expansion of the DNA net. Is Canada heading toward a DNA database for the entire population? Should the state have this power?

The second criticism emerges from jurisprudence. I contend that the DNA system is a system not of evidence but of proof. The charisma of genetic science is such that DNA has power beyond other forms of evidence, that its presence in the courts is almost always decisive. This can be a public good, but its effects on the administration of justice may not be. DNA evidence tends to allow a circumvention of certain legal principles and rules of evidence that are based in fundamental social values and that are designed to set limits on the authority of the state over individuals. Individual protections, framed as fundamental rights such as the right of bodily integrity, the right against self-incrimination, the right to a fair trial, the right to presumption of innocence, and the right against unreasonable search and seizure, are all now being challenged by practices such as invading the body for samples, mass testing of populations, genetic fishing expeditions, the use of genetic profiles to betray subjects, and the redefining of unreasonableness as a matter of physical discomfort rather than social rights. Increasingly, justice is being redefined as the identification of the guilty individual rather than the maintenance of a principled legal system. In Habermas's (1998) terms, the distance between facts and norms in the law widens as an empirical, factual emphasis marginalizes the moral content of law.

This leads to the third criticism. The moral content of law is arguably necessary if law is to maintain its legitimacy as a form of authority. The elevation of scientific expertise in the courtroom over that of lawyers marks a technicalization of the judicial process. As legal principles of fairness are eroded in favour of scientific identification of offenders, the ritual nature of justice disappears (Durkheim, 1893). A focus on efficiency and cost-effectiveness further contributes to this deritualization of justice; increasingly, determinations of guilt or innocence are made in laboratories rather than in the public arena of the courtroom. This may have the opposite effect of that intended by justice authorities. Ultimately, they hope to employ DNA typing and banking to produce a greater degree of ontological security in the public. Surveys show that public regard for the criminal justice system is consistently low and that levels of fear of crime are quite high. This condition can be useful to state agents seeking greater levels of authority, but it can also lead to a questioning of the state's competence to carry out its crime control function. DNA evidence is offered up by the state as a sign that it is still able to formulate strategies for enhancing crime management. However, if this can only be accomplished by reducing the ethical content of the law, the question arises: Can we trust our technical experts to act in ethical ways? This problem is at the heart of the risk society.

7 Conclusion: Toward Genetic Justice

In 1992, a woman in the small town of Kipling, Saskatchewan, went to the local RCMP station and told them that her doctor, John Schnee-berger, had administered a stupefying drug during an examination and then sexually assaulted her. In 1997 he was accused again of doing the same to a teenage patient. These shocking accusations were diffi-cult for local people to believe. Schneeberger was a South African doc-tor who had set up practice in the town a few years earlier. He was a model citizen – a community leader and a family man. Three times, RCMP officers obtained blood samples from him, but DNA from the samples did not match that of the semen samples from the victims. However, a DNA sample from one of the doctor's hairs did match the semen samples. A scientific mystery was developing that was worthy of a television drama. Eventually, a forensic technician noticed that the blood provided by Schneeberger seemed old, as if it had been removed from his body much earlier. On further investigation, police discov-ered that the doctor had surgically inserted a small tube of another man's blood into his arm prior to each blood test. Because he was a doctor, he had been allowed to self-administer the blood test; there he was able to draw the blood from the tube rather than from his own vein. New tests confirmed that DNA from his own blood matched that of the semen sample, and he was convicted of administering a stupefy-ing drug, sexually assaulting two women, and obstructing justice. He received a six-year sentence.

The Schneeberger case involved a medical professional with a great deal of sophisticated knowledge about DNA identification. However, other criminals are beginning to adapt to new, DNA-based forms of crime detection. Police in the United States have already reported a number of such developments: rapists wearing masks, gloves, and condoms; burglars wearing protective shoe covers, rape victims being forced to wash away DNA evidence, and prisoners caught tutoring one another on how to spread other people's blood and semen around crime scenes to trick forensic analysts (New Hampshire Police Standards and Training Council, 2000). These cases indicate the degree to which DNA testing and banking have already become integral to crime management. They also indicate that criminals can and will develop tactics to evade the 'ultimate identifier.' Genetic justice will not end crime; however, it will change how crimes are carried out and detected. Developments such as these naturally lead one to think about the future of 'genetic justice.' In this chapter I consider the impact that DNA testing and banking are having on criminal justice and the implications that genetic justice holds for the future of crime control. To this end, I return to the four central questions that motivated this study: How have DNA testing and banking entered the criminal justice system? How has the technology been defined, normalized, and secured within the public sphere? What impacts has it had on criminal justice? Finally, what will be its future effects?

How have DNA testing and banking entered the criminal justice system?

DNA testing and banking are entering the justice system in the general context of a risk society. They are at the centre of a network that socially organizes the technology into a knowledge system, a technical system, and a political force. The network that supports DNA typing and banking in Canada includes the National DNA Data Bank (NDDB), the regional RCMP forensic laboratories, the provincial laboratories in Ontario and Quebec, municipal and provincial police departments, federal and provincial solicitors general and justice departments, the criminal courts of Canada, the FBI and the U.S. Department of Justice, victims' groups, the media, equipment suppliers, and many others. Much of the work of this network, however, is not about managing the technology itself, but rather about managing the risks posed and defined by the technology.

When new technologies are introduced into a social context, dangers are generated for institutionalized authorities because they cannot gauge public reaction with certainty, nor can they predict the actions of all the actors involved in the socio-technical network. In the early stages of a new technology, its conceptual edges are still visible and it is open to critique. During the late 1980s and early 1990s, DNA typing came under attack from two directions. The first critique arose within the scientific community itself around the issue of how to calculate population genetics estimates of potential mismatches. The second critique emanated from the Supreme Court of Canada, which upheld common law restrictions on the use of DNA evidence and the need for consent from the accused. Questions about the scientific accuracy of DNA testing and institutional uncertainty about the legal viability of the evidence, which could be gathered only by invading, social subjects' bodies, had to be addressed before a viable technology for crime management could be produced.

Another issue when new technologies are being produced is how the public will respond. In a risk society, members of the public grow increasingly reflexive in their relationship to expert knowledge. During times of rapid social change, they feel a high level of ontological insecurity with regard to governmental institutions and risk-based expertise. If genetic experts themselves disagree over how to ascertain DNA matches, how can this knowledge be trusted when judicial decisions are being made? Could DNA testing and banking lead to intrusions on privacy and generally increase levels of social surveillance? Clearly, the public must be reassured that the state is aware of the risks posed by the technology and is acting to address these risks. At the same time, in our current social context, the public needs to be reassured that the state is acting to control crime. Despite a general decline in the crime rate, the public is highly anxious about crime; this is a sign of the public's uneasiness about the social changes that are occurring in late modernity. I contend that crime has come to symbolize the uncertainties of modern everyday life in general; as a result, crime control has been politicized. This provides the state with an opportunity to look like it is controlling the risks of crime by developing new strategies and technologies of surveillance, predetection, and identification. Thus, DNA testing and banking have emerged as important technologies in the government's arsenal of security.

In risk societies, security through biotechnology is based on processes of 'biogovernance.' These processes are characterized by privatization, politicization, objectification, normalization, and responsibilization. Biogovernance is oriented toward managing biotechnologies by organizing them within a governmental framework of risk management. Each type of biotechnology – DNA typing, cloning, gene therapy, genetic modification of organisms, and so on – foregrounds particular elements of biogovernance, but all of the elements are present to some extent. Currently, biogovernmental processes of DNA typing and banking are emphasizing normalization and objectification techniques to secure the public. DNA technology is somewhat unique among biotechnologies in that its politicization is occuring between and within expert knowledge communities such as law, science, and journalism, rather than in the public sphere. I suggest that normalization processes within the policy debates and media trial coverage have depoliticized the risks posed to the public by DNA typing and banking and have framed the issue as one of instrumental objectification. To date, DNA testing in Canada has been managed by governments rather than by the private sector. There are signs, however, that the private sector may soon play a larger role in DNA testing. Meanwhile, privatization as an element of neoliberal governance is having an impact by importing the language of 'McDonaldization' into the DNA socio-technical system. Responsibilization is also largely a future potential; it is just now beginning to take effect, with notions of subjectivity – in particular criminal subjectivity – beginning to incorporate genetic determinism as an important element.

How have DNA typing and banking been defined, normalized, and secured within the public sphere?

Related to the question of how DNA testing and banking enter the criminal justice system is the question of how the conceptual edges of this technology have been blunted and how the social conditions of its reception have influenced this process. In chapter 2 I argued that the current social, technological, and legal environments in Canada are highly conducive to an acceptance of DNA typing and banking. In the early 1990s, when the technology was first coming into wide use, levels of fear of crime were already very high, partly as a result of the hyper-reality of media representations of crime, and also as a result of the general ontological insecurity of late modernity. DNA testing seemed a promising weapon in the war on crime. Combined with all of this was a growing acceptance of surveillance technologies in public and private spaces, a result of advances in information technologies that allowed for the 'informating' of populations. For example, shoppers' transactions are now being recorded instantly in databases, and this information is being added to the data flows of our society. This is not an Orwellian form of surveillance because it does not involve submission to the gaze of another person, it does not seem to directly violate our individual sovereignty. It is easy to forget that databases are still *owned* by someone. People have become accustomed to this form of surveillance; in this sense, a DNA data bank is simply one more database, and one that is easier to tolerate because it does not include responsible citizens.

Our technological context throughout the 1990s and into the 2000s has been characterized by a fascination with the discoveries of genetic science. This is a charismatic science that evokes a sense of wonder at the possibilities it has opened up and the powers it bestows on its practitioners. People are far less afraid than they were in the 1970s that genetic science could contaminate nature. The success of the Human Genome Project seems to have opened up the possibility for improving public health as well as identification techniques. In terms of their applications in criminal justice, genetic technologies fit well with the 'culture of the trace' that characterizes perceptions of crime scenes and criminal bodies. For the past two hundred years, criminalists have been developing ever more precise means for linking crime scene traces to the bodies of criminals. It may be that with DNA testing, the ultimate linking technology has been found. Given how unequivocal DNA matching can be, it has replaced fingerprinting as the most certain way to identify a perpetrator. DNA traces contain an essence of the person, an essence that is missing from biometric forms of measurement, and for this reason it is having a powerful influence on judicial decisions. The debates over population genetics have been resolved, and the technology is becoming more and more refined, and as a result, the sense of certainty about DNA has increased significantly in a relatively short time.

The third contextual factor of note relates to how DNA technologies have been received in law. An important factor here is the common law doctrine of bodily integrity and how it restricts the state's ability to interfere with a citizen's control of his or her body and the information from that body. By the early 1990s this doctrine had already been eroded to some extent. The Supreme Court had by then upheld the right to bodily integrity in a number of cases involving police seizure of medical samples, a woman's right to an abortion, and the right not to be subject to injury; however, there were no cases focusing specifically on the seizure of DNA material from within a suspect's body until 1997, when in *R. v. Stillman* the Supreme Court upheld the accused's right to be free from excessive use of force to seize bodily samples. However in that case the Supreme Court was applying old law; *Stillman* involved a crime that had been perpetrated before the passage of the DNA warrant provisions, which simply overrode notions of bodily integrity.

Social, technological, and legal conditions in Canada at the beginning of the 1990s made possible a positive reception for DNA typing and banking. In 1994 the federal government could begin its consulting and legislative processes with some confidence that DNA testing and banking would enjoy broad support both from the public and from governmental stakeholders. Yet, the process was still risky; calls for severe restrictions on the application of this technology could be anticipated even if protest over the very idea would not be a serious threat.

During the consultations that led to the passage of the 1995 DNA warrant provisions and the 1998 data bank provisions in the Criminal Code, the government limited the terms of debate to questions about the form the warrant and banking legislation should take; it also defined the central problem as one of privacy. On that basis, the loudest calls for caution came from the Privacy Commissioner and the Canadian Bar Association (CBA); both these bodies recommended retaining only digital information about DNA codes rather than physical specimens and called for a limit on the range of offences included. Women's groups and other groups that tried to raise broader social issues were marginalized (for example, the Vancouver Rape Relief and Women's Shelter). In contrast, the Canadian Police Association (CPA) and victims' rights groups argued that the proposed legislation was not tough enough. These groups contended that samples should be taken and stored at time of arrest and that the list of designated offences should be broad enough to ensure maximum community protection. In this way, the range of the debate was set in the policy arena. The basic issue was how to balance individual privacy rights with the need for public safety.

Around the same time, the media trials of Guy Paul Morin and David Milgaard were underway. Press coverage of both cases generated a particular image of the shortcomings of the existing criminal justice system. From the level of stubborn government ministers to the level of vindictive police investigators, there appeared to be a shocking abuse of discretion as well as decisions based on subjective opinion rather than objective fact. The media narratives of these cases invited readers to place themselves in the role of victims of a justice system that was apparently out of control. According to this narrative, the problem was too much subjective discretion and the solution was DNA testing, along with more bureaucratic oversight. After all, DNA had exonerated both Morin and Milgaard.

The policy process and the media coverage worked in tandem to normalize DNA testing and banking in the public sphere. Both drew from a problem frame that resonated with the enabling conditions of late modern Canada. The policy process hegemonically framed the limits of debate. Policy stakeholders agreed that the key issue was genetic privacy. As long as an offender's DNA fingerprint was not distributed outside the criminal justice system, his or her Charter rights would not be violated. Public fears of invasion of privacy could be assuaged by legislative safeguards and electronic security systems. DNA testing and banking could be legitimated in the policy discourse by emphasizing the charismatic and objective nature of genetic science, the socially valuable goals of administrative efficiency and cost effectiveness, and the public security benefits of living in a surveillance society. Journalists went farther even than this, by highlighting the consequences of an ineffective criminal justice system. These consequences could be avoided by importing scientific expertise into the system in the form of DNA testing and by holding justice experts more closely to account. The end result was the same as in the policy process – the call went out for the greater objectivity that biotechnology could provide.

Thus, even before the DNA socio-technical network became fully operational in criminal justice, the presumption had been planted that it was objective – or at least more objective than non-scientific forms of evidence. Ever since, the challenge for lawmakers and forensic technical experts has been to secure the technology within the public sphere by ensuring that this reputation is maintained and enhanced. Legislative safeguards around privacy and techniques circulating the DNA trace through the technology of forensic laboratories constitute a regime of practice that is increasingly closed to outside criticism as a result of processes of expert boundary maintenance. The 'black box' of DNA testing has been closed by a set of technologies of distance that remove from view the intrusions of subjective judgments and the scientific controversies that expose elements of human interpretation in DNA matching analysis.

Various technologies of distance are being used to objectify DNA testing. First, in its publications, the NDDB in Ottawa provides a standard narrative of the testing process. The DNA trace circulates through a highly automated system to produce a bar code–like map, which can then be matched to a crime scene bar code. The process seems relatively simple and straightforward; no mention is made of problems that can arise in the sample collection phase at messy crime scenes, of the role other actors play in the socio-technical network, of the potential for technical error, or of the role played by human operators in determining matches. Second, the forensic community itself has developed the standards for measurement error and has thus erased from view the measurement variabilities that can result from different levels of competence and care. It is humans who compare two autorads and estimate the acceptable variation in length between them, and mistakes can be made. Measurement error can also arise during statistical calculations of false matches within a given population. Related to this is a third technology of distance – laboratory accreditation from outside bodies such as the Standards Council of Canada. If the laboratory meets the accreditation body's standards, its results are assumed to be trustworthy and beyond question. Finally, a fourth technology of distance relates to how errors are dealt with when they occur. Within the forensic science community, a general strategy is to individualize the problem and place the blame on individual technicians for being careless or exercising poor judgment. Mistakes are not allowed to reflect on the socio-technical system in general, although when an error becomes public, it is a risky time for the network. This was the case, for example, when Morin's lawyers found that the Ontario Centre of Forensic Sciences had lost and contaminated crime scene evidence. Very quickly, Stephanie Nyznyk was blamed for the problems, and any systemic problems were downplayed. However, the Kaufman Report refused to completely accept this and suggested that there were broader problems at the centre.

Together, these technologies of distance establish a boundary between expert and non-expert abilities to interpret DNA matches. They narrow the grounds for critiquing the socio-technical network to questions of objectivity and privacy, which the system's principal definers have determined are the bases for public insecurity around this technology. Through these practices, objectification is produced. With DNA testing and banking, objectification is essential if the technology is to be normalized and if the public is to perceive it as safe.

What are the impacts of DNA testing and banking on the operation of the criminal justice system?

Much of the debate over the potential negative effects of DNA on criminal justice has centred on questions of genetic privacy. This is not really a relevant question at this stage of the technology, though it may become relevant in the future. At present, there are much more pressing questions regarding biotechnology's impacts on criminal justice. Overall, these impacts can be characterized as having an instrumental rationalizing effects on the system – effects that lead to normative questions about the balance we want to strike between instrumental and value rationalities in criminal justice. From the very beginning, the potential for DNA testing and banking to bring about greater efficiency in crime management was recognized and promoted, but at the same time there was always an assumption that it would be simply another form of evidence, albeit an especially powerful form. However, DNA testing and banking have become more than that now that the justice system is adapting itself to meet the needs of the technology rather than the other way around.

In cases involving DNA evidence, the courtroom as a field is becoming increasingly scientized; this has required lawyers and judges to change their habitus. Court functionaries must learn the language of genetic science in order to understand the evidence and to properly adjudicate. Scientific capital is becoming as important as legal capital. This places the defendant at a disadvantage. Police forensic laboratories generally work for the prosecution; defence lawyers must often acquire the scientific capital themselves since most of their clients cannot afford private DNA tests. The resulting imbalance has become one of the main axes of current politicization within the DNA testing and banking socio-technical network.

Furthermore, DNA evidence is instrumentalizing judicial decisions. Judicial decisions regarding sampling orders on conviction are leaning strongly toward a permissive standard that ensures a maximization of sampling. Questions of intrusiveness are addressed using a language of physical rather than social intrusiveness. For the most part, courts are accepting DNA evidence gathered in questionable ways, as well as DNA evidence of questionable evidentiary value. All arguments for limiting the use of DNA evidence on the basis of the Charter have failed. The result has been a shift in the level of caution paid to ensuring that the judicial system errs on the side of the defendant.

Combined with trends in judicial decision making are provincial government and police calls for expansion of the DNA net. Ontario is the leader on this issue; its Attorney General is publicly encouraging the federal justice minister to close 'loopholes' in the legislation by adding more offences. The CPA and Toronto's police chief have both called on the government to expand the list of designated offences to include, among others, prowling, child pornography, and drug-related offences. In 2005 the federal government will be reviewing the legislation, and expansion of offences is one of the items up for review.

Instrumental rationality is also evident in the police tactic of conducting DNA sweeps of communities in order to eliminate residents as suspects and, it is hoped, catch the perpetrator. This practice bypasses traditional techniques of identifying and investigating likely suspects, by treating entire communities of people as suspects open to seizure of bodily substances. To date, there have been three broad-scale DNA sweeps in Canada: Vermilion, Alberta; Port Alberni, British Columbia; and Sudbury, Ontario. In each case, police asked men in the community to submit to DNA testing and hundreds of tests were conducted. In Port Alberni, the perpetrator was identified; in the other two sweeps, no one has been caught. Large-scale DNA sweeps are becoming increasingly common in the United States and in Britain and other European countries.

A final actor involved in the instrumentalization process is the private forensic laboratory. Private laboratories constitute only a small industry in Canada; however, there is evidence that they will be playing a greater role in future criminal investigations. Their operations are cheaper and faster, which makes them attractive options for police, prosecutors, and defence lawyers, especially in cases involving more minor offences. Furthermore, the NDDB is entering the private sector by developing technologies for licensing to other forensic laboratories. Governments are looking to form more partnerships with the private sector, and it is likely that some of these will be between public and private laboratories.

To date, these have been some of the major impacts of DNA testing and banking on the criminal justice system. But what are the broader implications of this rationalization process? I suggest that as DNA typing and banking are normalized, objectified, and depoliticized in the public sphere, the danger rises that agents of state control will be empowered beyond what is acceptable in a democracy. Police DNA dragnets are a disturbing development; more disturbing still is that communities are willing to submit to them. It is normal for people to want criminals, especially violent criminals, to be caught. However, there has been no reasoned public discussion about this means of catching them, and there is a danger that as DNA testing technology is normalized, mass testing of the public will be normalized along with it. There needs to be more discussion about how appropriate this technique is.

Part of the appeal of mass DNA testing arises from the charisma of genetic science itself. Genetic evidence enjoys great power in the courts and is becoming a system of proof rather than a form of evidence. Its presence in a case is often decisive, leading to guilty pleas and unchallenged evidence. As a result, the legal rules designed to ensure systemic fairness may be too easily bypassed by this new system of proof. Bodily integrity, the right against self-incrimination, the rules against police 'fishing expeditions,' and the presumption of innocence are being eroded in order to accommodate biotechnology. This technology is useful for identifying individual perpetrators, but it is not friendly toward the legal principles designed to ensure systemic fairness in the face of overwhelming state power.

The power of DNA evidence, combined with its effects on evidentiary rules, may well lead to problems in the future. DNA is already creating a rift between facts and norms in the justice system. As judicial decisions in cases involving DNA evidence come to be based more on technique, the moral bases for those decisions may sometimes become less clear, especially if the DNA system's scope continues to expand to encompass more and more non-violent offences. To some extent, DNA testing and banking by its very efficiency may end up producing its own forms of ontological insecurity as the value rationality of the justice system erodes in favour of efficient and increasingly easy access by state agents to the social body's genetic material.

The Future of Genetic Justice

Much of the discussion about the future of genetic justice focuses on two fears: that the DNA system will continue to expand, and that biotechnology will one day allow scientists to determine behavioural and physical propensities, which in turn will be used to stigmatize individuals and deny them access to institutional resources such as insurance and employment. That the DNA net is expanding has already been demonstrated; at this point, however, genetic predetection of behavioural tendencies remains only a future possibility. That said, developments in criminological research in Canada and elsewhere are generating an openness to the idea that criminality may have some genetic basis. This is where biogovernmental processes of responsibilization enter the justice system and prepare us for future representations of criminality based on genetic characteristics.

Even in the absence of proof of genetic causation, a new representation of criminality is emerging in North America. Dario Melossi (2000) characterizes shifting representations of criminality over the course of modernity as oscillating between two ideal types that correspond to broader shifts in social conditions. On the one hand is an attitude of 'sympathy' toward criminals that emerges in periods of social fragmentation and rapid change. During these periods – for example, during the turn of the last century, the 1920s, and the 1960s – organic intellectuals define society as plural and conflictual (2000: 296). This fragmentation is combined with good economic conditions, optimism about the future, a dominant liberal ideology, and low imprisonment rates. In these conditions, public discourse defines criminals as innovators fighting a corrupt system, and people view punishment as a means to rehabilitate offenders and to experiment with new modes of social reintegration. At some point, social fragmentation reaches an intolerable limit and elites begin calling for a reorganization of social solidarity based on hierarchy, centralized authority, and a unified moral order. Representations of criminality shift from sympathy to 'antipathy'; the criminal becomes a public enemy who is a threat to the moral order. The source of criminality is redefined as internal to the individual criminal rather than as a product of his or her interactions with the social environment. Punitive measures and imprisonment rates increase, and political rhetoric emphasizes concepts such as 'nation' and 'community.' This approach to criminality characterized the era of nation-state formation in the early nineteenth century, the Great Depression of the 1930s, and the period from 1973 until today (2000: 297).

Evidence of such a shift in Canada can be found in the changes that have occurred over time in discussions about parole. For example, the Fauteux Report (1956), which resulted in the establishment of the Canadian National Parole Board in 1959, justified parole in this way: 'Parole is a well recognized procedure which is designed to be a logical step in the reformation and rehabilitation of a person who has been convicted of an offence and as a result, is undergoing imprisonment ... It is a transitional step between close confinement in an institution and absolute freedom in society' (51). The report went on to quote from the United Nations' 1954 publication 'Parole and After-Care':

[Parole] is a socially just procedure because it enables society to play an auxiliary role in the readjustment of the individual who may have become a criminal partly through shortcomings in society itself. It may serve as a proper means of mitigating excessively severe punishments imposed under the influence of aroused public emotions ... Finally it offers an opportunity to re-evaluate the role of institutional treatment and the relative merits of alternative, less punitive techniques' (52).

By the time of the Daubney Report (1988), *Taking Responsibility*, a review of the parole process in Canada, a very different discourse had developed. Parole was now viewed not as a social responsibility, but rather as an individual privilege to be earned by the offender:

> The Committee believes that parole is a privilege that must be earned. The Committee agrees with the Honourable Brian Smith, former Attorney General of B.C., who said: 'I do not mean that you earn parole because you happen to be a nice manageable inmate who handles the guards well and is polite. I do not mean it at all. I mean that you earn your entitlement to parole because you have demonstrated in some material way that you are prepared to change the way you behave and the way you interact with society. You may do that by demonstrating that you wish to learn a trade or an occupation. While you are in custody, you work at that. You demonstrate that when you get out, you do not intend to go back to pushing drugs or whatever you were in there for, but that you intend to work and want to work. It is not by telling a parole officer that you do, but you demonstrate it by having already shown that you can do so.' (1988: 191)

Melossi (2000: 308) refers to contemporary criminological theory, represented by the Daubney Report, as 'revanche criminology,' drawing from Eric Hobsbawm's (1994) assertion that the current period of social crisis began with the energy crisis of 1973. This traumatic check on Western economic growth marked the beginning of a conservative shift that has affected all social sectors. From this point onward, Western economies underwent massive organizational restructuring, rising unemployment, and a harsh disciplining of the working class. Alongside these economic developments, incarceration rates reached levels never before seen. These rates achieved their pinnacle in the United States, where by the end of the 1990s, a significant proportion of those at the bottom of the socio-economic/racial hierarchy were passing through the correctional system, often as a result of the 'war on drugs.'

Melossi's ideal types of sympathy and antipathy toward criminals provide a useful framework for thinking about shifts in representations of, and responses to, criminality. The idea that the current 'revanche' criminology is a response to late modern shifts in the mode of production is well-established in sociological theory. In analysing the increase in Canadian incarceration rates in the 1980s, Michael Mandel argues that the increase in punitiveness is a response by judges, as agents of ruling elites, to the ongoing economic downturn at the end of the twentieth century (1995: 253). This increase is an attempt to discipline and contain the potentially disruptive underclass as its prospects decline. Bauman (2000) extends this argument to suggest that the high-tech, high-security prisons in the United States reflect a new mode of managing the global underclass produced by the global economy – immobilization and separation from the mainstream.

Yet there is something unsettling about this increased punitiveness, even to those with a highly conservative perspective. High levels of incarceration imply that massive numbers of people no longer are participating in the organic solidarity of modernity. More and more people must be compelled to participate in our institutional structures, or, they must be isolated in order to protect those structures. Rituals of justice no longer demonstrate the ongoing enforcement of social norms; they are performed too often to serve that purpose – so often in fact, that crime is no longer viewed as functional but rather as pathological. Increasingly, authorities find themselves having to rely on force to maintain social order; no longer are they able to operate through legitimated legal-rational institutional processes. This indicates that our normal mode of authority is breaking down.

In this context of increased class antipathy and declining levels of solidarity and trust, the emphasis of social governance changes. Piet Strydom (1999: 31) contends that since the 1970s there has been a shift in the 'master frame' of modernity from a discourse of rights and justice to one of responsibility. Although he is referring specifically to discourses about the relationship between society and nature, I argue that the same applies to the discourse about the relationship between society and the individual. Risk society is characterized by an individualization of responsibility for risk management and by a need to constantly demonstrate that sense of responsibility as a condition of access to the networks of inclusion in society. In a society characterized by a lack of trust at all levels, demonstrating a sense of responsibility becomes very important.

One demonstrates this responsibility through acceptance and enactment of middle-class values regarding work and consumption, through the self-control and striving for self-actualization that can be accomplished through labour, through the acquisition of goods and services, and through the market. The deviant and the criminal are the ones who are unable or unwilling to be responsible by this definition. As was discussed in chapter 6, deviants are placed in networks of exclusion, where they are subjected to more authoritarian forms of social control such as policing and imprisonment. This is the crimefare system, which is used to manage the least salvageable elements of the old welfare underclass. Those who show the potential to enter into networks of inclusion become subject to systems of workfare and welfare that attempt to discipline them away from cultures of dependency and criminality and toward the necessary entrepreneurship of the self. Having been disciplined, they will be able to enter the labour market and the consumer market.

In terms of criminal justice, there are at present two forms of crime management. Garland defines these as a criminology of the self and a criminology of the other (1996). Criminology of the self refers to the responsibilization of individual citizens, who are required to organize their lives in such a way as to reduce the likelihood of being victimized. Criminology of the other refers to processes by which criminals are demonized in late modernity – by which they are characterized as irresponsible. In both cases, the focus is on the self and the individualization of crime and crime management. In the present era, criminality is defined as an individual and internal process. Irresponsibility is seen to proceed from non-social bases.

Defining criminality in terms of responsibility or refusal to be responsible has become an enabling condition for biological definitions of criminality. Why do certain people refuse to adopt the characteristics of a responsible citizen of late modernity? Social science has been unable to answer that question. As criminologist Diana H. Fishbein (1990) states: 'Given similar environmental and sociocultural experiences, why does only a subgroup engage in antisocial and sometimes violent behavior? Sociological research has well established the link between particular adverse environmental and social conditions, but has been unable to explain individual differences in vulnerability to these conditions' (42).

This need to move away from aggregate toward individual understandings of criminality proceeds from a basic assumption that is becoming increasingly prominent among criminologists: a handful of male criminals are responsible for most crimes of violence. If we can develop prediction models that identify these natural criminals at an early age, we will be able to significantly reduce violent crime rates (Gibbs, 1995: 102).

Biologists take two general approaches with regards to the biological basis for violent criminality. Some consider the question from the perspective of sociobiology. Simply stated, sociobiology – an approach developed by biologist Edward O. Wilson in the 1970s – extends population biology and evolutionary theory into studies of social organization and behaviour. Wilson points out that scientists and philosophers face the same question: 'What is man's ultimate nature' (1978: 1). He quickly reduces this question to one of understanding the human mind, and then further reduces it to one of understanding the workings of the human brain. Human nature can be understood by studying how our brain evolved to promote the survival and reproduction of the individual's genes: 'No species, ours included, possesses a purpose beyond the imperatives created by its genetic history' (1978: 2). In terms of ethics and morality, this means that human values and emotional 'responses 'have been programmed to a substantial degree by natural selection over thousands of generations' (1978: 6).

The implications of these assumptions for aggressive and violent behaviour have since been explored by other sociobiologists. Michael Ghiglieri points out that in human societies, success in spreading one's genes is the ultimate motivation for violent behaviour: 'Murder is coded in our DNA, just as it is in the genes of our close ape cousins' (1999: 154). From this, he draws a number of conclusions:

> Homicide is an instinct coded by sexual selection into the human male psyche in a design that prompts men to kill (1) to *expand* their personal gains leading to reproductive advantage or (2) to keep major gains they have already made. Women, meanwhile, usually kill to *protect* their personal security or reproductive future. Clearly, the implication here is that whereas violence by women is finite and more predictable in perceived self-defense (however twisted), men's violence tends to be more infinite and opportunistic. (1999: 154)

Murder occurs in a world of reproductive competition in which the winners decide our genetic heritage. From this perspective, men are driven to expand their reproductive success and women are motivated by the need to protect themselves to ensure they can continue to reproduce. Consequently, men are more inclined toward homicide than women.

Randy Thornhill and Craig Palmer in *A Natural History of Rape* (2000) provide a sociobiological explanation for rape that is along the same lines as Ghiglieri's analysis of murder:

Human rape arises from men's evolved machinery for obtaining a high number of mates in an environment where females choose mates. If men pursued mating only within committed relationships, or if women did not discriminate among potential mates, there would be no rape. The two leading evolutionary hypotheses for the existence of human rape behavior are (1) that rape is an incidental effect (a by-product) of men's adaptations for pursuit of casual sex with multiple partners and (2) that rape is an adaptation in and of itself. (2000: 190–1)

According to Thornhill and Palmer, more research needs to be conducted to determine which hypothesis is most correct. In the meantime, sociobiologists contend that social science explanations should be dismissed because they are ideologically motivated as well as inconsistent with evolutionary theory. This is especially true of feminist theories, which assert that rape is motivated by power rather than lust (2000: 124). From the perspective of sociobiology, all men are potential murderers and rapists. Social conditions in which sexual partners are limited or in which women have the power to select their mates will bring out these natural tendencies: 'People who murder do so deliberately based on their own personal decisions favoring their own ultimate self-interests. They do not murder because they themselves are hapless victims of a society gone haywire' (Ghiglieri, 1999: 133).

The second approach to establishing a biological basis for criminal violence proceeds from developments in genetic science and is not as indebted to evolutionary theory or primate studies. Over the past decade in the United States, researchers have conducted several important studies in the search for biological markers that can be used to identify individuals as prone to criminal violence. A number of possibilities have been identified: high levels of testosterone, low heart rates, 'inhibited' temperament resulting from variable amounts of the neurotransmitter norepinephrine and the stress-regulating hormone cortisol, high levels of manganese in the body, and low levels of the neurotransmitter serotonin. But there is a problem with all of these markers: groups that exhibit them produce a high number of false positives. That is, most of these individuals do *not* become criminals, which means that, direct links between genetic characteristics and criminality cannot be scientifically established. Perhaps future research will establish more reliable markers.

In terms of this research, the most promising marker of potential violent behaviour seems to be serotonin. In the summer of 2002, researchers at the University of Wisconsin, Madison, announced that they had found a direct link between serotonin levels and violent behaviour. This research drew from a line of research dating back to 1993, when Dutch researchers studied a family that had a multigenerational criminal history. The family was found to suffer from a genetic defect that determines the production of the enzyme monamine oxidase A (MAO A), which breaks down excess amounts of the neurotransimitters serotonin, dopamine, and norepinephrine in the brain. In further studies involving mice, researchers found that when the gene that produced MAO A was turned off, the mice became impulsive and fearless. When their brains were examined, they were found to have nine times the normal amount of serotonin. Yet there remained the problem of false positives: most people with abnormal MAO A levels lead ordinary, non-criminal lives. Something else had to be involved in pushing some of these people into criminal behaviour.

This is where the Wisconsin researchers entered the scene. They started from an observation made by social scientists: violent inmates were often abused as children, but a history of abuse is not in itself a predictor of future criminality. So is some combination of MAO A deficiency and abuse associated with criminal behaviour? Drawing from a longitudinal study begun at the Dunedin School of Medicine in New Zealand in 1972, the Wisconsin team gathered genetic material from 442 participants in the study and examined the data on their histories of abuse, criminal convictions, and evidence of violent and antisocial behaviour such as bullying, stealing, persistent fighting, and disobedience to authorities as adolescents. They found that 12 per cent of the abused children had the genetic coding for low MAO A levels and that these individuals accounted for roughly 50 per cent of their generation's convictions for violent crimes in New Zealand (Wilson, 2002: 48). The combination of low MAO A levels and abuse magnified the odds of criminality by nine times. Researchers hypothesize that high levels of MAO A may promote trauma resistance and account for why many individuals in abusive environments do not become criminals. Research of this sort is continuing and is opening up the possibility of developing drug therapies to treat aggression as a disease. This seems to be the goal of many biological researchers (Raine, 1993).

With respect to biological bases of crime, studies of genetic variation and brain chemistry seem to be displacing sociobiology. Genetic research promises a more precise and objectified understanding of criminality; sociology is more nebulous, and the factors it identifies are ultimately untreatable. As well, sociobiology has been tainted by its socio-political implications; for example, it has been used in studies that have claimed a correlation between low IQ and an individual's presence in the 'underclass' (Herrnstein and Murray, 1994: 520–2). From works such as *The Bell Curve*, the implication has been drawn that African Americans in the United States occupy the lower rungs of the socio-economic ladder because they generally have lower IQs and are not as 'evolved' as other groups. According to these works, this also accounts for the high levels of crime within that group. In the wake of the uproar around this claim, biologists in the United States have basically stopped including minorities in biological studies of criminality (Gibbs, 1995: 106).

Given the assumptions of sociobiological and genetic approaches to crime, certain solutions present themselves. The question is how to distinguish those whose criminality is a product of the social environment from those incorrigibles who are not genetically disposed to learn responsible behaviours that would enable them to enter networks of inclusion. Sociobiology provides prescriptions for those who rationally choose to commit acts of violence. For Ghiglieri, violence as an evolutionary strategy can be overcome in two ways:

> The first process is to teach children, all children, from day one, self-control, self-discipline, and self-responsibility in a world where we ourselves show that offensive violence is wrong. We must make the teaching of fairness, justice, and human values our primary goals. Boys becoming young men must already have been socialized with these deep human values (in a palatable form, more or less as Boy Scouts of America wishes to do) *by their parents*. Second, we must decide to cooperate to make felonious violence – rape, murder, offensive war, genocide, and terrorism – not only 'not pay' for the perpetrator but also reap pain. In short, to stop violence, we must decide that our justice is *lex talionis* justice. (1999: 256)

First, through personal will and socialization, we must learn a sense of responsibility. Second, we must harshly punish violent behaviour to ensure that criminals, as rational actors, decide that the costs outweigh the benefits. Rational violence, Ghiglieri argues, can be controlled by properly training individuals to pursue peaceful means to achieve their personal ends. But what of non-rational violence?

The power of genetic approaches is that they offer the possibility of managing those who cannot learn to adopt civil behaviours. If we can determine the chemical processes involved in producing non-rational violence, we will be able to predetect and pre-empt such violence by removing individuals from social environments that trigger the dysfunction – by treating their condition as a manageable disease, perhaps through drug therapies or even gene therapy. However, despite some claims to the contrary, scientists have not yet clearly demonstrated direct links between genes and behaviours, nor are they close to gene therapies or even drug therapies for genetically motivated violence. For now, this vision of crime control remains part of the genetic imaginary; even so, it has powerful implications for risk management. It fits well with current representations of criminality as predatorial, internal to the individual, and threatening to the moral order of society. Sociobiological explanations correspond with Garland's criminology of the self, in which the individual citizen is seen as responsible for preventing his or her own victimization and in which each person is seen as a potential criminal. Genetic explanations correspond with the criminology of the other, which defines criminals as a limited set of evil predators who cannot be rehabilitated and must be very strictly controlled; if human beings can be reduced to their genes, a person's character cannot change and the person who has shown himself or herself to be a danger will always be a risk.

What would a genetic justice system look like if based on notions of genetically determined violence? There are a number of possibilities. Steven Friedland contends that it would introduce an element of 'propensity determinism' into judicial decisions and in this way change our notions of criminal responsibility (1998: 334). Courts would be involved in determining the extent to which a criminal act was the result of a genetically based drive programmed into the perpetrator. Systems would be developed for classifying genetic predispositions according to degree of aggressiveness or other abnormalities. Predictions of dangerousness and prescribed treatments would become part of the sentencing process, which would also consider mitigating factors and defences. Friedland imagines a number of subsidiary effects:

> The police would create new strategies of investigation based on the genetic propensities of suspects. When pulled over for speeding, an individual could be asked for a driver's license, registration, and genetic propensities card. When a fight at a bar occurred, the investigating officers could run a genetics check on the participants. Discovery of an accused's genetic propensities would be sought in a wide variety of criminal cases and be made available through computer files for fast, nationwide refer-

encing. A cadre of 'dangerousness' experts, ready to testify about their expertise at trial, would develop. This group would offer a different approach to dangerousness than that of the psychologically oriented psychiatrists and psychologists of today. At sentencing, the length of the defendant's sentence might be affected by his or her 'dangerousness quotient.' Rehabilitation would be relegated to an official secondary status and would be oriented toward those individuals whose genes indicated they could be most influenced by environmental factors. Incarceration would be recognized for what it has already become in many settings – merely a means of separating dangerous individuals from the rest of society. Genetic predispositions would also become increasingly important at the parole stage, while the prisoner's conduct in prison would lessen in importance. (1998: 337)

The power of propensity determinism would be its powers of predetection and prediction – the ultimate goals of all risk management technologies. However, this approach would also likely lead to certain problems in the administration of justice. Given the charisma of genetic science and the deference paid to genetic researchers, a tendency might develop to accept overly simplistic answers to complex questions about criminality – something we already see happening in sociobiology. The interactions between the human body and the environment are too complex for deterministic explanations, which tend to remove environment from the equation. In terms of how this applies to justice, the law in its application has never been fully amenable to quantitative analysis. Despite the current public desire for objective answers to questions of facts and guilt, scientific findings cannot always provide the best answers, factually or morally. Public pressures can lead scientists to make premature generalizations, as happened in the XYY chromosome research of the 1960s and 1970s, and as is arguably happening now in the MAO A research based on one family. Also, in terms of predetection, there may be a tendency to treat 'genetic violence' as a foregone conclusion that requires immediate treatment in the form of moral regulation.

A second effect could be a shift in traditional conceptions of criminal responsibility and how criminal law should react to criminals. For centuries, the yardstick for measuring an act in criminal law has been moral blameworthiness. This is what distinguishes criminal law from civil law, which focuses on questions of efficiency and consequences. Criminal law also functions on the principle of due process, which involves predictable and fair procedures for interrogating criminal charges.

Finally, criminal law assumes that the individual is responsible for his or her own conduct. The law defines the individual as possessing free will and as making choices in how to act. External influences on behaviour are only rarely accepted as valid reasons for criminal behaviour. The only such influences the law accepts are a handful of physiological conditions (such as epileptic seizures and reflex responses) and a short list of psychological ones (such as insanity, automatism, and battered woman's syndrome). Generally, actors who are shown to have been in their right mind are held responsible for their conduct. Free will is central to notions of justice. As Durkheim pointed out, free will justifies the punishment of crime and allows the community to engage in rituals of norm reinforcement. Once crime is redefined as a disease, society loses this central basis for social solidarity and may resist the evacuation of the moral content of the law.

One example of the negative public reaction to offenders defined as diseased, innately deviant, and non-rehabilitatable can be found in the problems that arise when pedophiles are released from prison. Bobby Gordon Oatway was released to a Toronto halfway house in 1996 after serving two-thirds of three concurrent ten-year sentences for two counts of buggery and bestiality, three counts of gross indecency, and one count of rape. The community around the halfway house mobilized against his presence there. A city councillor, Dennis Fotinos, led the campaign against Oatway, declaring, 'He should be in jail for the rest of his life. We're saying, "Look, this isn't right." You have to make this right. This man has to be put behind bars where he will no longer be a danger to society. He's living in an area that is literally two blocks away from five schools. It's like saying: "Here's a fire that's raging in this guy. We're just going to add some fuel to it and tempt him a little"' (in Welsh, 1996: A7). Residents protested outside the halfway house every day with placards reading, 'Mommy, mommy, make the bad man go away.' Thousands of photographs of Oatway's face were plastered on walls and windows throughout the neighbourhood.

In the case of Owen Dulmage, a seventy-seven-year-old pedophile released to return home to Ottawa in 1999, the police distributed a letter to residents of the neighbourhood:

> It is difficult to balance the rights of the offender against the rights of the community ... I am in receipt of current assessment reports that caution that Mr. Dulmage remains a high risk to re-offend upon his release ... Our school resource officers will be speaking with officials in the local schools

to apprise them of the situation. Please understand we are not suggesting Mr. Dulmage will re-offend, and I have every confidence and hope he will not attempt any contact with young children ... Any violation of the terms of probation will be dealt with swiftly and with zero tolerance. I would ask that you remain vigilant and not vengeful. (McRae, 1999: 7)

The letter and the immanent release of Dulmage prompted Earl McRae, a local newspaper columnist to state: 'Owen Dulmage, incurable pedophile, should never be released back into the community; they should be locked away until they die in a "treatment centre" for their ilk' (1999: 7).

That sentiment can also be encountered in academic circles. Amitai Etzioni (1999) examined the 'Megan's laws' in many American states, which require that released sex offenders report to local police every time they move somewhere. After analysing conflicting reports on recidivism rates, levels of compliance to Megan's laws, rates for pedophilia and other sexual offences in the United States, and assessments of the likelihood that serial sexual offenders can be rehabilitated, he concluded that the best solution to this social problem would be to create isolated, walled communities for repeat sexual offenders where they would live out their lives away from potential victims and free of the social stigma they face when they re-enter communities.

Both in public discourse and in criminological discourse, there seems to be a sense that pedophiles cannot be rehabilitated, that they have to be permanently isolated in some way. Even Clayton Ruby, a high-profile criminal defence lawyer and advocate for defendants' rights, commenting on the Oatway case, contended that pedophiles should be permanently institutionalized, but within a civil system rather than a criminal one:

It seems to me that if this fellow is a mentally ill pedophile and a danger to the public, then there ought to be a civil commitment. He should be committed under the Mental Health Act. That's what you do when there's a danger to the public. It's not a criminal process, it's a civil process. But the civil hospitals don't want them because it will crowd their wards and they don't have a budget for it. (in Welsh, 1996: A7)

From this perspective, the response is to medicalize the problem and then use the medical system to incarcerate incurable offenders. There appear to be two options currently available: criminal incarceration or medical incarceration. Until a medical therapy is widely available:

such as castration of sexual offenders (which has been resorted to in the past) or the return of the death penalty, the problem of people 'naturally' inclined toward certain deviant behaviours will continue to grow, especially if researchers find genetic links to violence and sexual deviance. But there is more to the issue than that. Public anger is not simply about protecting children from pedophiles. It is also about ensuring that adequate punishment is dealt out. A disease model of crime does not satisfy this requirement; it does not provide moral satisfaction that a person is suffering for his or her crimes. The distinction between a disease model of treating certain offenders and a moral model of criminal punishment could form the basis for a new politicization of justice issues within the genetic justice system.

Once again, all of this resides in the genetic imaginary, the sense that we already live in a society in which we can scientifically attribute behaviours to definite genetic characteristics and in which we have the capacity to intervene in the genetic make-up of individuals. However, for now, the concept of genetic justice refers only to DNA testing and banking. Arguably, these technologies are the first step in the development of a broader genetic justice and carry with them a great weight of expectation with regard to their ability to improve crime management. Currently, however, they do not enable predetection and therefore do not satisfy the ultimate goal of risk management in criminal justice. Nevertheless, DNA testing and banking may have some predictive power, not through a reading of genetic codes, but rather by socially coding an individual as someone with a sample in the NDDB. I contend that one of the primary social effects of DNA banking is that it codes individuals who are risky and who must be monitored in terms of their access to networks of inclusion, especially if they are violent and/or sexually deviant.

What is the future of DNA testing and banking, and of genetic justice, in Canada? Much of the groundwork for the future is already in place. In 2005 the federal Parliament will review the DNA banking legislation in the Criminal Code, and it is likely that the list of designated offences will continue to expand to include more and more non-violent offences. Mass DNA testing will continue as a strategy of crime detection and will become increasingly normal. Court processes will continue to be scientized as DNA evidence becomes a central element in both violent and non-violent cases. Crime itself may become scientized as criminals learn techniques for evading DNA identification.

The search for links between genetic make-up and criminal behaviours will continue, and if scientists discover them, the function of DNA testing and banking will change to some extent. DNA banking will become a wider social process in which individuals are tested and banked at birth. This is already happening to some extent in the United Kingdom where a national 'biobank' has been established. Currently, it is voluntary for new mothers to donate a sample of their babies' genetic material to the biobank, but the government is asking doctors to encourage mothers to do so. In the United States, the former federal Attorney General, Janet Reno, asked a national commission to study the legality of taking DNA samples from everyone arrested, rather than just those convicted of violent offences (Tracy and Morgan, 2000: 668). In Nebraska and West Virginia, police are authorized to store samples at particular universities, with personal identifiers removed. It seems a small step to allow genetic research on these samples, since doing so would not violate prisoners' privacy (Kimmelman, 2000: 212). There is a tendency for the use of DNA data banks to spread, given their strong record for identifying perpetrators. If links are ever clearly established between criminal behaviour and genetics, it will be difficult, within a risk society, to resist requiring all new-born children to contribute samples for testing for genetic propensities toward crime. This would not be a matter of parents' choice, but rather a matter of moral regulation by the state and the public. Communities would not feel safe knowing that potential criminals might be living undetected in their midst. Perhaps something equivalent to Megan's law would develop for those at risk of committing genetically motivated violence.

In some ways this scenario seems far-fetched. Yet the enabling conditions are already present in Canada. Excessive fear of crime, the desire on the part of the public and the state to objectify criminal justice, laws that have supplanted the notion of bodily integrity with an increasing openness of the citizen's body to state sampling, the normalization of this sampling within public and legal discourse, the absence of restrictions on mass DNA testing and the willingness of communities to participate in it, the growing number of calls for expansion of the DNA net, the absence of political debate, the potential for private-sector growth in DNA testing, the charisma of genetic science, the openness of the courts to DNA evidence, the claims of scientists searching for genetic causes of crime, shifts in representations of criminality toward genetic causation, and notions of individual responsibilization in crime management – all of these factors, I argue, are creating the conditions for a genetic justice system. To date, there have been few critiques of DNA testing and banking. Once the novelty of the technology wears off, it will become simply another unremarked part of the background of criminal justice. It is important, however, to map out the processes by which this is happening and the language by which it is being legitimated. DNA testing and banking have moved the criminal justice system toward greater levels of control by the state and away from ideals about individual rights. The state is demonstrating its ability to control crime by enhancing its power over the citizen's body. The long-term implications of this shift must be continuously monitored from the perspective of democratic values.

Notes

1. Introduction: Risk, Biogovernance, and the Genetic Imaginary

1 A good example of recent strategies of population management was the 1999 announcement by the Ontario government that it intended to establish a system of identification cards. In the Speech from the Throne that year, the Ontario government proposed that all residents of the province should carry 'smart cards' which would involve the use of either retina scans or electronic fingerprints to identify the bearer and give him or her access to government services. The Ontario government had previously proposed a similar plan in 1995, based on a Toronto police program to identify welfare recipients by electronically scanning their fingerprints, but it was abandoned due to privacy concerns and the costs involved. Since the 1999 throne speech, this second attempt has also been placed on hold (Mackie, 1999; A1).

2 This is certainly one of the primary tasks of the Canadian Biotechnology Advisory Committee, which has been established as an arm's length body to advise the federal government on biotechnology issues. As well, the Minister of Industry co-ordinates a board of government ministers to oversee the development of policy initiatives relating to biotechnology. The first paragraph of the Canadian Biotechnology Strategy Online website sets out the business priorities of the government's strategy: 'Although wide-spread interest in biotechnology issues is a recent phenomenon, the Government of Canada first identified biotechnology as an important economic sector and a key enabling technology to support economic growth and international competitiveness in the 1970s.'

3 It is interesting to compare two American-based organizations, the Council for Responsible Genetics and the Biotechnology Industry Organization, each of which has published its own 'bill of rights' concerning research and

development in biotechnology. They illustrate the language gap that exists in political discussions about biotechnology. The Council for Responsible Genetics includes the following ten points:

- All people have the right to preservation of the earth's biological and genetic diversity.
- All people have the right to a world in which living organisms cannot be patented, including human beings, animals, plants, microorganisms and all their parts.
- All people have the right to a food supply that has not been genetically altered.
- All indigenous peoples have the right to manage their own biological resources, to preserve their traditional interests.
- All people have the right to protection from toxins, other contaminants, or actions that can harm their genetic makeup and that of their offspring.
- All people have the right to protection against eugenic measures such as forced sterilization or mandatory screening aimed at aborting or manipulating selected embryos or fetuses.
- All people have the right to genetic privacy including the right to prevent the taking and storing of bodily samples for genetic information without their voluntary informed consent.
- All people have the right to be free from genetic discrimination.
- All people have the right to DNA tests to defend themselves in criminal proceedings.
- All people have the right to have been conceived, gestated, and born without genetic manipulation.

These rights can be contrasted to those set out in the Biotechnology Industry Organization's 'Bill of Rights for Bioentrepreneurs':

- Right to intellectual property protection.
- Right to education, employment and training.
- Right to funding for basic research and technology transfer.
- Right to a modern, science-based regulatory system.
- Right to a fair tax structure and long-term incentives.
- Right to legal protection.
- Right to employ qualified international employees.
- Right to fair financial market regulation.
- Right to representation (Feldbaum, 1998: 18).

While the second of these bills is couched in the language of rights, it is clearly about the distribution of financial, regulatory, legal, and property responsibilities and is ultimately about determining who is responsible for the various risks involved in the research and development of biotechnology. The former of the two bills falls squarely within traditional human and animal rights discourse and is about the protection of natural rights and the assurance of just outcomes. On many points, the two statements of rights have diametrically opposed interests.

4 An example of one such encounter occurred in January 2000 as government and industry representatives from around the world met in Montreal to draft a treaty governing genetically modified foods. This biosafety protocol, named the Cartagena Protocol after the location of a previous meeting, allows rejection of food imports if there is evidence that they may be dangerous to human health. Under this treaty, shipments containing GMOs must be clearly labelled. The meeting in Montreal, which lasted a week, was marked by constant protest by anti-GMO activists from around the world. After a week, the *Montreal Gazette* was prompted to remark in a headline: 'The bio-battle of words. Activists won the propaganda war with clever words and images. The serious-looking guys in suits never stood a chance' (Abley, 2000, B1, B4). The article recounts the various strategies utilized by both sides to gain public and media attention. It is clear from the story that there was little contact between the activists and the delegates other than an incident at a press conference when a member of the Quebec-based protest group, Les Entartistes, threw a pie in the face of the conference chairperson.

2. Creating the Conditions of Possibility: Scientific, Social, and Legal Contexts

1 In this case, a witness to a murder identified the perpetrator as an African-American named Will West. Police located a Will West and arrested him. The arrest was supported by the fact that a Will West had served time in Leavenworth Prison and the anthropometric measurements of the suspect matched those recorded for the prisoner. However, the arrested man claimed innocence and asserted that he had never been to prison. Luckily, authorities had fingerprinted the prisoner and found that the suspect's fingerprints did not match. When they located the ex-convict Will West, they found that they had arrested the wrong man. This case came to signify the power of fingerprinting as an identification technique and the pitfalls of relying on anthropometry.

2 The Dominion Police was a national police force in Canada in the late nine-

teenth and early twentieth centuries. In 1920 it amalgamated with Canada's other national police force, the North West Mounted Police, to form the Royal Canadian Mounted Police.

3 Mullis immediately turned his attention to the market potentials of his technology, founding a company that will produce cards and jewellery containing DNA cloned from celebrities, as well as cards containing DNA from various primates as a way of illustrating evolution to school children (Nelkin and Lindee, 49).

4 For example, a police program targeted at the elderly – a population seen by the police as vulnerable to crime – urges risk reduction strategies such as turning the telephone ringer down to the lowest setting because a ringing telephone indicates the occupant is not at home, carrying an empty wallet as well as the regular wallet, and never going out in public without a buddy (see Ericson and Haggerty, ch. 12).

5 In the 1985 report, the Law Reform Commission of Canada recommended that warrants be available for the following procedures:

- Inspection of the body for the purpose of detecting identifying features, which might be concealed from view, in the nature of tattoos, wounds, scars, and so forth.
- Inspection of the body and/or body cavities of the subject, not involving the probing of the body or body cavities of the subject, for the purpose of ascertaining whether the subject is carrying or concealing an 'object of seizure.'
- Forensic physical examination by a qualified medical practitioner.
- The photographing of the subject, not involving the exposure of the subject's private parts.
- The taking of prints or impressions from any exterior part of the subject's body.
- The taking of hair combings, brushings, or clippings from the subject.
- The taking of scrapings or clippings from the subject's fingernails.
- The removal or attempted removal of residues or substances from the external body of the subject by means of washings, swabs, or adhesive materials.
- The taking of saliva samples from the subject for purposes other than the detection of intoxicating substances.
- The search for, removal of, or attempted removal of, 'objects of seizure' concealed within the subject's body cavities, by a qualified medical practitioner.
- The making of dental or bite impressions.
- The seizure of any clothing concealing the subject's private parts.

3. Framing DNA: Negotiating the DNA Warrant and Data Bank System in the Public Sphere

1 Designated offences in *The DNA Identification Act* are now section 487.04 of the *Criminal Code* and include the following:

Primary Offences:
Approaching, entering, etc. a prohibited place
Threats or violence
Harboring or concealing
Piratical acts
Hijacking
Endangering safety of aircraft or airport
Seizing Control of ship or fixed platform
Using explosives
Participation in activity of terrorist group
Facilitating terrorist activity
Commission of offence for terrorist group
Instructing to carry out activity for terrorist group
Harboring or concealing (Terrorism)
Sexual interference
Invitation to sexual touching
Sexual exploitation
Incest
Offence in relation to juvenile prostitution
Infanticide
Murder
Manslaughter
Causing bodily harm with intent
Assault with a weapon or causing bodily harm
Aggravated assault
Unlawfully causing bodily harm
Sexual assault
Sexual assault with a weapon
Aggravated sexual assault
Kidnapping
Hostage taking
Attack on premises, residence or transport of internationally protected person
Attack on premises, accommodation or transport of United Nations or personnel

Explosive or other lethal device
Rape
Sexual intercourse with female under fourteen and between fourteen and
    sixteen
Sexual intercourse with feeble-minded, etc.
Sexual intercourse with step-daughter, etc.

Secondary Offences
Bestiality in the presence of or by child
Child pornography
Parent or guardian procuring sexual activity
Indecent acts
Causing death by criminal negligence
Causing bodily harm by criminal negligence
Dangerous operation causing bodily harm
Dangerous operation causing death
Failure to stop at scene of accident
Impaired driving causing bodily harm
Impaired driving causing death
Assault
Torture
Assaulting a peace officer
Robbery
Breaking and entering with intent
Mischief that causes actual danger to life
Arson – Disregard for human life
Arson – Own property
Arson
Setting fire to other substance

2 It is important to note that *obiter dicta*, even from the Supreme Court of
   Canada, are not binding on subsequent courts.
3 By the time of the appeal, scientists had developed mitochondrial DNA testing, which does not require a root from the hair in order to obtain a DNA
   sample. The trial court's basis for its decision to overturn the hair root provisions of the act no longer existed.
4 It is interesting to examine who was involved in the consultation process. In
   conjunction with the RCMP, the Department of Justice, and Correctional
   Services Canada, the Solicitor General began the consultation process by
   mailing out more than 750 letters and consultation documents and a further

550 upon request (Solicitor General, 1996b). Between 6 February and 17 June, consultation sessions were held in all of the provinces and territories. During the course of the national consultations, 106 organizations were represented, while 67 written submissions, often from the same organizations, were received. Of those who presented briefs at the consultation sessions, 51 (48 per cent) represented police organizations; 21 (20 per cent) represented provincial government agencies, most commonly divisions of provincial Justice departments and Solicitor General offices; 12 (11 per cent) represented provincial and federal correctional services; 6 (6 per cent) represented medical and scientific laboratories, both public and private; 13 (12 per cent) represented privacy and human rights organizations, including provincial and federal privacy commissioners; 2 (2 per cent) represented women's organizations; and 1 (0.9 per cent), the Canadian Bar Association represented a defence lawyer's perspective. Viewed in this way, the overwhelming majority of presentations were from police, justice, and corrections agencies – 84 out of 106 (79 per cent). Those raising critiques of the plan from the perspective of privacy, ethics, and individual rights numbered 16 (15 per cent), with the remainder representing forensic laboratories. Of the written submissions, 69 per cent were from police, justice, and corrections agencies, as well as one victims' rights group (46 out of 67); 24 per cent were from privacy and human rights organizations, including women's organizations, and the Canadian Bar Association (16 out of 67); and the remainder were from medical and scientific laboratories (6 out of 67 or 9 per cent).

5 The methodology for the framing analysis conducted here involved the following steps. The first step was to identify all of the relevant publicly available documents through extensive library and website searches. For policy documents, the Solicitor General's report, *Establishing a National DNA Data Bank: Summary of Consultations* (1996b), provides a listing of the groups involved in the consultation process. Also, a number of secondary sources refer to major government publications in this area. Finally, keyword searches on the Internet led to a number of crucial government and non-government policy-related documents on the issue. For Canadian print media coverage, on-line periodical indexes for the period between 1994, the beginning of the policy process, and 1999, one year after the passage of the DNA data bank provisions, uncovered fifty newspaper articles and two newsmagazine articles on the specific topics of DNA warrants and the DNA data bank.

The second step in the analysis was to develop a protocol of questions with which to approach the texts in order to unpack their power/knowledge implications. How are DNA testing and banking first spoken in the docu-

ments? How are they situated in terms of what has come before? What is the
cast of characters defined as important to the process? What forms of expertise are included/excluded in defining the issues and conducting the
debates? Who are the primary definers in the media coverage? What hap-
penings become cogent for framing the event? What narrative emerges
across the media texts? What central images, metaphors, tropes, and keywords are significant in figuring the technology? How is the process of
adopting the technology resolved, if it has been resolved? Armed with these
general questions, repeated reading of the documents allows one to bring to
the surface the metaphors, characters, contestations, and negotiations that
occur across the texts and to observe how they resolve into conceptual categories. Applying this method, five frames emerge from the policy and media
texts: privacy, surveillance, correcting the flaws of the justice system, the
objectivity of genetic science, and the need for administrative efficiency.
These became the narrative forms that grew out of the policy discussions
and their coverage in the media as governmental decision-makers and journalists negotiated the biogovernmental implications of new genetic identification technologies in Canada.

6 See for example, *In re: West Virginia State Police Crime Lab*, 438 S.E. 2d 501 (W.
  Va. 1993). In this case, Fred Zain, a forensic serologist was convicted of misconduct in over 130 criminal cases.

4. Corrective Justice: Media Events and Public Knowledge of DNA in the Criminal Justice System

1 In this intense media trial, Lyle and Erik Menendez were ultimately convicted of first-degree murder in 1996, for the shooting of their parents.
2 Sergeant Michalowsky was never put on trial because of his poor health.
3 Donald Marshall had also been wrongly convicted of murder a few years
  earlier.
4 The first of these was the case of Wilbert Coffin, a Quebec prospector convicted in 1953 of the murder of three American hunters. He loudly proclaimed his innocence, leading the Cabinet to pose a hypothetical question
  to the Supreme Court: Given that Coffin had been denied leave to appeal to
  the Supreme Court, how would the court have decided if it had heard such
  an appeal? The court responded that it would have had no reason to overturn the conviction. Coffin was hanged in 1956. The second case was that of
  Steven Truscott. In 1959, the fourteen-year-old Truscott was sentenced to
  hang for the murder of a twelve-year-old girl. In 1967, the Supreme Court re-
  examined the trial evidence and new submissions. The trial verdict was not

overturned, but Truscott was paroled two years later. He was later exonerated by DNA evidence.

5. Opening and Closing the Black Box: DNA Typing as a Regime of Practice

1 In 1998, Swissair Flight 111 crashed off the coast of Nova Scotia, killing all 229 passengers and crew.
2 For details see the NDDB website: http://NDDB-BNDG.ORG/ pri_secu_e.htm.
3 For example, the 14 March 2001 NDDB newsletter includes the following 'urgent' message about fingerprints:

> Please remember that index fingerprints must be included on the back of the #3800 collection card.
> While the index fingerprints may appear to be unnecessary paperwork, they are critically important because they are the only verifiable link between the biological sample and the identity of the donor. If, for example, bar codes have been mixed up, or other administrative errors have occurred, the biological sample can still be positively linked to the correct offender through the index fingerprints on the sample collection card. The Halton Regional Police Service suggests turning the collection card upside down will place the fingerprint squares closer to the edge of the table, making it easier to take a clear print. The NDDB does not mind 'upside down' fingerprints. The important thing is to please include them!

4 For example, in Nebraska and West Virginia, offenders' DNA samples are stored in universities, opening the door to research on these samples (Kimmelman, 2000)

6. From Crime Control to Crime Management: DNA and Shifting Notions of Justice

1 See for example Mike Davis (1990) and also Roger Burrows (1997), both of whom argue that contemporary metropolises are characterized by fortress zones requiring authorization to access.
2 Although the Canadian test for determining the admissibility of new scientific evidence is taken from *R. v. Mohan*, Canadian courts often cite the American test. Initially, in the United States, the *Frye* test was the standard, based upon the 1923 decision of *Frye v. United States* where the court held that scientific evidence is admissible if it is generally accepted as valid by the

scientific community. In the 1993 decision in *Daubert v. Merrell Dow Pharmaceuticals*, the United States Supreme Court held that the 1975 enactment of the *Federal Rules of Evidence* overturned the *Frye* test and that judges and juries cannot defer to the scientific community's acceptance of evidence. They are required to make an independent determination of the reliability and probative value of the evidence to determine whether the reasoning or methodology underlying the testimony is scientifically valid. The court set out four factors to consider: (1) whether the theory or techniques can be or have been tested; (2) the extent to which there has been peer review and publication of the theory or techniques; (3) the known or potential error rate and the existence and maintenance of standards controlling the technique's operation; and (4) the general acceptance of the methodology or technique in the scientific community.

Judges, lawyers, and juries are not normally trained to make scientific determinations, and the general consensus among American judges and scholars is that the shift from the *Frye* rule to the *Daubert* rule has made it easier to get scientific evidence admitted to the courtroom. It has also made the whole process more difficult for trial court judges (Rothstein, 1999: 120), which may be the reason for the trend toward admitting complex evidence. Nevertheless, the discourse of the courtroom is becoming increasingly scientized.

3 In Canada, the number of primary designated offences committed each year numbers around 19,000, while the number of secondary offences numbers close to 100,000. Therefore, the National DNA Data Bank estimates that 'as partners in the police and legal communities become more familiar with the legislative requirements, the total number of samples collected annually should rise significantly' (NDDB Annual Report, 2001, 17).

Bibliography

Abley, Mark. 2000. 'The Bio-Battle of Words.' *Montreal Gazette*, 29 January, B1.

Altheide, David. 1992. 'Gonzo Justice.' *Symbolic Interaction* 15(1): 69–86.

– 1996. *Qualitative Media Analysis*. London: Sage.

– 1997. 'The News Media, The Problem Frame, and the Production of Fear.' *Sociological Quarterly* 38(4): 647–68.

Andreas, Peter. 1998. 'The Rise of the American Crimefare State.' *Queen's Quarterly* 105(1): 49–56.

Appleby, Timothy. 1997. 'DNA testing may clear The Fugitive.' *Globe and Mail*, 18 September, A12.

Astroff, Robert. 1996. 'Identity Crisis: The *Charter* and Forensic DNA Analysis in the Criminal Justice System.' *Dalhousie Journal of Legal Studies* 5: 211–35.

Atkins, Eric. 2000. 'Ontario Moving to Strengthen DNA Databank.' *Lawyers Weekly* 20(27).

Bassan, Daniela. 1996. 'Bill C-104: Revolutionizing Criminal Investigations or Infringing on *Charter* Rights?' *University of Toronto Faculty of Law Review* 54: 246–92.

Bauman, Zygmunt. 1987. *Legislators and Interpreters: On Modernity, Post-Modernity, and Intellectuals*. Cambridge: Polity Press.

– 1999. *In Search of Politics*. Stanford: Stanford University Press.

– 2000. 'Social Issues of Law and Order.' *British Journal of Criminology* 40: 205–21.

Beck, Ulrich. 1992. *Risk Society: Towards a New Modernity*. London: Sage.

Benjamin, Cynthia, and Dean Weston. 2000. 'The Gene Machine: Contemplating the Impact of DNA Technology on Criminal Justice and Society.' In J. Roberts (ed.), *Criminal Justice in Canada: A Reader*, 57–68. Toronto: Harcourt Brace.

Bindman, Stephen. 1997. 'DNA testing program to battle bum raps.' *Montreal Gazette*, 21 July, A1, A2.

Bourdieu, Pierre. 1987. 'What Makes a Social Class? On the Theoretical and Practical Existence of Groups.' *Berkeley Journal of Sociology* 32: 1–18.

Bourdieu, Pierre, and L.J.D. Wacquant. 1992. *An Invitation to Reflexive Sociology.* Cambridge: Polity Press.

Bovard, James. 2000. 'Rise of the Surveillance State.' *American Spectator* 33(4): 68–9.

Brodsky, G. Greg. 1993. 'DNA: The Technology of the Future Is Here.' *Criminal Law Quarterly* 36: 10–39.

Brummett, Barry. 1990. 'Mediating the Laws: Popular Trials and the Mass Media.' In Robert Hariman, ed., *Popular Trials: Rhetoric, Mass Media, and the Law*, 179–193. Tuscaloosa: University of Alabama Press.

Burrows, Roger. 1997. 'Virtual Culture, Urban Social Polarisation and Social Science Fiction.' In Brian Loader, ed., *The Governance of Cyberspace*, 38–45. New York: Routledge.

Byk, Christian. 1999. 'Law and the Cultural Construction of Nature: Biotechnology and the European Legal Framework.' In Patrick O'Mahony, ed., *Nature, Risk and Responsibility: Discourses of Biotechnology*, 147–64. New York: Routledge.

Canada NewsWire. 2001. 'Time running out for federal government to close loopholes in DNA data bank.' 8 September. www.newswire.ca/.

Canadian Bar Association. 1996. *DNA Data Banking.* Ottawa: National Criminal Justice Section, Canadian Bar Association.

Canadian Centre for Justice Statistics. 1999. *The Juristat Reader.* Toronto: Thompson Educational Publishing.

Canadian Police Association. 1998a. *Brief to the Standing Committee on Legal and Constitutional Affairs Regarding Bill C-3.* Ottawa: Canadian Police Association.

– 1998b. *Media Release: CPA Denounces Liberal Decision to Proceed on Flawed DNA Data Bank Bill.* Ottawa: Canadian Police Association.

Canadian Press. 1995. 'DNA results cast doubt on murder count.' *Montreal Gazette*, 21 January, A10.

– 1996. 'Soaring demand prompts expansion of Canada's Biggest DNA lab (Centre for Forensic Sciences in Ontario).' *Canadian Press Newswire*, 13 May.

– 1997a. 'National data bank would store DNA.' *Montreal Gazette*, 2 October, A18.

– 1997b. 'Cold trail in murder mystery.' *Montreal Gazette*, 21 December, A5.

– 1998. 'Jessops have hope: new DNA databank could catch killer: Christine's mother.' *Montreal Gazette*, 11 April, A14.

– 2001. 'Ontario DNA Crime Bank Leads Country.' *Toronto Sun*, 14 May.

Carcknel, David. 2000. 'Police get new Powers to take DNA samples.' *National Post*, 11 December, A9.

Carlson, Daryl-Lynn. 2001. 'Testing on Trial.' *Canadian Lawyer*, February, 37–41.

Castel, Robert. 1991. 'From Dangerousness to Risk.' In G. Burchell, C. Gordon, and P. Miller, eds., *The Foucault Effect: Studies in Governmentality*, 281–98. Chicago: University of Chicago Press.

Chermak, Steven. 1998. 'Police, Courts, and Corrections in the Media.' In F. Bailey and D. Hale, eds., *Popular Culture, Crime, and Justice*, 87–99. Belmont, CA: West/Wadsworth.

Chiricos, Ted, Sarah Eschholz, and Marc Gertz. 1997. 'Crime, News and Fear of Crime: Toward an Identification of Audience Effects.' *Social Problems* 44(3): 342–57.

Chisholm, Patricia, and Sharon Doyle Driedger. 1995. 'Righting a wrong: After ten years and two trials, a murder conviction is overturned by new DNA evidence.' *Maclean's*, 6 February, 60–1.

Christie, Nils. 1994. *Crime Control as Industry: Towards Gulags, Western Style*. London: Routledge.

CNN.com. 2001. 'Demand for DNA testing creating national backlog.' 30 August, www.cnn.com/2001/LAW/o8/29/dna.backlog/index.html.

Cohen, Lynne. 2001. 'Criminal Law and Forensic Services.' *Canadian Lawyer*, May, 46–51.

Cohn, Marjorie, and David Dow. 1998. *Cameras in the Courtroom: Television and the Pursuit of Justice*. Jefferson, NC: McFarland and Company.

Cole, Simon. 1998. 'Witnessing Identification: Latent Fingerprinting Evidence and Expert Knowledge.' *Social Studies of Science* 28(5/6): 687–712.

Council for Responsible Genetics. 2000. *The Genetic Bill of Rights*. www.gene-watch.org/bill_of_rights_text.html.

Cox, Wendy. 1995. 'Modern science gave Morin his freedom.' *Winnipeg Free Press*, 24 January, A3.

– 1998. 'Commons panel eyes DNA bank legislation.' *Halifax Chronicle Herald*, 4 February, A16.

Coyle, Jim. 1995. 'A bizarre case for our criminal justice system.' *Vancouver Sun*, 17 January, A13.

Crimtac. 2001. *DNA Databases – The International Experience*. www.crimtac.gov.au/dnainternational.htm.

Daemmrich, Arthur. 1998. 'The Evidence Does Not Speak for Itself: Expert Witnesses and the Organization of DNA-Typing Companies.' *Social Studies of Science* 28(5/6): 741–72.

Dahlgren, Peter. 1992. 'Introduction.' In P. Dahlgren and C. Sparks, eds., *Journalism as Popular Culture*, 1–23. London: Sage.

Daisley, Brad. 1993. 'DNA evidence – It makes headlines in criminal trials, but lawyers use it in custody and immigration cases, too.' *Lawyers Weekly*. 12(40). www.lexis.com/research/retrieve?_m=fa26f288039c0aa0d61e8d0e6187 bbd5&docnum=24

Daubney, David. 1988. *Taking Responsibility: Report of the Standing Committee on Justice and Solicitor General on Its Review of Sentencing, Conditional Release and Related Aspects of Corrections*. Ottawa: Queen's Printer.

Davis, Mike. 1990. *City of Quartz*. London: Verso.

Deleuze, Gilles. 1992. 'Postscript on the Societies of Control.' *October* 59: 3–7.

Department of Justice (Canada). 1994. *Obtaining and Banking DNA Forensic Evidence*. Ottawa: Department of Justice.

– 1998. *Fact Sheet: DNA Sampling*. Ottawa: Department of Justice.

– 2002. *DNA Data Bank Legislation: Consultation Paper*. Ottawa: Department of Justice.

Department of Justice (United States). 2002. *Prison and Jail Inmates at Midyear 2001*. Washington: Bureau of Justice Statistics.

Derksen, Linda. 2000. 'Towards a Sociology of Measurement: The Meaning of Measurement Error in the Case of DNA Profiling.' *Social Studies of Science* 30(6): 803–45.

Drucker, J. Susan, and Janice Platt Hunold. 1990. 'The Claus von Bülow Retrial: Lights, Camera, Genre?' In Robert Hariman, ed., *Popular Trials: Rhetoric, Mass Media, and the Law*, 133–47. Tuscaloosa: University of Alabama Press.

Dunn, Mark. 1995. 'Innocent for 10 years: DNA testing proves man didn't kill girl.' *Winnipeg Free Press*, 24 January, A3.

Durkheim, Émile. 1964. *The Division of Labor in Society*. New York: Free Press (originally published 1893).

Edelman, Murray. 1993. 'Contestable Categories and Public Opinion.' *Political Communication* 10: 231–42.

Einsiedel, Edna. 1997. *Biotechnology and the Canadian Public: Report on a 1997 National Survey and Some International Comparisons*. Calgary: University of Calgary.

Entman, Robert. 1993. 'Framing: Toward Classification of a Fractured Paradigm.' *Journal of Communication* 43: 51–8.

Ericson, R., P. Baranek, and J. Chan. 1989. *Negotiating Control: A Study of News Sources*. Toronto: University of Toronto Press.

Ericson, Richard, and Kevin Haggerty. 1997. *Policing the Risk Society*. Toronto: University of Toronto Press.

Etzioni, Amitai. 1999. *The Limits of Privacy*. New York: Basic Books.

Fauteux, Gerald. 1956. *Report of a Committee Appointed to Inquire into the Principles and Procedures Followed in the Remission Service of the Department of Justice of Canada*. Ottawa: Queen's Printer.

Federico, Ricardo. 1990. 'The Genetic Witness: DNA Evidence and Canada's Criminal Law.' *Criminal Law Quarterly* 32: 204–28.

Feldbaum, Carl. 1998. 'A Bill of Rights for Bioentrepreneurs.' *Nature Biotechnology* 16, supplement, 18.

Fennell, Tom. 1997. '"I'm sorry, Paul."' *Maclean's*, 1 July, 20–1.

Fishbein, Diana. 1990. 'Biological Perspectives in Criminology.' *Criminology* 28: 41–72.

Fishman, Mark. 1980. *Manufacturing the News*. Austin: University of Texas Press.

Foucault, Michel. 1979. *Discipline and Punish*. New York: Vintage.

Fraser, Nancy, and Linda Gordon. 1992. 'Contract versus Charity: Why Is There No Social Citizenship in the United States?' *Socialist Review* 22(3): 45–67.

Friedland, S. 1998. 'The Criminal Law Implications of the Human Genome Project: Reimagining a Genetically Oriented Criminal Justice System.' *Kentucky Law Journal* 86: 303–66.

Gamson, William. 1989. 'News as Framing.' *American Behavioral Scientist* 35: 157–61.

Garland, David. 1996. 'The Limits of the Sovereign State: Strategies of Crime Control in Contemporary Society.' *British Journal of Criminology* 36(4): 445–71.

General Social Survey, 1999. 'Cycle 13: Victimization.' Ottawa: Statistics Canada.

Gerbner, George, Larry Gross, Michael Morgan, and Nancy Signorielli. 1980. 'The Mainstreaming of America: Violence Profile no. 11.' *Journal of Communication* 30: 10–29.

Ghighlieri, Michael. 1999. *The Dark Side of Man: Tracing the Origins of Male Violence*. Reading, MA: Perseus Books.

Gibbs, W. Wayt. 1995. 'Seeking the Criminal Element.' *Scientific American*, March, 9, 10, 102–9.

Giddens, Anthony. 1985. *A Contemporary Critique of Historical Materialism*, Volume 2, *The Nation-State and Violence*. Berkeley: University of California Press.

– 1990. *The Consequences of Modernity*. Cambridge: Polity Press.

– 1991. *Modernity and Self-Identity: Self and Society in the Late Modern Age*. Cambridge: Polity Press.

Gitlin, Todd. 1980. *The Whole World Is Watching: Mass Media in the Making and Unmaking of the New Left*. Berkeley: University of California Press.

Goldfarb, Ronald. 1998. *TV or Not TV: Television, Justice and the Courts*. New York: New York University Press.

Gordon, Colin. 1991. 'Governmental Rationality: An Introduction.' In G. Burchell, C. Gordon, and P. Miller, eds., *The Foucault Effect: Studies in Governmentality*, 1–51. Chicago: University of Chicago Press.

Graber, Doris. 1980. *Crime News and the Public*. New York: Praeger.

Grange, Michael. 1997. 'Police back plan to use DNA bank in crime fight.' *Globe and Mail*, 20 January, A1, A6.

Gray, Jeff. 2001. 'Rock unveils anti-cloning bill.' *Globe and Mail*, 4 May, www.theglobeandmail.com.

Habermas, Jürgen. 1971. *Toward a Rational Society*. London: Heinemann.

– 1989. *The Structural Transformation of the Public Sphere*, trans. T. Burger and F. Lawrence. Cambridge, MA: MIT Press.

– 1998. *Between Facts and Norms: Contributions to a Discourse Theory of Law and Democracy*, trans. William Rehg. Cambridge, MA: MIT Press.

Hall, Neal. 1994. 'Rapist linked to Milgaard case walks free today.' *Vancouver Sun*, 26 May, A3.

Hallin, Daniel. 1985. 'The American News Media: A Critical Theory Perspective.' In J. Forrester, ed., *Critical Theory and Public Life*, 121–46. Cambridge, MA: Harvard University Press.

Harmon, Rockne. 1993. 'Legal Criticisms of DNA Typing: Where's the Beef?' *Journal of Criminal Law and Criminology* 84(1): 175–88.

Herman, E.S., and N. Chomsky. 1988. *Manufacturing Consent*. New York: Pantheon.

Herrnstein, Richard, and Charles Murray. 1994. *The Bell Curve: Intelligence and Class Structure in American Society*. New York: Free Press.

Hobsbawm, Eric. 1994. *The Short Twentieth Century 1914–1991*. London. Abacus.

Holmgren, Janne, and John Winterdyk. 2001. 'DNA Evidence: Balancing the Scales of Justice.' *LawNow*, October/November, 11–13.

Hubbard, Ruth, and Elijah Wald. 1993. *Exploding the Gene Myth*. Boston: Beacon Press.

Industry Canada. 1998. *Canadian Biotechnology Strategy: An Ongoing Renewal Process*. Ottawa: Government of Canada.

Jang, Brent. 1994. 'Report clears Saskatchewan's handling of Milgaard; Probe found no evidence to back convicted killer's claims to innocence.' *Montreal Gazette*, 17 August, A12.

Jasanoff, Sheila. 1998. 'The Eye of Everyman: Witnessing DNA in the Simpson Trial.' *Social Studies of Science* 28(5/6): 713–40.

Jenish, D'Arcy. 1997. 'How did it happen? Truth remains elusive at the Morin inquiry.' *Maclean's*, 10 March, 19.

Joseph, Ann, and Alison Winter. 1996. 'Making the Match: Human Traces, Forensic Experts and the Public Imagination.' In Francis Spufford and Jenny Uglow, eds., *Cultural Babbage: Technology, Time and Invention*, 93–214. London: Faber and Faber.

Kaplan, Jonathan M. 2000. *The Limits and Lies of Human Genetic Research: Dangers for Social Policy*. New York: Routledge.

Karp, Carl, and Cecil Rosner. 1991a. 'The Milgaard story: A body in the snow, a life in penitentiary.' *Vancouver Sun*, 12 December, A4.

– 1991b. *When Justice Fails: The David Milgaard Story*. Toronto: McClelland and Stewart.

Kay, Jonathan. 1999. 'Big Brother can't resist watching.' *National Post*, 4 October. www.nationalpost.com.

Kaye, David. 1993. 'DNA Evidence: Probability, Population Genetics, and the Courts.' *Harvard Journal of Law and Technology* 101(7): 101–71.

Kerr, Joanna. 2000. 'Building the Future of DNA Technology: RCMP's DNA Data Bank Sets a World Standard.' *RCMP Gazette* 62(5/6): 21–4.

Kevles, Daniel. 1997. *In the Name of Eugenics: Genetics and the Uses of Human Heredity*. Cambridge, MA: Harvard University Press.

Kimmelman, Jonathan. 2000. 'Risking Ethical Insolvency: A Survey of Trends in Criminal Databanking.' *Journal of Law, Medicine and Ethics* 28: 209–21.

Kirkey, Sharon. 2000. 'Suicidal thoughts linked to faulty gene: Study could lead to blood test to find mutation.' *Ottawa Citizen*, 29 January, A17.

Kite, Melissa, and Richard Ford. 2000. 'Blair orders DNA register of criminals.' *Times* (London). 1 September. www.the-times.co.uk/news/pages/tim/2000/09/01/timnwsnws01037.html.

Kubanek, Julia. and Fiona Miller. 1997. *DNA Evidence and a National DNA Databank: Not in Our Name*. Vancouver: Vancouver Rape Relief and Women's Shelter.

Kuhn, Thomas. 1964. *The Structure of Scientific Revolutions*. Chicago: University of Chicago Press.

Laframboise, Donna. 1992. 'Scales of justice out of balance.' *Toronto Star*, 30 November, A25.

– 1995. 'When justice is blind, so is science.' *Toronto Star*, 30 January, A17.

Lander, Eric. 1993. 'DNA Fingerprinting: Science, Law, and the Ultimate Identifier.' In D. Kevles and L. Hood, eds., *The Code of Codes: Scientific and Social Issues in the Human Genome Project*, 191–210. Cambridge, MA: Harvard University Press.

Law Reform Commission of Canada. 1984. *Investigative Tests* (Working Paper 34). Ottawa: Supply and Services Canada.

– 1985. *Obtaining Forensic Evidence*. Report 25. Ottawa: Supply and Services Canada.

– 1991. *Recodifying Criminal Procedure*. Report 33. Ottawa: Supply and Services Canada.

Lawyers Weekly. 26 February 1993, 12(40). www.lexis.com/research/retrieve?_m=fa26f288039c0aa0d61e8d0e6187bbd5&docnum=19

Leonard, Jack. 2001. 'Using DNA to trawl for killers.' *Los Angeles Times*, 10 March, A1.

Levy, Harlan. 1996. *And the Blood Cried Out: A Prosecutor's Spellbinding Account of the Power of DNA*. New York: Basic Books.

Levy, Harold. 1994. 'DNA tests still not hard evidence in court.' *Toronto Star*, 14 October, A21.

– 1995. 'How can Morin still be on suspect list? Police reluctance to exclude Guy Paul Morin raises new questions about justice and fairness.' *Toronto Star*, 10 February, A17.

Lewis, C.S. 1947. *The Abolition of Man: Or, Reflections on Education with Special Reference to the Teaching of English in the Upper Forms of School*. New York: Macmillan.

Lewontin, R.C. 1995. *Biology as Ideology: The Doctrine of DNA*. Concord, ON: Anansi.

Loew, Franklin. 1991. 'Animal Agriculture.' In B. Davis, ed., *The Genetic Revolution: Scientific Prospects and Public Perceptions*, 118–31. Baltimore: Johns Hopkins University Press.

Lupton, Deborah, and John Tulloch. 1999. 'Theorizing Fear of Crime: Beyond the Rational/Irrational Opposition.' *British Journal of Sociology* 50(3): 507–23.

Lussier, Marie. 1992. 'Tailoring the Rules of Admissibility: Genes and Canadian Criminal Law.' *Canadian Bar Review* 71: 319–56.

Lyon, David. 1994. *The Electronic Eye: The Rise of Surveillance Society*. Minneapolis: University of Minnesota Press.

Mackie, Richard. 1999. 'Ontario's ID plan spurs privacy fears.' *Globe and Mail*, 22 October, A1.

Maienschein, Jane, James Collins, and Daniel Strouse. 1998. 'Biology and Law: Challenges of Adjudicating Competing Claims in a Democracy.' *Jurimetrics* 38 (Winter): 151–81.

Makin, Kirk. 1997a. 'Lawyer at Morin inquiry takes apart "garbage evidence."' *Globe and Mail*, 19 July, A1.

– 1997b. 'System does fail, wrongly jailed stress.' *Globe and Mail*, 17 December, A12.

– 1998. *Redrum the Innocent*. Toronto: Penguin.

Mandel, Michael. 1995. 'The Great Repression: Criminal Punishment in the Nineteen-Eighties.' In N. Larsen, ed., *The Canadian Criminal Justice System*, 241–93. Toronto: Canadian Scholar's Press.

Marx, Gary. 1988. *Undercover: Police Surveillance in America*. Berkeley: University of California Press.

May, Kathryn. 1999. 'Majority immune to biotech health scare: Willing to take risks.' *National Post*, 24 July. www.nationalpost.com.

Mazlish, Bruce. 1993. *The Fourth Discontinuity: The Co-Evolution of Humans and Machines*. New Haven: Yale University Press.

McArthur, Keith. 1997. 'DNA data-bank bill to be retabled.' *Globe and Mail*, 12 September. www.globeandmail.ca.

McIlroy, Anne. 2000. 'Canadians wary of genetically altered food.' *Globe and Mail*, 23 January, A2.

McRae, Earl. 1999. 'What the hell kind of justice is this?' *Ottawa Sun*, 10 November, 7.

Melossi, Dario. 2000. 'Changing Representations of the Criminal.' *British Journal of Criminology* 40: 296–320.

Morris, J. 1997. 'Central DNA data bank's effectiveness questioned' *Halifax Chronicle Herald*, 10 April, A10.

National Commission on the Future of DNA Evidence (United States). 1999. *What Every Law Enforcement Officer Should Know about DNA Evidence*. National Institute of Justice, United States Department of Justice. www.ncjrs.org/nij/DNAbro/id.html.

National Council of Welfare (Canada). 2000. *Justice and the Poor*. www.ncwcn-bes.net/htmdocument/reportJustice&Poor/reportjusticepoor/repjustice-poor.htm.

National DNA Data Bank of Canada. 2001a. *Newsletter: March 14th, 2001*. http://NDDB-BNDG.ORG/updates/n_5_e.htm.

– 2001b. *Annual Report 2000/2001*. Ottawa: Royal Canadian Mounted Police.

– 2002a. *Statistics: May 14, 2002*. http://NDDB-BNDG.ORG/stats_e.htm.

– 2002b. *Annual Report 2001/2002*. Ottawa: Royal Canadian Mounted Police.

– 2003. *Statistics: January 13, 2003*. www.nddb-bndg.org/stats_e.htm.

Nelkin, Dorothy. 1993. 'The Social Power of Genetic Information.' In D. Kevles and L. Hood, eds., *The Code of Codes: Scientific and Social Issues in the Human Genome Project*, 177–90. Cambridge, MA: Harvard University Press.

Nelkin, Dorothy, and M. Susan Lindee. 1995. *The DNA Mystique: The Gene as a Cultural Icon*. New York: W.H. Freeman.

Nelkin, Dorothy, and L. Tancredi. 1994. *Dangerous Diagnostics: The Social Power of Biological Information*. Chicago: University of Chicago Press.

Neufeld, Peter. 1990. 'DNA evidence may be used in Legere trial.' *Fredericton Telegraph Journal*, 11 August, 3.

– 1993. 'Have You No Sense of Decency?' *Journal of Criminal Law and Criminology* 84(1): 189–202.

New Hampshire Police Standards and Training Council. 2000. 'Articulable Suspicion (Electronic Edition).' October 2000. www.justiceworks.unh.edu/ Email/Justiceworks/News/oct2000.pdf)

Nichols, Mark. 1995. 'DNA on Trial: Genetic tests are a powerful tool in deciding guilt or innocence.' *Maclean's*, 6 February, 56–7.

Novas, Carlos, and Nikolas Rose. 2000. 'Genetic Risk and the Birth of the Somatic Individual.' *Economy and Society* 29(4): 485–513.

O'Malley, Pat. 1992 'Risk, Power and Crime Prevention.' *Economy and Society* 21(3): 252–75.

– 1996. 'Risk and Responsibility.' In A. Barry, T. Osborne, and N. Rose, eds., *Foucault and Political Reason*, 189–208. London: UCL Press.

Osborne, Richard. 1995. 'Crime and the Media: From Media Studies to Postmodernism.' In D. Kidd-Hewitt and R. Osborne, eds., *Crime and the Media: The Post-modern Spectacle*, 25–48. London: Pluto Press.

Overstall, Richard. 1999. 'Mystical Infallibility: Using Probability Theorems to Sift DNA Evidence.' *Appeal Review of Current Law and Law Reform* 5: 28–37.

Papoff, Lawrence. 1996. 'DNA evidence can be devastating to defence.' *Lawyers Weekly*, 1 November, www.lexis.com/research/retrieve?_m=fa26 f288039c0aa0d61e8d0e6187bbd5&docnum+12

Plischke, Helen. 1995a. 'Mounties check DNA to hunt mystery rapist.' *Edmonton Journal*, 12 May, A1.

– 1995b. 'The blooding of a prairie town.' *Ottawa Citizen*, 13 May, A3.

– 1996a. 'Process of elimination: Mass DNA testing in hunt for rapist.' *Edmonton Journal*, 14 June, A1.

– 1996b. 'Vermilion rapist nocturnal, loner, RCMP tells 200.' *Edmonton Journal*, 19 June, A6.

Pomerance, Renee. 1995. 'Body of Evidence: Section 487.01 of the *Code*, Bodily Integrity, and Searches of the Person.' *Journal of Motor Vehicle Law* 7: 143–77.

Poster, Mark. 1996. 'Databases as Discourse: or, Electronic Interpellations.' In David Lyon and Elia Zureik, eds., *Computers, Surveillance, and Privacy*, 175–92. Minneapolis: University of Minnesota Press.

Priegert, Portia. (1994) 'Banking convicts' DNA studied.' *Winnipeg Free Press*, 21 September, A5.

Privacy Commissioner of Canada. 1992. *Genetic Testing and Privacy*. Ottawa: Privacy Commission of Canada.

– 1995. *Response of the Privacy Commissioner of Canada to Department of Justice Consultation Paper, Obtaining and Banking DNA Forensic Evidence*. Ottawa: Privacy Commission of Canada.

– 1997. *Annual Report*. Ottawa: Canada Communications Group.

– 1998. *Remarks to the Standing Committee on Justice and Human Rights Concern-*

ing Bill C-3, the DNA Identification Act. Ottawa: Privacy Commission of Canada.

Propp, Vladimir. 1968. *Morphology of a Folktale*. Austin: University of Texas Press.

Rabinow, Paul 1992. 'Artificiality and Enlightenment: From Sociobiology to Biosociology.' In J. Crary and S. Kwinter, eds., *Incorporations*, 234–52. New York: Zone.

Raine, Adrian. 1993. *The Psychopathology of Crime*. San Diego, CA: Academic Press.

Rapp, Rayna. 1999. *Testing Women, Testing the Fetus: The Social Impact of Amniocentesis in America*. New York: Routledge.

Recer, Paul. 1997. 'FBI on DNA: Better than fingerprints.' *Halifax Chronicle Herald*, 27 December, C6.

Regalado, Antonio. 2000. 'The Great Gene Grab.' *Technology Review* 103(5): 48–55.

Rose, Nikolas. 1993. 'Government, Authority and Expertise in Advanced Liberalism.' *Economy and Society* 22(3): 283–99.

– 2000. 'Government and Control.' *British Journal of Criminology* 40: 321–39.

Rothstein, Mark. 1999. 'The Impact of Behavioural Genetics on the Law and the Courts.' *Judicature* 83(3): 116–23.

Sacco, V. 1982. 'The Effects of Mass Media on Perceptions of Crime.' *Pacific Sociological Review* 25: 475–93.

Sanders, Clinton, and Eleanor Lyon. 1995. 'Repetitive Retribution: Media Images and the Cultural Construction of Criminal Justice.' In J. Ferrell and C. Sanders, eds., *Cultural Criminology*, 25–44. Boston: Northeastern University Press.

Schichor, David. 1997. 'Three Strikes as a Public Policy: The Convergence of the New Penology and the McDonaldization of Punishment.' *Crime and Delinquency* 43(4): 470–92.

Schlesinger, Hank. 1999. 'Your Body Is Your ID.' *Popular Science*. January, 56–9.

Schmitz, Cristin. 1995. 'DNA warrants give police sweeping new powers." *Lawyers Weekly*, 21 July. www.lexis.com/research/retrieve?_m=fa26f288039 c0aa0d61e8d0e6187bbd5&docnum=77).

– 1998. 'Should vandals give DNA samples?' *Lawyers Weekly*, 20 March.

Schneider, Howard. 1997. 'Conviction of innocent man spurs questions about double jeopardy in Canada.' *Washington Post*, 22 June, A24.

Schudson, Michael. 1982. ' The Politics of Narrative Form: The Emergence of News Conventions in Print and Television.' *Daedalus* 111: 97–113.

– 1989. 'The Sociology of News Production.' *Media, Culture and Society* 11: 263–282.

Sherman, Rorie. 1993. 'DNA Unraveling.' *National Law Journal*, 1 February, 1.

Shragge, Eric (ed.). 1997. *Workfare: Ideology for a New Underclass*. Toronto: Garamond Press.

Sinha, Gunjan. 1999. 'DNA Detectives.' *Popular Science*, August, 48–52.

Solicitor General of Canada. 1996a. *Establishing a National DNA Data Bank: Consultation Document*. Ottawa: Solicitor General.

– 1996b. *Establishing a National DNA Data Bank: Summary of Consultations*. Ottawa: Solicitor General.

– 1998a. *Basic Facts about Corrections in Canada*. Ottawa: Correctional Service Canada.

– 1998b. *Speaking Notes for the Hon. Andy Scott, M.P., Solicitor General of Canada, to the Standing Committee on Justice and Human Rights, Bill C-3, National DNA Data Bank*. Ottawa: Solicitor General.

– 1998c. *Speaking Notes for the Honourable Andy Scott, M.P., Solicitor General of Canada, to the Senate Committee on Legal and Constitutional Affairs, Bill C-3, DNA Data Bank*. Ottawa: Solicitor General.

Sparks, Richard. 1992. *Television and the Drama of Crime: Moral Tales and the Place of Crime in Public Life*. Buckingham: Open University Press.

Statistics Canada. 2001. *General Social Survey, Cycle 13: Victimization*. Ottawa: Statistics Canada.

Strauss, Stephen. 1998. 'Legal spin on DNA sways jury, studies say.' *Globe and Mail*, 17 February, A9.

Strydom, Piet. 1999. 'The Civilization of the Gene: Biotechnological Risk Framed in the Responsibility Discourse.' In Patrick O'Mahony, ed., *Nature, Risk and Responsibility: Discourses of Biotechnology*, 21–36. New York: Routledge. 36.

Surette, Ray. 1990. 'Media Trials and Echo Effects.' In Ray Surette, ed., *The Media and Criminal Justice Policy: Recent Research and Social Effects*, 177–82. Springfield, IL: Charles C. Thomas.

– 1996. 'News from Nowhere, Policy to Follow: Media and the Social Construction of Three Strikes and You're Out.' In David Shichor and Dale Sechrest, eds., *Three Strikes and You're Out: Vengeance as Public Policy*. Thousand Oaks, CA: Sage.

Thanh Ha, Tu. 1995. 'DNA-testing bill passed.' *Globe and Mail*, 23 June, A1, A7.

Thompson, William. 1997. 'A Sociological Perspective on the Science of Forensic DNA Testing.' *University of California, Davis Law Review* 30(4): 1113–36.

Thornhill, Randy and Craig Palmer. 2000. *A Natural History of Rape: Biological Bases of Sexual Coercion*. Cambridge, MA: MIT Press.

Tracy, Paul, and Vincent Morgan. 2000. 'Big Brother and His Science Kit: DNA Databases for 21st Century Crime Control.' *Journal of Criminal Law and Criminology* 90(2): 634–90.

Tuchman, Gaye. 1978. *Making News: A Study in the Construction of Reality.* New York: Free Press.

Turney, Jon. 1998. *Frankenstein's Footsteps: Science, Genetics and Popular Culture.* New Haven: Yale University Press.

Tyler, Tracey. 1997. 'DNA clears Milgaard.' *Toronto Star,* 19 July, A17.

– 1998a. 'Blinded by science: How forensic evidence put Guy Paul Morin behind bars for a murder he didn't commit.' *Toronto Star,* 29 March, F1.

– 1998b. 'The expert who just forgot.' *Toronto Star,* 29 March, F4.

– 1998c. 'DNA testing unusual tool.' *Toronto Star,* 19 October.

Valkenburg, Patti, and Marguerite Patiwael. 1998. 'Does Watching Court TV Cultivate People's Perceptions of Crime?' *Gazette* 60(3): 227–38.

Van Dijck, José. 1998. *Imagenation: Popular Images of Genetics.* New York: New York University Press.

Victims of Violence (n.d.). *DNA Search Warrants.* www.victimsofviolence.on. ca/dna.htm.

Vienneau, David. 1997. 'Supreme Court justice invited rapist to confess to Gail Miller slaying.' *Toronto Star,* 19 July, A17.

Walklate, Sandra. 1998. 'Excavating the Fear of Crime: Fear, Anxiety or Trust?' *Theoretical Criminology* 2(4): 403–17.

Welsh, Moira. 1996. 'Where should pedophiles live? No easy answer for dealing with child molesters once they're free.' *Toronto Star,* 1 April, A7.

Williamson, Larry. 1990. 'The Saga of Roger Hedgecock: A Case Study in Trial by Local Media.' In Robert Hariman, ed., *Popular Trials: Rhetoric, Mass Media, and the Law,* 148–63. Tuscaloosa: University of Alabama Press.

Wilson, E.O. 1978. *On Human Nature.* Cambridge, MA: Harvard University Press.

Wilson, Jim. 2002. 'Criminal Genes.' *Popular Mechanics* 179(11): 46, 48.

Wright Mercer, Sheryl. 1995. 'From Loops and Whorls to The Double Helix: A Century of Fingerprinting.' *Canadian Lawyer,* May, 24–7.

Yourk, D. 2002. 'Fantino calls for greater DNA sampling: Police chief wants Ottawa to expand list of selected crimes and relax collection laws.' *Globe and Mail,* 8 May, A22.

Zuboff, Shoshana. 1988. *In the Age of the Smart Machine: The Future of Work and Power.* New York: Basic Books.

Cases Cited

Cloutier v. Langlois (1990) 1 S.C.R. 158 (S.C.C.).

Daubert v. Merrell Dow Pharmaceuticals (1993) 113 S. Ct. 2786 (U.S.).

F(S) v. Canada (Attorney General) (1998) 11 C.R. (5th) 232 (O.C.J. – Gen. Div.).

Fleming v. Reid (1991) 4 O.R. (3d) 74 (O.C.A.).

Frye v. United States (1923) 293 F. 1013 (D.C. Cir.).

Hunter v. Southam (1984) 2 S.C.R. 145 (S.C.C.).

In re West Virginia State Police Crime Lab (1993) 438 S.E. 2d 501 (W. Va.).

Laporte v. Laganière (1972) 8 C.C.C. (2d) 343 (Que. Q.B.).

Marcoux and Solomon v. R. (1975) 24 C.C.C. (2d) 1 (S.C.C.).

New York v. Castro (1989) 545 N.Y.S. 2d 985 (Sup. Ct.).

R. v. Anderson (2001) O.J. No. 1346 (O.C.J.).

R. v. Beare (1988) 2 S.C.R. 387 (S.C.C.).

R. v. Borden (1994) 3 S.C.R. 145, 92 C.C.C. (3d) 404 (S.C.C.).

R. v. Briggs (2001) O.J. No. 3339 (O.C.A.).

R. v. Brighteyes (1997) 199 A.R. 161 (Alta. Q.B.).

R. v. Brochu (2000) O.J. No. 3635 (O.S.C.J.).

R. v. Brosseau (2001) A.J. No. 1510 (Alta. Prov. Ct.).

R. v. Bruhm (2001) N.W.T.J. No. 77 (N.W.T. Terr. Ct.).

R. v. Colarusso (1994) 1 S.C.R. 20 (S.C.C.).

R. v. Creighton (1993) S.C.R. 3, 83 C.C.C. (3d) 346 (S.C.C.).

R. v. D.M.F. (2001) S.C.C.A. No. 604 (S.C.C.).

R. v. Dwyer (2000) O.J. No. 4683 (O.C.J.).

R. v. Dyment (1988) 2 S.C.R. 417 (S.C.C.).

R. v. Eakin (2000) O.J. No. 1670 (O.C.A.).

R. v. Feeney (2001) B.CJ. No. 311 (B.C. C.A.).

R.v. Gillis (2000) O.J. No. 4431 (O.C.J.).

R. v. Greffe (1990) 55 C.C.C. (3d) 161 (S.C.C.).

R. v. Isbister (2002) A.J. No. 246 (Alta. C.A.).

R. v. Jordan (2002) N.S.J. No. 20 (N.S.C.A.).

R. v. Larsen (2001) B.C.J. No. 820 (B.C.S.C.).

R. v. Legere (1994) 35 C.R. (4th) 1, 95 C.C.C. (3d) 139 (N.B.C.A.).

R. v. McCraw (1991) 3 S.C.R. 72, 66 C.C.C. (3d) 517 (S.C.C.).

R. v. Metcalfe (1993) 41 M.V.R. (2d) 308 (Alta. Q.B.).

R. v. Mohan (1994) 2 S.C.R. (S.C.C.).

R. v. Morgentaler (1988) 1 S.C.R. 30, 37 C.C.C. (3d) 449 (S.C.C.).

R. v. Murrin (1999) B.C.J. No. 2715 (B.C.S.C.).

R. v. Murrins (2002) N.S.J. No. 21 (N.S.C.A.).

R. v. Nguyen (2002) O.J. No. 3 (O.C.A.).

R. v. Parent (1988) 46 C.C.C. (3d) 414, 91 A.R. 307 (Alta. Q.B.).

R. v. Pelletier (1989) 50 C.C.C. (3d) 22 (Sask. Q.B.).

R. v. Penney (2001) N.J. No. 320 (Newfoundland Prov. Ct.).

R. v. P.R.F.; R. v. Hendry; R. v. G.A.M.; R. v. W.D.W. (2001) O.J. No. 5084 (O.C.A.).

R. v. Rennie (2002) B.C.J. No. 10 (B.C.C.A.).

R. v. S.A.B. (2001) A.J. No. 1202 (Alta. C.A.).

R. v. S.F. (2000) O.J. No. 60 (O.C.A.).

R. v. Stillman (1995) 97 C.C.C. (3d) 164 (N.B.C.A.).

R. v. Stillman (1997) 1 S.C.R. 607 (S.C.C.).

R. v. Terceira (1998) 38 Ontario Reports (3d) 175 (O.C.A.).

R. v. Turner (2001) N.J. No. 104 (Newf. S.C.).

R. v. Van Osselaer (1999) B.C.J. No. 3141 (B.C.S.C.).

R. v. Wise (1992) 1 S.C. R. 527, 70 C.C.C. (3d) 193 (S.C.C.).

R. v. Wong (1990) 3 S.C.R. 36, 60 C.C.C, (3d) 460 (S.C.C.).

R. v. Xie (2000) A.J. No. 817 (Alta Q.B.).

Rodriguez v. British Columbia (Attorney General) (1993) 3 S.C.R. 519, 85 C.C.C. (3d) 15 (S.C.C.).

Index